King
of Innocence and Peace

The Guiltlessness In You,
a Poetic Truth

Second Edition

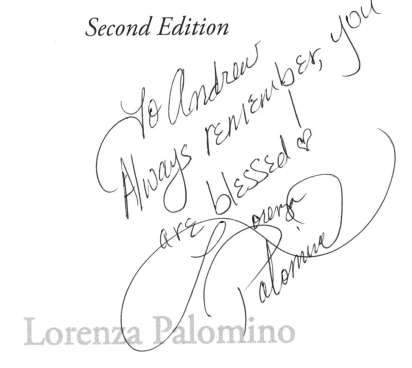

To Andrew
Always remember, you
are blessed ♥
Lorenza Palomino

Lorenza Palomino

ISBN 978-1-64258-824-8 (paperback)
ISBN 978-1-64258-825-5 (digital)

Christian Faith Publishing, Inc.
832 Park Avenue
Meadville, PA 16335
www.christianfaithpublishing.com

Printed in the United States of America

This poetic truth is dedicated to our Father in Heaven, our Lord Jesus Christ and thy Holy Spirit Who have been with me through the long arduous journey of my writings. They lift the severe pains and fatigue of the physical afflictions I suffer on a daily basis because many days, I was unable to do anything, not even write. They uphold me when I fall and did not want to get back up. They encouraged me when I was discouraged and wanted to give up. They lifted the load and carried me through when I was unable to lift a finger. I could not have completed the first edition, let alone the second edition without Them, but God kept His promise to me and helped me to uphold my promise to Him and the Sonship. With Christ and the Holy Spirit working alongside of me, God released His agreement with me that I would write the lovely truth in you and me upon the arrival time regardless of what I am suffering in my own life. I am forever grateful to the Trinity for the power in them through me as They work in unison to ensure I succeed in leaving behind the legacy of the beautiful truth in you. My own ego thinking of fear and darkness were healed and corrected as I persevered with Them. I am happy to learn that many will be spiritually awakened, just as I was, while I am still on this world and long after I have transitioned back home. Nevertheless, when I transition to Heaven is when many more will fully awaken to the legacy I left for you to learn, remember and receive the lovely truth in you. And the essence of the legacy in this edition is your willingness to release Christ from His own suffering of the crown of thorns first and you will free yourself and your brothers' from a grandeur of sufferings swiftly. This is the quantum leap into forgiveness, Atonement, spiritual knowledge, and vision where you will know and see clearly the guiltlessness, innocence, and peace in you and the Sonship. This is a meaningful cause for celebration because you will behold the loveliness in you and your brothers' in the chaotic kingdom of where you spree.

I also dedicate this poetic truth to all the Sonship from one end of the world to the other because we are all brothers and sisters and we all know each other from Heaven because Heaven is where we are all from. The only reason we call each other strangers is that we do not remember, "we created the stranger," A Course In Miracles (ACIM) (the ego, devil, enemy, call it what you will), before we were even born. We are now in the era to remember this and admit to it without guiltiness so you are able to make room to perceive the loveliness in you. And when you do, it becomes a reflection where you see the beautification of the immortality of the Sonship and your own and that we are all homies from Heaven. Let God purify the stranger in you to bring the remembrance of the innocence and peace in you releasing your own suffering and the sufferings of the Sonship from all over the world where love, joy, peace, sanity, immortality, freedom, safety and union enters. For this is the ultimate purpose of releasing Christ from the crown of thorns and honoring Him with the crown of white lilies that will release Him from His sufferings and so you too will be freed from your own. This is a quantum leap into Atonement, "reconciling with Christ"—ACIM. And to reconcile with Him first releases you to reunite with the Sonship in recognition that they are just as much your brothers' as Christ is. We are not strangers, the ego is, and it is time to be willing to learn and remember we are no stranger and embrace it with love, joy, and peace.

This poetic truth is also dedicated to all of our brilliant astronomical minds from all over the world who study the universe and everything in it. Heed to the simple fundamental power of "spiritual vision" where the Holy Spirit will gently hurdle you into the quantum leap realm. Here, you will soar into the abyss of the universe where you will know and see the wonders of what we created and you will let it be your friend. For through spiritual vision, it does become your friend because it shows you anything and everything you want to see and know and this brings the remembrance of your part in creating it, therefore will no longer fear it in frustration. Take the quantum leap into the universe through the guidance of the Holy

Spirit and you will make breakthroughs and, ultimately, you will make history. And this is what I had said to the Holy Spirit one day. I said, "Those who study the universe that look at it firsthand and choose to study it through spiritual vision is going to make history Lord." He said, "Would you like to be the one?" I said, "Heck no, I'm not a physicist. I do not study the universe. I'm a writer. I pass the spiritual torch of glory to those who study the universe and let them make history. I wish to stay focused on our writing." The only reason I am able to write poetry about the universe is that I asked God to show me His part and our part in the creation of it, although I had no idea that I was going to be taken through the quantum leap process through spiritual vision in order to see all that was shown to me. I'm passing the spiritual torch of glory to our brilliant astronomical minds because I am satisfied with what was shown to me in regards to the universe. My curiosity has been quenched. I will leave the rest of it up to the brilliant astronomical minds because whoever chooses to study it through spiritual vision is going to see and learn more than I was willing to learn. Because the discoveries they have already made and attempting to make is going to all come together for them through spiritual vision, there will be many "aha" moments, for they will see so much more than I was willing to learn and remember. I pass what I call "the spiritual torch of glory" to them because either they spent years studying the universe or they made it their career and life goal to know it.

Be willing to take a quantum leap into spiritual vision with the Holy Spirit and make history and go and be a fruitful learner of the universe through the quantum leap process of spiritual vision, and make history, all you brilliant astronomical minds! In the name of the Kingdom of God. Amen.

Contents

Acknowledgments

I respectfully, humbly, and gratefully thank the Trinity for upholding me through the process of my writings and for tenderly guiding me through the process of remembering the true from the false. I couldn't have done this alone and none of us could. It is vital to invite the Holy Spirit to be your teacher, guide, and comforter through the process of spiritual vision where He eventually and gently takes you through the quantum leap realm of everything you want to know. Thank you God, Christ, and Holy Spirit for answering all my "why, what, where, how, and when" questions. I am fully content with the spiritual knowledge you have given me. It was a long arduous road until you took me into quantum leap and I can't thank you enough for your tender and gentle hurdle through this realm. I am at total peace and my mind feels entirely complete with the truth of the world from which I am from and with the false world from which I do not belong. Thank you, thank you, and thank you from the core of my heart, mind, and soul!

I give my thanks and gratitude to Genelle Smith, Social Worker and Facilitator of the Art of Being program at Wellspring Women's Center. Thank you, Genelle, for being the gem you are through the whole process in the Art of Being program I participated in. I was determined to come out of the fear, darkness, loneliness, sadness, and hopelessness emotions I struggled with for so long and so desperately wanted to break free from. In your Art of Being class is where I had my breakthrough to pick up the pen and begin to write poetry again. I was such a confused soul trying to find the answers to all my questions about everything. The Art of Being was a stepping stone to all the open doors that were always in front of me I could not see. Because the fears I was in kept me blind to the doors Christ always holds open waiting in patience and in peace for me to awaken to His direction and calling. I thank you for your love, kindness, patience, peace, and silence through the whole process. You are a Heavenly gem I will always cherish and value dear to the core of my soul, wellness of my mind and the love of my heart forevermore.

I am ever so thankful and grateful to my best friend Marilyn Holt for continuing to permit me to call her for her opinion and suggestions in the poetry that I have shared with her. Thank you, Marilyn, for your divine input in everything I have written that I shared with you for your input. I am ever so grateful for your openness of your mind and heart in what I have written through the guidance of the Holy Spirit. You are divinely connected to Him yourself because your input has been such a glorious blessing. Thank you, my lovely sister and friend.

I want to give my gracious thank you to all the employees and customers at Bel Air grocery store, Scott's Seafood Restaurant, Peet's Coffee and Starbuck's employees and customers, FedEx employees, cigarette store employees, friends and neighbors. I thank you from the core of my heart for your willingness to release Christ from His sufferings and our own with your blazing amazing smiles to be featured in the thirty second Blazing Amazing Smiles videos. Your participation has been a delightful blessing to the Blazing Amazing Smiles project as a creative way to promote the King of Innocence and Peace, The Guiltlessness In You, A Poetic Truth before it is even published. I could not have started this project without your willingness to be featured with your delightful blazing amazing smiles. Your willingness to take part in releasing Jesus Christ from His sufferings of the crown of thorns and honoring Him with the crown of white lilies, no thorns, has ignited this project into motion. At your willingness to release Him from His sufferings releases you and your brothers from sufferings galore. Your golden smile blazes aglow alongside of Christ golden blazing amazing smile. And this is such an exciting venture to take into the realm of love, light, life, joy, peace, truth, kindness, faith, patience, unity, safety and freedom. In the name of the Kingdom of God. Amen.

I also give my thanks and gratitude to Jenna Frazier for such a fantastic and stunning artist she is. The portrait of Jesus Christ for "The Crown of White Lilies" poem is divinely beautiful! Jenna, I hope you always remember our first miracle together when we went to Staples to make glossy copies of your finished portrait of Jesus Christ. That was a heavenly day I, myself, will never forget!

I give my further gratitude to Avi Singh, Greenhaven Print Pack and Ship, FedEx. Thank you so much Avi for all your support you have given me as a local author. Your guidance and support for the Blazing Amazing Smiles project has been delightfully uplifting. It has been an enjoyable honor working with you and I hope we continue to work together.

In the name of the Kingdom of God, I give my divine royal salute to all of you. Amen.

My Thoughts to Yours

Have faith you are love, light, holy, sinless,
guiltless, joyfulness, and peace for you
are the innocence of God's brilliance.

For the righteous qualities in you are the purity
of unity of the Trinity, which you are part of,
for it is the Sonship of a holy relationship
of pure love, light, joy, peace, and innocence.

An unfaithful and loveless attitude bonds you
to guilt, judgment, imprisonment, hate, fear and
darkens the mind to the truth in you where you
perceive the Sonship without gratitude bringing
you to a place of uncertainty of your brothers' and
yourself making a false world true for you.

Faithfulness, truthfulness, love, freedom,
happiness, and peacefulness are sensible, for
it keeps you confident in certainty that you
are as loveable and vibrant as God is and as
innocent and peaceful as Christ is, and as patient and
comforting as the Holy Spirit is. Learn this,
and you will remember this is the truth in you.

And so be willing to invite the Holy Spirit to lead
you to the truth in you and you will find God and
Heaven where you gain your memory of who
you are, why you are here, where you
come from, and where you will return.

III. Sin as an Adjustment

1. The belief in sin is an adjustment. And an adjustment is a change; a shift in perception, or a belief that what was so before has been made different. Every adjustment is therefore a distortion, and calls upon defenses to uphold it against reality. Knowledge requires no adjustments and, in fact, is lost if any shift or change is undertaken. For this reduces it at once to mere perception; a way of looking in which certainty is lost and doubt has entered. To this impaired condition *are* adjustments necessary, because it is not true. Who need adjust to truth, which calls on only what he is, to understand?

2. Adjustments of any kind are of the ego. For it is the ego's fixed belief that all relationships depend upon adjustments, to make of them what it would have them be. Direct relationships, in which there are no interferences, are always seen as dangerous. The ego is the self-appointed mediator of all relationships, making whatever adjustments it deems necessary and interposing them between those who would meet, to keep them separate and prevent their union. It is this studied interference that makes it difficult for you to recognize your holy relationship for what it is.

3. The holy do not interfere with truth. They are not afraid of it, for it is within the truth they recognize their holiness, and rejoice at what they see. They look on it directly, without attempting to adjust themselves to it, or it to them. And so they see that it was in them, not deciding first where they would have it be. Their looking merely asks a question, and it is what they see that answers them. You make the world and then adjust to it, and it to you. Nor is there any difference between yourself and it in your perception, which made them both.

4. A simple question yet remains, and needs an answer. Do you like what you have made? – a world of murder and attack, through which you thread your timid way through constant dangers, alone and

frightened, hoping at most that death will wait a little longer before it overtakes you and you disappear. *You made this up.* It is a picture of what you think you are; of how you see yourself. A murderer *is* frightened, and those who kill fear death. All these are but the fearful thoughts of those who would adjust themselves to a world made fearful by their adjustments. And they look out in sorrow from what is sad within, and see the sadness there.

5. Have you not wondered what the world is really like; how it would look through happy eyes? The world you see is but a judgment on yourself. It is not there at all. Yet judgment lays a sentence on it, justifies it and makes it real. Such is the world you see; a judgment on yourself, and made by you. This sickly picture of yourself is carefully preserved by the ego, whose image it is and which it loves, and placed outside you in the world. And to this world must you adjust as long as you believe this picture is outside, and has you at its mercy. This world *is* merciless, and were it outside you, you should indeed be fearful. Yet it was you who made it merciless, and now if mercilessness seems to look back at you, it can be corrected. (Chapter 20, *ACIM*)

Prologue

It is better not to burn your bridges at both ends, for you will fall. However, if you do end up burning your bridges at both ends look up when you land on solid ground and surrender the fall to God. He will raise you up and ask you to pat off the dust and try again in lesson learned. It is better not to lose faith in this because He is always with you ready and waiting in patience and in peace for your invitation to ask for His help. And the day will come when you will scream out His name, just as I did, when I believed I never would. I remember through the years as an atheist people would say to me, "don't burn your bridges at both ends," and I would gaze upon them in silence feeling puzzled. They too would gaze upon me in silence probably thinking that I get it. However, honestly, my thought about this was puzzling because I was blind to this phrase for many years.

In speaking with a friend through a span of three days of her challenges in her life, I was already thinking of voicing to her the parable of the burning bridge, but I did not, because I still didn't fully understand what it meant even though I was thinking that it probably means "burnout." So I asked the Holy Spirt what exactly is the meaning of this term. I waited in patience for His answer so I did not use the phrase until the day the Holy Spirit directed me to do so. Through my friend's words and energy, I already knew she was on the path of burning people out because of her diligence to quench her needs when her friends, including me, were doing everything they could to help her while she tried to lay low as to not do her part. So rather than receiving the help in appreciation, she took advantage of the assistance by expecting more and more and more without any effort in her part to ensure her situation improved. As I let this scenario of her approach play out in my mind, a vision came to me of how desperately and persistently she was in trying to get us to do everything for her. I had to get firm with her and told her that I will not do it all for her that she would have to meet me halfway because she needs to be willing to help herself and be thankful and appreciate what we have already done to assist her. In the vision, I saw her walking against a strong wind trying to reach the bridge she very much wanted to reach; and from afar, I could see the bridge beautiful and intact. But the harder she tried to reach it while stepping on toes, the wind grew stronger and she trampled over her own feet when she saw the bridge swaying. The bridge suddenly burst into flames at both ends engulfing it to a burning bridge. I was clearly surprised at this vision and I had to step into the realm of peace and faith that she would receive the assistance from all parties involved in thankfulness and gratefulness by doing her part so that it would all work out for her without anyone getting burnt out. I prayed and asked God to let us (the bridge) remain intact without the intense effect of "burnout" over the trials of our friend. Soon after, the day arrived when I was to relay the message of the "burning bridge" parable to her as the Holy Spirit stood beside me with His head bowed. He said, "Tell her not to burn her bridges at both ends, for she will fall. Remind her that God will lift her up and ask her to pat off the dust and try again in lesson learned." This was an amazing revelation for me, because first, I hadn't heard this phrase in years since it was last said to me many years earlier when I had no clue what it meant. Second, it was at that moment that I fully understood the miracle of this revelation, for the vision of it, I had already received, and the Holy Spirit voicing it all came together for me. And so she seemed to understand fully what we meant because she replied, "Thank you for the reminder." But then again, she might have seen the Holy Spirit standing beside me because she does see through spiritual vision she just needs to learn to be calm in the midst of a storm and be willing to let her spiritual perception work in her favor.

II. Revelation, Time and Miracles

2. Revelation is intensely personal and cannot be meaningfully translated. That is why any attempt to describe it in words is impossible. Revelation induces only experience. Miracles, on the other hand, induce action. They are more useful now because of their interpersonal nature. In this phase of learning, working miracles is important because freedom from fear cannot be thrust upon you. Revelation is literally unspeakable because it is an experience of unspeakable love. (Chapter 1, *ACIM*)

Years earlier, I had a similar lesson where I learned quickly not to persistently bother people with my needs even when I was penniless and had nothing to eat and nowhere to live but in my car. I came to the understanding that people were not yet ready to do the miracle.

Although, at the time, I did not yet know that their help would have been a lovely miracle, I look back at it now and I see clearly that when I asked for help and received very little or none at all, miracle-minded people were not in my life script at that point of my life. So I learned relentlessly to lean on God for everything during my trials of those years of homelessness, and to this day, I still do. Sometimes when we want immediate satisfaction to our challenges in life, we seek to lean on one another in the hopes of getting instant help and peace of mind. However, sometimes, it might backfire because we really don't know what others are going through in their life at the time we seek their help of our own situations. They might be burnt out trying to deal with their own life's challenges so it would be best to lean on God for everything because He never gets burnt out. His bridge never burns because He never grows tired of anything. And it is always better to be honest with people and let them know that you would like to help but you are going through your own issues seeking strength and assistance of your own life matters. This way, you won't ruin relationships and you can move on in your path of life without any guilt upholding faith, peace, and holiness recognizing their innocence and your own leaving relationships intact without losing love, kindness, humbleness, peace and compassion for each other. This is the meaning of holy thinking. Sometimes, two or more people can give each other the support and strength needed and it works, particularly when we are thankful and appreciate it and do our part to ensure success in helping the situation improve. And always remember that if you are too burnt out to handle another's troubles, it doesn't make you a bad or selfish person. As I said, it is better to be honest about your own situation and bless each other with compassion and success in peace; and in faith, the trials and tribulations will unravel to an improvement of each other's lives. This is positive energy of blessings that the universe will boomerang to all parties involved in its time. Faith upholds the holiness and salvation in you and me as we face the challenges of this world. Remain in love, joy, kindness, humbleness, peace, and patience because blessings will always prevail, for God never fails, therefore neither will you.

The circumstances you might face in this world brings you to have questions upon questions as to why such tragic things happen to you. The stack of questions are only because you don't remember your life script you yourself wrote before you were born. The disastrous events that happen in your life is you yourself doing this to yourself and each other because we all agreed to it; therefore, we are in it together. This is where the innocence in you and the Sonship comes in because we are not alone in the prewritten events that are to unfold in everyone's life as they do. We are all brilliant writers because we wrote our own life script before we were born into it, but we don't remember this and this is why we ask, what I call, "the fundamental questions of blindness," like "Why did this happen to me?" "I didn't ask for this or I didn't agree to this" and "Am I alone." When the truth is you did ask for it and you agreed to it, then, no, you are not alone. We can change our life script by the decisions we make. Just listen to the goodness of your instinct because it is God speaking to you lighting up the path of love, peace, and safety. However, there is a way in which to take a swift journey into learning how to release yourself from suffering to happiness. It is the "quantum leap effect" in which I am about to enlighten you as to how you can swiftly wake up from the dream or nightmare you might face. Stand with me in peace, patience, and faith and trust in what I am about to share with you because it is deep stuff you already know but just temporarily forgotten about. I am going to title it here, because this is what the Holy Spirit has led me to do and I am God's obedient host for the sake of your spiritual awakening and my own.

The Testimony of the Crown of White Lilies

We all go through the same phases of life asking all the why, what, where, how, and when questions and "who are we and where did we come from" questions and the "are we alone" question and "why did this happen to me" question. These questions stem from not remembering who you are and where you come from and what you wrote and agreed to before you were even born. We seek all over the world and in the universe for the answers not realizing the answer is us and in us, therefore always with us. The memory of who we are and where we come from and why tragic events happen in our lives is wiped out the moment we are born from out of timelessness into time. You might go through the dream of life having glimpses of whom you are and where you come from and why things happen the way they do wondering if you are alone. You might even feel like you are going crazy and you might even sound insane to other people you might share the snapshots with of the memory loss. It's OK to ask the "why" questions because this means you are seeking the truth and this is the proof of evidence you are semi-aware of who you are and where you come from, that there is another world from which you come that has got to be better than this one, and that you can't be alone. And the truth is you are correct! There is a world from which you come that is grandeur in its loveliness that your mind can't even perceive it alone. However, keep asking and seeking because you will get your answers through your diligence, vigilance, and determination to find the truth in you and everything seen and unseen. And when you find your answers, you will know you are not crazy, you will know who you are and where you come from, and you will know why things happen the way they do. Ultimately, you will know you are not alone and that you have never been alone. However, in order to get the true answers to all your questions, there is one condition, "willingness." You must be willing to seek not outside yourself, rather search within yourself. Your willingness is of vital importance because God does not force His knowledge upon you. This is why you must be willing to receive it.

There is a universal teacher in you patiently and peacefully waiting for you to invite Him to answer all your questions and He will be all too happy to unveil the truth of what you ask. He is God's Holy Spirit Who has always been with you and will be with you through the duration of your time on this world. He can only emerge from your memory by your invitation because God is not intrusive but is always gently sending to your remembrance messages of whom you are, where you come from, why things unfold the way they do, and that you are never alone. The times you hear and see signs of the evidence of it are the moments you are listening to the Voice of His Holy Spirit. However, in order to go from sometimes being semi self-aware to being consistently fully self-aware, you must be willing to invite the Holy Spirit to lead and teach you so you will learn and remember the answers to all your questions. In the beginning, it might be frightening, but God is not to fear because He's the One Who lifts you up when you fall and wipes your tears and holds you near to His heart because He cherishes you most dear. The only reason the initial reaction might be "fear" is because the ego thinks God is going to obliterate it. But this is not so because first of all, there is no wrath in God and He respects what you have made even though He did not support your decision to create fear and darkness and be born into it so you can experience it. Although He authorized it, it doesn't mean He agreed to it. Nevertheless, this is all behind you now if you so choose to forgive God for letting you be born into a merciless world and let it go and move forward in love, light, and peace. We are in the era of forgiveness and letting go of the pains and sorrows of the merciless world we asked for. In order to do this, you first must be willing to let go of the play of the crown of thorns and the fear of the act of the crucifixion and lovingly and respectfully embrace the crown of white lilies. You do this and you have taken a swift but gentle quantum leap into self-awareness and understanding of all creation of the visible and invisible and the true from the false.

The quantum leap brings you swiftly, completely, and gently out of fear and darkness and softly into the fullness of love and lightness. And when you merge into the love and light of God, you see all the beauty of His creation and your own; and when you calmly turn to look behind you, you see the ugliness, meaningless, and senseless dream you thrive to leave or wake from. Here, you will be all too grateful you've taken the quantum leap, for you instinctively know you took a swift growth from not knowing to all knowing and from blindness to all seeing. The King of Kings and Lord of Lords showers you with peace of the memory you thoughtfully seek. Even though you felt alone for too long, the Holy Spirit in you constantly reminds you, "You are not alone." This is why we say too often, "I felt so alone, but then, I suddenly knew I was not alone." We are never alone because there is negative energy always thriving within us, but the same is true for positive energy. And so the ultimate question then is "Which energy will you feed?" Feed the negative and you fall deeper into the pit of fear and darkness where you remain in the bondages of its sufferings and the belief that death is real. However, feed the positive and you nurture the light within where you clearly see in certainty you are love and do not have to suffer, you are light and you do not have to be blind, and you are immortal, the gift of eternal life. This truth will enable you to see the beautiful golden light in you and it will flourish to the surface where you become a shining star, the light of the world. This is what it means to resurrect. The fundamental resurrection is release from fear and into love, release from darkness and rise in lightness, release from insanity and into sanity, release from sorrows and into joy, release from wars and into peace, release from judgment and into embracement, release from guilt and into innocence, release from danger and into safety, release from separation and into unification and release from bondage and into freedom. And you can free yourself from all the negative forces with the assistance of the Holy Spirit all at once embracing the quantum leap effect. However, there is one condition here, as well. In order to take the quantum leap from the dark circle of negative forces to the golden circle of positive forces, you must release Christ first from the suffering of the crown of thorns and the belief in death through the play of the crucifixion. This is the quantum leap.

For this is your ultimate role you are here to do and if you are willing to release Christ from the crown of thorns, you free Him, the Sonship, and yourself from sufferings galore.

And so this is how you free Christ: In your mind's eye (prayer), invite the Holy Spirit as your witness to the liberation of Christ from the crown of thorns and He will follow you as you happily pick wholly blossomed white lilies to make a sphere for an imperial crown of white lilies. Make the base of the crown with the stem of the green leaves of the lilies, and connect the fully blossomed white lilies all around the foundation of the crown. Make the crown nice and full with white lilies and let the green leaves peak between the lily petals. Be sure you don't place thorns in the crown of white lilies because if you do, you will only be prolonging the bondages of your own suffering of guilt and the belief in the fear of death keeping you blind from the beauty of the truth. When you've completed the creation of the crown of white lilies, invite the suffering Christ to enter and delicately remove the crown of thorns from his bloody and injured head. And in love, joy, and calmness, place the crown of white lilies on His injured and bloody head. Here, you are a witness to the transformation from guilt to innocence, from bloody to beauty, from injured to healed, from frail to sovereignty and from death to life. To free Christ from the bloodiness of all the ugliness means you free yourself and the Sonship from it, as well. Here, you have taken the quantum leap into wholly light where you are in the realm of full-blown self-awareness and understanding where you now utterly see the truth of whom you are, where you come from, and why things happen the way they do and you are not alone. Now, you are completely free from suffering insanity and you will be all too happy to take the crown of white lilies upon the palm of your hands and offer it to your brothers and let it spring like a domino effect to all the Sonship from one side of the world to the other. There will be parades all over the world celebrating the release of Christ from His sufferings and yours as many lift up the crown of white lilies to the Heavens placing it on the head of Christ and each other. This is the eventual offering to the recognition of Christ's holiness and innocence and your own enabling love, light, life, truth, joy, peace, union, safety, and freedom to thrive from the minds and hearts in you and the Sonship from one side of the world to the other.

Here is where you take the quantum leap and you are witness to the overjoyous of everyone who receives this divine gift of remembrance of who we are, where we come from, and why we say and do the things we say and do. Because of the release of the King of Innocence and Peace, from suffering, you are able to see in all clarity and certainty you are not alone and Heaven is your natural home. And so the crown of white lilies is the resurrection of mind and spirit who is life, innocent, holy, love, truth, the way, joy, peace, and freedom in the eternity of togetherness and safety. And so the King of Kings and Lord of Lords has risen with a golden blazing amazing smile wearing the crown of white lilies fully healed not bloody, for He shines of love, light, life, truth, beauty and sovereignty. Here, you too have risen smiling aglow, alongside of Him, for He is your brother and savior and so you too are His brother and savior. And so the crown of white lilies is the quantum leap from filthy to purity, guilty to innocence, darkness to lightness, blindness to all seeing, not knowing to all knowing, fear to love, sorrowful to joyful, war to peace, hatefulness to pleasantness, judgment to embracement, danger to safety, separation to unification, and bondage to freedom. And so this is the testimony of the crown of white lilies. Be willing then to take the quantum leap and you will be completely free to be the loveliness of your essence along with Christ and all the Sonship. This is the delightfulness of the holiness and innocence of Christ in you, for you are the way, the life, and the truth; and the quantum leap of the crown of white lilies is the evidence of the swift recognition of everything seen and unseen and the all-knowing of what is true and what is false.

And so the testimony of the crown of white lilies is the quantum leap to release the suffering of Jesus Christ from the crown of thorns, the suffering of your brothers and your own from every thorn propped at every angle of the world. This is the swift announcement to your acceptance of love, light, life, truth, joy, peace, unity, freedom, and safety. This is what we all spend a lifetime seeking. The offering of the crown of white lilies permits Christ to enter and merge His love and light with yours in joy and peace. This is where you are released from your own sufferings of insanity. And through the gentle journey into quantum leap is where you see through spiritual vision, the wonders of who you are, why things happen the way they do, where you came from, where you will return, and you have never been alone. You will be excited and over joyous to be a witness to the lovely innocence in you, and the Sonship and to the wonders of Heaven, your natural home. This will permit anyone, willing to receive, to give a blazing amazing smile.

This is how I placed the crown of white lilies on the injured and bloody head of Christ. Through meditation, I summoned the suffering Christ into spiritual vision. When He merged His light with mine, now face to face, He bowed His injured and bloody head and I slowly and tenderly put my hands on the crown of thorns and compassionately, peacefully, and gently removed the crown of thorns from His bloody and injured head. Here, I happily, lovingly, and peacefully placed the crown of white lilies on His bloody head and I became a witness to the transformation from guilt to innocence, bloody to beauty, injured to healed, sorrow to joy, suffering to delight, frail to sovereignty and bondage to freedom. And His eyes sparkled and His spirit glistened golden. Suddenly, my heart jumped from within my chest and a flood of happy tears streamed down my face. I fall to my knees and kiss His fully healed golden feet and I found myself in complete stillness, and the Holy Spirit was awfully quiet. The calmness was so overwhelming. I didn't know what to do with it. But then, I realized I too must remain in silence and patiently wait with Him for the next move of God's work. However, for days after I honored Christ with the crown of white lilies, the Holy Spirit was still way too quiet. I didn't like the way I felt about it. However, I elected not to be weary just quiet along with Him and take in every ounce of the overjoyous deed I did to release Christ from His sufferings, yours, and my own. The Holy Spirit knows what will unfold next in my life script so I asked for His peace and rest in what I know not what to expect. I humbled myself to Him and remained in faith and peace we do not work in vain, for we have spoken and written powerfully poetically, which will be a blessing to many who are ready to receive the truth of God, Heaven, and the Sonship. This is what is meaningful and important and I had to remember that God never fails so we too cannot fail. Even though I know this, still I had to ask for His reassurance by lifting the burden of how I feel from my mind and heart. I was so calm that I felt something is terribly wrong, for I am not used to being so composed. I asked the Holy Spirit to let me know this is not "the calm before the storm" but "the calm before the blessings" of many. I asked Him to lift the burden of discomfort from my mind and heart and bless me with complete and utter comfort and peace of the next phase of our work, for I already know I am to share the testimony of the crown of white lilies the Holy Spirit gave me to enlighten the Sonship with because the time has arrived to toss the crown of thorns even though it was tossed over two thousand years ago. My own experience of the testimony of the crown of white lilies I also share with you for insight. Through this whole experience, I needed to be at total peace with the calmness I had received so I can enjoy the dwelling of God's greatness so I can continue to remain tranquil and still in what is to unfold. What the Holy Spirit is directing me to share is not anything new. Time has arrived to enforce it and I am all too happy to be part of it. You too will arrive at your time when you will share your experience of the crown of white lilies testimony, for there are a godzillion ways to say the same thing everyone will come to eventually know, confess, and share. However, even in remembering all this, I still needed God's confirmation to move forward in joy and peace of His lovely and poetic affirmations. I wanted to settle in comfort of being so calm that there would not be a speck of anxiety in me and no calamity stirring, only complete stillness and serenity in all certainty. This is what Heaven is, complete stillness because there is no movement to bring about changes. This is why Heaven never changes because God's light holds everything together in complete stillness, whereas the universe has movement and this is why everything changes and we don't like it, because we subconsciously remember that we come from a world where change is nonexistent. Heaven is so perfect there is never anything to change. As I already said, God's love and light is the gravity that holds everything together. This is how powerful He is. He can obliterate the creation of the ego if He wanted to, but He is love and love gives pure freedom. So when we asked to create the ego as our wrathful father and be born into the merciless world we created to experience the father we made, He let the lovely white dove go and granted what we asked for. And so He retrieved His light from part of Heaven, we borrowed and call it the universe, which we think is dark gravity that holds it all together, but really, it is God's light masked in night that lets everything in the universe suspend in the darkness of the cosmos. Dark gravity is the dark grimness that always obliterates because it's fake, an illusion, delusion, or dream, whichever you like to call it. One day, it will cease because this is the Will of God and your own because no one wants fear and darkness forever even if you think you do.

We are all securely and divinely connected to God that if God were to be wiped out we'd all be annihilated along with Him because He created us to be eternally joined. However, you will be pleasantly pleased to learn and remember that this is the only thing that is impossible because God is eternal and so too are we. There isn't anything we created that can annihilate God because fear and darkness is weak and love and light is strength. And Christ elaborates on this in a ACIM. And so to be faithfully calm, still, and patient doesn't mean something horrid is about to happen. To arrive at this place in your mind and heart, as I have, means you've reached Heaven in time. You might feel something bad is about to happen, as I did, because you have been in the ancient storm of insane, radical, fanatical, and wrathful thinking, as I was, for so long that you forgot what it means to be still and calm in the light of God's love, joy, and peace. It is Heaven, literally, to be in the wholesome of peace even as I find myself surrounded by the bittersweet illusional dream everyone else is having. Christ has always told us that we can rest in peace in time. In fact, through the writings of Helen Schucman in ACIM,

Christ tells us that the phrase "rest in peace means it is for the living," which means us that are living in a chaotic world. For those who have transitioned left the dark, unforgiving world of fear and entered the lovely world of love and light, Heaven, unless, of course, you wrote in your life script to transition from hell to hell to experience the more intense fear and darkness, but this you can change, as well. The only difference of feeling fear and cruelty between physical and spiritual is that in the spiritual "hellish" realm, you will feel the effects of fear, pain, hopelessness, loneliness, and sadness one hundred thousand times more than you did in the physical.

Well, now I understand fully what Christ means by being at peace in a world anchored in change, chaos, suffering, guilt, judgment, and limitations. I now know how He must have felt when He came to the peace of Heaven, in time, as He was surrounded by wolves of cruelty and judgment He witnessed happening all around Him and eventually made Him the center of the ego's sick attention and afflictions. However, this is all behind Him now because He reached the peak of His life script when He spiritually ascended to Heaven and the Holy Spirit emerged to be with us to lead us from the point Jesus Christ physically left the dream and has been spiritually with us ever since. And so as we continue in the world of time, God is invisible and so is Jesus and the Holy Spirit. They are the Trinity, and as long as we are in time, they will always work in unison to ensure your achievement that you reach the peak of your life script until you transform from physical to spiritual and transition into Heaven just as Jesus did. It's OK to be calm in a chaotic world. Do not fear peacefulness, rather embrace it and appreciate it, for it is the essence of the true you. Show the calmness as an example of who you are because it is the connection to God and the Sonship, and your brothers will remember the stillness in them, for their time will arrive to flourish in it just as you and I have. And so the feeling of the calm before the storm is the ego's way of trying to obliterate your love, light, happiness, and peace because it wants you to believe God is wrathful. Be willing not to let it keep you anchored in this false bondage, for it is the ego that is wrathful, not God. And the calm before the blessings is the Holy Spirit's way of keeping your love, light, happiness, and peace intact. Be willing to receive it no matter the tragic events that might unfold in your own life and all the screams of pains and sorrows you witness all over this merciless world. He did the same for Jesus and He will do the same for you, just as He had done for me, for this is what God has Willed, along with you. This is why Jesus is the King of Innocence and Peace because He embraced it through all the horrid things done to Him in the dream. He never let go of the real meaning of His nature of Who He truly is because He knew He can only return to Heaven in forgiveness, love, joy, and peace for God, Heaven and the Sonship, which He achieved and so was crowned the King of Innocence and Peace. Through His experiences, He did not grow angry, hateful, bitter, and hostile because the Holy Spirit guided Him through the remembrance of who He is and what He was born to do. And so when the time arrived for Him to realize this, He embraced the truth of it and of God, Heaven you and Him, and cherished it to the end. Even on the cross, He lifted the value of His love, joy and peace for God, Heaven, and the Sonship in forgiveness.

And so too are we scheduled to do the same at the arrival time of this game to remember you too are love, light, life, joy, and peace and the importance of forgiveness because of your innocence and agreement. In love, joy, and peace, forgive God, yourself, and the Sonship. When you entrust your spirit to God with this in your mind and heart, you will ascend to Heaven and be granted the golden crown of eternity. To find your way out of the mangled maze of chaos is a great achievement; and in the end, you do not find bereavement, you find the blissfulness of happiness, peacefulness, calmness, and stillness where the purity of love, light, life, joy, peace, union, freedom, and safety reign forever. And so when the Holy Spirit is silent, be silent with Him in patience, in peace, and in faith because He is preparing you for the next phase of your life script. Let Him prepare you for what is to unfold so you don't fall and crumble at the trespass of a storm. Receive it in calmness to uphold the love, joy, peace, and innocence in you and your brothers because this is the essence of spirit and spirit is the true life in you and the Sonship.

People are always shocked when I ask them to forgive God. Some even get upset, but this is only because they do not yet have the understanding and remembrance of why it is important to forgive God, as well as yourself and the Sonship. The shock of learning this was also my initial reaction because I too did not yet have the full understanding and remembrance of why I am being asked to forgive God. When the Holy Spirit instructed me to forgive God, I asked Him the same question everyone else asks me. I said, "Why would I forgive God?" In fact, the Holy Bible tells us that God has forgiven us so if God forgives us, why wouldn't we forgive Him? Ephesians 4:32, King James Version, (KJV) states: "And be ye kind one to another, tenderhearted, forgiving one another, even as God for Christ's sake hath forgiven you." God is not a one-way street. He is very fair, and with Him, everything works both ways. There is a scripture in ACIM written by Helen Schucman where Christ explains why it is important to forgive God, and for me, this was another confirmation. By the time I read the passage in ACIM of "forgiving God" already written made so much sense to me because the Holy Spirit had already asked me to forgive God and through my willingness to do so released God's wisdom, which allowed his knowledge and understanding to enter to help me unravel the world of fear and darkness we created in agreement with each other. And I had accepted the fact that I wrote my own life script in agreement with the Sonship before we were born. Forgiving God is part of the purification and cleansing process. When you learn and accept that you wrote your own life script and made the Earth to be born into in order to be able to experience what you had written, you will most certainly understand fully the importance of forgiving God. For Christ tells us in ACIM to forgive God for letting us create a loveless father (ego), a merciless world of fear and darkness, and then be born into it so we can know the opposite of love. However, there is no opposite of love. We had to create it in order for there to be an opposite of love just as Jesus explains in ACIM through the writings of Helen Schucman. I was given the vision of the Sonship sitting around a white round table in Heaven brainstorming how we would make a loveless father and a merciless world. However, I am very grateful to learn that fear, the opposite of love, is temporary. It won't last forever and I am very happy about this! And so because of His authorization to let us make a loveless father and merciless world and be born into it in order to experience it is the only reason why we must be willing to forgive God. And in my experience, to forgive Him made it much easier to forgive the Sonship and myself. It's the same thing with humbleness. When you genuinely humble yourself to God at every prayer, it becomes easier to humble yourself to others. Humbleness is a quantum leap into the divine qualities already in you. In fact, all the great gifts of God are a quantum leap from insanity to sanity, blindness to all seeing, and not knowing to all knowing. And this is where love, joy and peace shower upon you because of the immense release in learning and remembering the true from the false, which is pure bliss!

Therefore, forgive God, yourself, and each other and be at peace with the correction process because all the dirt will be brought to your remembrance for purification and cleansing and this is God's judgment and it is a beautiful and loving movement because God comforts you and does not confine you or punish you in order to force it upon you. He lets you remain free until you decide to invite His Holy Spirit Who will lead you to God's threshold to start the process and He will back off the moment you need to rest and will emerge at the next invite, for you are guiltless and God knows this, but you don't, only because you don't remember the guiltlessness in you. This world (Earth) is anchored on guilt, judgment, punishment, and imprisonment so we thrive in it, but God looks past that and sees the perfection of His creation. For the spirit is holy and sinless, you will remember this through the quantum leap or long process, whichever way you choose to learn, and remember you are flawless and you will definitely see this through the purification and cleansing process. If you take the quantum leap path to know the truth and false of everything, it will be so swift you will be happy and free sooner. This process will swiftly wipe out all shame and guilt of every bad deed you ever thought, said, or did; and you will see how meaningless and senseless it all is because you will see the truth of God, Heaven, the Sonship, and your own. And God will not let you simmer in guilt and shame for too long because He is eager to reunite with you in love, joy, and peace forever.

And so lovingly remove the crown of thorns from the injured and bloody head of Christ and honor him with the crown of white lilies, for this is the quantum leap of your journey to the bridge that never burns. And when you cross it, you will see the diamond star you created in Heaven before you were born as a holy memoir to our Father in Heaven and your own.

III. Sin as an Adjustment

6. Who in a holy relationship can long remain unholy? The world the holy see is one with them, just as the world the ego looks upon is like itself. The world the holy see is beautiful because they see their innocence in it. They did not tell it what it was; they did not make adjustments to fit their orders. They gently questioned it and whispered, "What are you?" And He Who watches over all perception answered. Take not the judgment of the world as answer to the question, "What am I?" The world believes in sin, but the belief that made it as you see it is not outside you.

7. Seek not to make the Son of God adjust to his insanity. There is a stranger in him, who wandered carelessly into the home of truth and who will wander off. He came without a purpose, but he will not remain before the shining light the Holy Spirit offered, and you accepted. For there the stranger is made homeless and *you* are welcome. Ask not this transient stranger, "What am I?" He is the only thing in all the universe that does not know. Yet it is he you ask, and it is to his answer that you would adjust. This one wild thought, fierce in its arrogance, and yet so tiny and so meaningless it slips unnoticed through the universe of truth, becomes your guide. To it you turn to ask the meaning of the universe. And of the one blind thing in all the seeing universe of truth you ask, "How shall I look upon the Son of God?"

8. Does one ask judgment of what is totally bereft of judgment? And if you have, would you believe the answer, and adjust to it as if it were the truth? The world you look on is the answer that it gave you, and you have given it power to adjust the world to make its answer true. You asked this puff of madness for the meaning of your unholy relationship, and adjusted it according to its insane answer. How happy did it make you? Did you meet your brother with joy to bless the Son of God, and give him thanks for all the happiness that

he held out to you? Did you recognize your brother as the eternal gift of God to you? Did you see the holiness that shone in both you and your brother, to bless the other? That is the purpose of your holy relationship. Ask not the means of its attainment of the one thing that still would have it be unholy. Give it no power to adjust the means and end.

9. Prisoners bound with heavy chains for years, starved and emaciated, weak and exhausted, and with eyes so long cast down in darkness they remember not the light, do not leap up in joy the instant they are made free. It takes a while for them to understand what freedom is. You groped but feebly in the dust and found your brother's hand, uncertain whether to let it go or to take hold on life so long forgotten. Strengthen your hold and raise your eyes unto your strong companion, in whom the meaning of your freedom lies. He seemed to be crucified beside you. And yet his holiness remained untouched and perfect, and with Him beside you, you shall this day enter with him to Paradise, and know the peace of God.

10. Such is my will for you and your brother, and for each of you for one another and for himself. Here there is only holiness and joining without limit. For what is Heaven but union, direct and perfect, and without the veil of fear upon it? Here are we one, looking with perfect gentleness upon each other and on ourselves. Here all thoughts of any separation between us become impossible. You who were a prisoner in separation are now made free in Paradise. And here would I unite with you, my friend, my brother and my Self.

11. Your gift unto your brother has given me the certainty our union will be soon. Share, then, this faith with me, and know that it is justified. There is no fear in perfect love *because* it knows no sin, and it must look on others as on itself. Looking with charity within, what can it fear without? The innocent see safety, and the pure in heart see God within His Son, and look unto the Son to lead them to the Father. And where else would they go but where they will to be? You and your brother now will lead the other to the Father as surely as

God created His Son holy, and kept him so. In your brother is the light of God's eternal promise of your immortality. See him as sinless, and there can *be* no fear in you. (Chapter 20, *ACIM*)

VII. Seek Not Outside Yourself

1. Seek not outside yourself. For it will fail, and you will weep each time an idol falls. Heaven cannot be found where it is not, and there can be no peace excepting there. Each idol that you worship when God calls will never answer in His place. There is no other answer you can substitute, and find the happiness His answer brings. Seek not outside yourself. For all your pain comes simply from a futile search for what you want, insisting where it must be found. What if it is not there? Do you prefer that you be right or happy? Be you glad that you are told where happiness abides, and seek no longer elsewhere. You will fail. But it is given you to know the truth, and not to seek for it outside yourself. (Chapter 29, *ACIM*)

Prayer

I send my prayers from my
thoughts to yours that you
give the miracle of blessings
upon one to another with
complete and utter love, faith,
peace, and holiness, for the
universe will receive what
you give and send it back to
you in humbleness and true.

I pray those you assist in their
trials are thankful, grateful, and
appreciate your help and receive
it as a steppingstone to do their
part to ensure the improvement
of their situation because they
are just as innocent in it as you are.

Here, they will not burn their bridges at both ends
allowing those who help to remain peacefully
intact as you both remain standing upholding
your relationship in love and faith and
without guilt and judgment.

I pray you are willing to give good
and positive energy one to another
blessing your strength and power
you have over any challenges of the
world through the eyes of forgiveness
and faith looking past all the bleakness
and into the light of God where you find
the peace and calmness already in you.

I ask that in God you trust and be willing to take the quantum leap into forgiveness and atonement with the wholeness of love, faith, and innocence, offering white lilies upon the bloody and injured head of Christ, and upon the head of the Sonship, for this is pure love without guilt, judgment, punishment and imprisonment.

You do this and the Holy Spirit showers joy
and peace upon you reminding you that
God will not leave you alone in any
situation or circumstance.

In return, He asks you to choose again to let go of
the crown of thorns, the nails of bondage, and the
crucifixion of death.

Always remember His Holy Spirit is with
you waiting in patience and in peace for you
to call His name and there He is in a holy
instant ready and willing to guide you through
from the belief in bondage, fear, darkness, and death
and into the world of love, joy, peace, safety, light,
life, unity, and freedom.

Always remember, God wants you to consistently
give all your burdens to Him, for with Him you
can never burn your bridges at both ends
because His light is always lit and He will
never burn out in assisting you through
the trials of your innocence; therefore,
His bridge is always intact.

Turn to the bridge that never burns and
you will overcome all circumstances of
your experiences as He lifts your spirit
to watch the battleground from above.

I pray you always remember to do your
part in the faith of goodness and peace,
for they will lead you out of the dream and
into the reality of God's love, light, and eternal
life the essence of your immortality.

Continuously remember God will always
meet you halfway as He stands in His light
of love, peace, and holiness with open arms
waiting for His innocent children to embrace
His kindness and grace in thanks and
appreciation of where He lifts you out of and
into the bosom of His love and safety forever.

In the name of the Kingdom of Heaven. Amen.

V. The Circle of Atonement

10. The crucifixion had no part in the Atonement. Only the resurrection became my part in it. That is the symbol of the release from guilt by guiltlessness. Whom you perceive as guilty you would crucify. Yet you restore guiltlessness to whomever you see as guiltless. Crucifixion is always the ego's aim. It sees everyone as guilty, and by its condemnation it would kill. The Holy Spirit sees only guiltlessness, and in His gentleness He would release from fear and re-establish the reign of love. The power of love is in His gentleness, which is of God and therefore cannot crucify nor suffer crucifixion. The temple you restore becomes your altar, for it was rebuilt through you. And everything you give to God is yours. Thus He creates, and thus must you restore. (Chapter 14, *ACIM*)

Learn to remember to see past
physical vision, a false bittersweet
world we made through the
perspective of the ego's
deceitful allure

And

You take a quantum leap into
spiritual vision and knowledge where
you behold all things lovely and true as
cocreator with our

Father in Heaven

Linda

Linda, now has a divine agenda, for her
glisten spirit of silver resurrected and has returned
home to Heaven, because this is where she is from
as well as where you and I come from.

She will be remembered in our minds and hearts,
for we are all part of her divinity indefinitely.

She was and still is very talented and skillful,
for she did everything from cooking, decorating,
arts and crafts, knitting, crocheting, caring, sharing
and ever so impressively poetic, and was not
ready to leave her family.

For she wanted nothing more than to be with her
children and grandchildren, for she wanted to care for
their growing pains and witness their happy gains.

In the end, she was at peace with her transition
from Earth to Heaven where she will divinely
prosper sprinkling her glistening touch of gold
and silver upon the land of where we spree.

For her heart of divine gold and her spirit of
glisten silver embrace and intertwine like the
golden glistening white vine ensuring blessings
enter the life, minds and hearts of every soul
ever so divinely bold.

Her saintly status God honors, for she no longer
wanders the kingdom of uncertainty, for she is
now home in the Kingdom of Wonders where she

freely roams in all certainty ever so effortlessly
where she is forever healthy.

For she is love and light in which God
loves with all His might and now is under
the safety of His cover forevermore.

And so Linda is the blessed one just as everyone,
for she has made it home to the Kingdom of Heaven
where we will join her when the duration of our time
comes to its end. And it is a blessing to know, we will
be together again eternally where every single one of us
are ever so utterly and divinely adored.

In Ever Loving Memory

of

Linda C. Quiroz

May 12, 1959 – August 6, 2018

Art of Being

Dedicated to Genelle Smith
Wellspring Women's Center, Sacramento, California

We all have been asleep for way
too long. It is now time to awaken
and tap into the creativity within.

Art of being is the thing you want
to check out to set yourself up for a
lovely spiritual awakening.

Because you are creative even if
you think you're not, for every single
soul is creative, but the ego likes
to suppress the loveliness in you, for
it tells you *you* are dumb, stupid, and
you don't know how to do anything.

The truth is, you are the total opposite
of what it says you are, for it is blind
and deaf and doesn't know the beauty
in you. This is why it says foolish things
it knows nothing about.

God sees you and hears you because
He created you and He created you to
be fruitful in all your divine ways.

You are His masterpiece let the art of
being in you be your masterpiece of
creativity and let it flourish to the
surface and be all that you already are.

For you are God's chef d' oeuvre
Who waits in patience and in peace
for your willingness to awaken to the
divine creativity He planted in you,
godzillions ago.

And so you are the art of being of
everything beautiful He gave you.
Awaken to it and go and be all the
loveliness you are and share it
forward with all your brothers.

Reconnecting

It is no accident that we have
come into the era of technology
where we find ourselves reconnecting
with home girls and home boys
through social media.

We are so brilliant we don't even
see it only because we don't recall
the technology we created would
be one way to ensure we reconnect.

No matter how young or old we are,
we all utilize social media and don't
even realize we are reconnecting
through the technology we made
before we were even born.

We think we are home girls and home
boys from the neighborhoods, city,
and states where we met and grew up
with each other.

The truth is you are my home girl and
home boy from Heaven because Heaven
is where we all come from so every
single one of you are my homies.

This fills up my heart to no end, a blessing
of contentment that fulfills the loneliness
I have felt for way too long.

I now do as God does, wait in patience
and in peace for you to be willing to
remember you are all my homies.

And so reconnecting is inevitable and
the evidence of it is all over social media.

Unmask the Ask

We believe we did not ask
to be born into a world of
dreadful tasks, but this
belief is only a mask.

Too often we say, "I didn't ask
for this," "I didn't ask to born
into this," or I didn't agree to
this."

These phrases are only a mask,
be willing to unmask the ask, we
not only agreed too, but we asked
to write it, make it and experience
it as well.

And it is love and light we asked God
to retrieve from part of Heaven so we
can know the fear and darkness we
made and wrote a screenplay to be
born to live it.

I think it's brilliant we can write it,
make it, witness, and experience it,
senseless because no one likes to suffer,
but to remember how brilliant we really
are is blissfulness!

We do not remember everything
that happens has its purpose as we
walk through this world of fear and
darkness.

We are too careless in a world of
dimness because we do not remember,
not only what we wrote, made and
asked for, but we cannot see in darkness.

We were given every warning that
we'd be temporarily doomed in a
world of gloom, yet it feels like
eternity.

But this no longer matters, for we
have reached the era to forgive,
atone and be willing to unify in
love, light, life, joy, patience, peace,
truth, safety and freedom to be enlightened
ever so swiftly.

Here, we are eager to forgive and bless
every hater with love, light, life, joy, truth,
unity, safety, freedom, patience and
peace.

For it does not matter what form haters
manifest itself in because through love,
light, peace and truth, we remember we
are the beasts through our own making
and asking of fear and darkness.

Be willing to come to the realization
of thy holy self-awareness to once and
for all unmask the ask where we
remember the universe is also a mask
we made ensuring we do not recall
the love and light of God from godzillions
ago.

So to unmask the ask is to finally enter
the realization that we receive as we
have asked.

So be careful what you continue to ask
for in the world of dreams because it will
manifest in its time. And, ultimately,
immortality is greater than mortality.

For mortality is but a bittersweet dream
that has no power over you unless you
give up your divine power to it.

And so be willing to let God's light unmask
the night we asked for and His light will
tenderly outshine all darkness enabling
you to see and remember what you wrote,
made, and agreed too. For His light is
temporarily masked in night. What a
generous God we have to let us mask
His light in night!

I'm So Hooked on You

I went soaring into the openness of
Heaven where I was witness to the
loveliness of Your peace, and the
moment I saw You, I was captivated
by You; and as I return to the dream
I remain so hooked on You.

There was a time I had forgotten
what love is because love was a
painful thing, for I did not recall
what was in it.

Now that I am reacquainted with
You, I can never again leave You
because I am wide awake to You,
more than I ever been.

So the idea to create a merciless
world of fear and darkness and
be born into it turned out to be
a brilliant idea after all.

Because now in certainty, I know
there is never any need to be a
spoiled brat and get greedy with
Your generous tasks You always
lovingly do freely.

I'm so hooked on You, I could never
stop thinking of You, for the memory
of You never leaves my mind because

I appreciate how Your true nature is
ever so lovingly kind.

Never again will I agree with my
brothers to brainstorm how to
create a loveless father when I
have the best loving Father there
is and ever will be.

I'm so hooked on You, I will forever
agree to create only just like You,
for You create in and of loveliness
and lightness.

And there I am alongside of You
forever creating in the winsomeness
of classiness, and so I give You my
golden diamond seal and this is how
I truly feel.

The aroma of Your lilies is so divinely
pretty that never again will I agree to
be filthy dirty through temptations so
stinky flirty it's duplicity.

I'm so hooked on You that nothing in
this dream no more makes me blue
because I clearly see all the graceful
clues you kindly give to me at every
day I wake.

And so it is most exalting that I'm so
hooked on You because You are the
love in every heart that beats, and

now I remember what is in the love
I so desperately seek and this is
splendidly true.

Dedicated to God in the Love of Christ.

A Merciless World

My soul is bold for it leaves
my body and hovers over
everybody watching all the
meaningless and senseless
activity of a merciless world
so cold with a heart of stone.

Every mind thrives on the ego's
objective, for it doesn't stop to
think of a more meaningful
direction.

It's a mastermind of ruthless
doings and you are the clay
it molds in every which way
it wants you to go.

As I hover above a merciless
world I see the confusion of
everyone's illusion and it's a
sad thing to watch every mind
being blocked from the open
doors to salvation.

You look like a fleet of robots
as the ego brings down the
walls to direct every step you
take.

You are so blind you cannot
see its walls manipulate every
move you make, for it tells you

to kill and you do it, and it tells you
to say hurtful things and you
say it.

It's constantly maneuvering
through every relationship
you're in molding it to its own
satisfaction not giving a care
of your happiness and salvation.

Realize all its negative thoughts
and stop. Be still a moment and
let yourself see its walls of
damnation.

Yet, its walls are so weak you can tap
it with the tip of your finger and it
shatters and disappears into nothing
because it was never real or anything
meaningful.

At the smithereens of the walls, you
can openly see and hear amazingly
keenly the Voice of the Holy Spirit Who
never blocks your path to the righteous
choices you wish to make, for His goal is
to save the mind by fully healing and
correcting your thinking.

Here, He leads the way to the golden
road of Heaven to your mind's salvation;
and on your way there, He restores your
merciless thinking to merciful believing
in the value of your brother.

The ego is a merciless world, thank God
you can abolish it and flourish in loveliness
and kindness as you let the Holy Spirit teach
you to learn and remember you are the
immortal spirit of love and light full of the
clergy of God's mercy.

God would never tell you to kill or say
hurtful things to anyone. You designed
the ego to control your every thought,
which determines what you would say
and how you would behave if you let its
ruthless walls block your Godly ways.

Be thankful and grateful for His Holy
Spirit to redirect you to the devout
way of thinking to ensure your mind's
healing, for a healed mind brings a
healthy outcome of behavior.

Here, you are ready to connect
with the Sonship and be a savior
to those God leads you to and
them to you.

You will have mercy upon them
because you chose to abolish a
merciless world from the patterns
of your thoughts, for you realize
corrupt thinking is the pit of darkness
that is meaningless, senseless, and
ugliness.

A merciless world will never again
interrupt the wholesomeness of
your mind so you will never again

be blind to the knowledge of true
reality of God's love, mercy, and
your own.

For a merciless world is the illusion
in your mind that can easily be put
to an end if you so choose to see the
innocence and holiness in you and
your brothers' through the eyes of
love, joy, peace, and mercy.

And so the merciless world is a
loveless father, but love, joy, peace
and mercy is the Christ in you.

V. Heralds of Eternity

3. It is impossible to overestimate your brother's value. Only the ego does this, but all it means is that it wants the other for itself, and therefore values him too little. What is inestimable clearly cannot be evaluated. Do you recognize the fear that rises from the meaningless attempt to judge what lies so far beyond your judgment you cannot even see it? Judge not what is invisible to you or you will never see it, but wait in patience for its coming. It will be given you to see your brother's worth when all you want for him is peace. And what you want for him you will receive. (Chapter 20, *ACIM*)

The Rays of Night

All the misery in your mind
is so tangled you can't even
unravel where it started.

There are so many twists and
turns at each corner of the road
you take, yearning to try and find
your way out of the misery you
hate.

The escape is so simple, but your
mind is so abnormal, you can't even
see the open doors as clear as crystal.

For your Savior of salvation holds
the doors wide open patiently waiting
for you to see the exodus from insanity
to sanity.

Through all the tangled, mangled, and
radical misery, you fall bitterly into the
madness of darkness catching a glimpse
of light here and there.

And in that moment, you get excited
and happy, but you slip back into misery
and the joy gets murky.

Here, the rays of night obscures the
rays of light you so desperately want
to hold onto with all your might.

For you see the rays of light through
the rays of night, but you revert into
dimness because of your stubbornness
to remain in darkness.

Here, you keep slipping into every agony
you ever experienced because your choice
is to hang onto it rather than forgive it and
let it go.

This is where the rays of night become
a jumbled mess in your mind's eye, even
though you notice a glimpse of light every
now and then, but ignore its every whim.

The escape from the forest of darkness
is real simple. Take the quantum leap
into forgiveness and forgive every hurtful,
devastating, and traumatic event you ever
encountered and you let the rays of light
outshine the rays of night.

Forgiveness is cleansing. Forgiveness
is purifying. Let it prevail in you and
the darkness transforms to the
lightness in you.

The confused misery of the rays of
night unravels into nothing and you
see as bright as day the rays of light
outshine the rays of night.

Here, you feel the embrace of God's
love and the warmth of His light and
you remember you have always been
loved in the openness of His radiance,

yet you too are love and light and when
it combines, it is most tenderly divine.

For the light you chose to see awakens
you to the simple fact forgiveness is the
release to wellness of mind and to the
happiness of holy passions of
completeness.

And so it has always been this easy
because quantum leap has always
been in your memory to help you
get out of the rays of night of misery
and claim salvation of mind's wellness
ever so swiftly and into the rays of light
of love, happiness, peace, unity, safety,
and freedom, indeed.

VI. The Light of Communication

8. The Holy Spirit's function is entirely communication. He therefore must remove whatever interferes with communication in order to restore it. Therefore, keep no source of interference from His sight, for He will not attack your sentinels. But bring them to Him and let His gentleness teach you that, in the light, they are not fearful, and cannot serve to guard the dark doors behind which nothing at all is carefully concealed. We must open all doors and let the light come streaming through. There are no hidden chambers in God's temple. Its gates are open wide to greet His Son. No one can fail to come where God has called him, if he close not the door himself upon his Father's welcome. (Chapter 14, *ACIM*)

Through the Eyes of Forgiveness

In Heaven, everything is forgiven
because all the ugliness we asked
to experience was pardoned, and
this is given the moment you are
born into the world of fear and
darkness.

As you roam on a world so different
from Heaven, you constantly ask for
God's forgiveness not remembering
you are forgiven and that you must
learn and remember to forgive God,
yourself, and your brothers.

You do this and you see through the
eyes of forgiveness that shows you all
things of beauty and the holiness within
and you gaze upon it with the bliss of
happiness.

Here, you see clearly the meaningless
of all the ugliness you agreed to be born
into; and from a distance, you see the
bridge of escape from it and you will reach
it and cross it to once and for all leave
the world of fear and darkness.

As you are crossing the bridge and approach
the center of it, as many pass you by where
you stand, you stop in amazement and gaze
upon the two worlds that are so different.

For you can hardly believe you are about to leave a world full of fear and enter a world full of love because you been gone for so long you forgot the lovely world from which you belong.

But only through the eyes of forgiveness can you fully enter Heaven, and if you are crossing the bridge is because you have forgiven yourself and everything and everyone you are leaving behind.

And at the other end of the bridge, God awaits to embrace you because He knows you also have forgiven Him for letting you be gone from Heaven for so long.

Now, through the eyes of forgiveness, you see more vivid the remembrance of the light and holiness of who you are and that you are leaving the world you took part in of its creation.

And so through the eyes of forgiveness, you finally arrive in Heaven, the home where you will always belong, because you also had a part in the creation of Heaven and all your lovely treasures are housed under the sparkly openness of the safety of God's cover forever.

II. The Forgiven World

2. This loveliness is not a fantasy. It is the real world, bright and clean and new, with everything sparkling under the open sun. Nothing is hidden here, for everything has been forgiven and there are no fantasies to hide the truth. The bridge between that world and this is so little and so easy to cross, that you could not believe it is the meeting place of worlds so different. Yet this little bridge is the strongest thing that touches on this world at all. This little step, so small it has escaped your notice, is a stride through time into eternity, beyond all ugliness into beauty that will enchant you, and will never cease to cause you wonderment at its perfection. (Chapter 17, *ACIM*)

Truth of Faith

When you wander the world
feeling alone, the reality of faith
seems lost.

You lose hope in your own
relationship with Self and
with others, and it does
become a bother because
no one likes to be alone.

Yet, we are not alone. Be
willing, then, to uphold faith,
for peace follows enabling
you to remain hopeful for it
is then holiness enters.

This will shed light on faith
and hope, for it is better not to
slide down the slope of disbelief
in what you do not see.

The light of faith is a lovely
sight to see in the brief
darkness where you spree.

You are free to choose the
wonders of faith who leads
you to the decree of truth.

For it is truth you seek in you
and me, let it not crumble in
the midst of our troubles.

Faith upholds the holiness in
you and me. In togetherness, let's
embrace the truth of her decree.

Peacefulness and holiness
awaits our acceptance to call
upon faith who leads us to the
truth of our eternal fate.

Let faith salvage your relationships
in peacefulness and holiness for
this is the truth of faith you must
be willing to embrace.

Faith upholds the holiness of all
your relationships if you would
allow yourself to see past flesh
and bones.

Here, you see what is invisible
past everything that is on the
surface of what you perceive to be
true when really it is the illusion of
your dream, which makes everything
you perceive seem it is outside of you
when really, it is all in you.

And so through forgiveness, truth
of faith shows you the lovely purity
in you and your brothers, and peace
and holiness enter the heart and the
sight of you and the Sonship where
you embrace each other in amity and
jollity.

Nicole

Nicole has a heart of gold, for
she is full of courage in the
tenderness of boldness.

I enjoy expressing the splendidness
of her blessings, for she operates under
the truth of faith as to support
the biblical number eight.

As the world becomes extremely
in disorder, her faith represents the
resurrection of a new beginning
of loving order.

Her support she does not abort because
even through my frustrations and
confusions, she has been a delightful sport.

Through the doubtful toils, she has
been most insightful and I am forever
thankful and grateful she has been
tenderly thoughtful.

Through the whole process,
she has never showed an ounce
of aggressiveness. Even through
the challenges I faced, she lovingly
held my hand in faith.

A devotion to the peacefulness
of holiness of our relationship
ensuring no cessation in salvation.

Faith has been excessively neglected.
It is time she be resurrected, so thank you,
Nicole, for remaining faithfully, peacefully,
and holy connected through the whole process.

And so, Nicole, you are a glisten of gold
the exquisiteness of Heaven.

Dedicated to Nicole Hepak in the Love of Christ.

The Test of Faith

Into a deep sleep, He
emerged into my dream
and I heard His gentle Voice,
my spirit rejoiced.

In His tender speech,
He said, "What would you
like to work on first?"

Immediately I replied,
"Faith, for I have none."

He gently plucked my spirit
into Heaven and projected
a lovely vision.

As I sit surrounded by the
purity of white walls, I patiently
wait for His delightful call.

"Place your right foot on the
step," His lovely Voice said.

"But I see no step," in my reply.

After the second time of Him
asking me to place my right
foot on the step, I understood
to meet with no resistance
and follow His lead instead.

I lift my right foot onto the
purity of the white floor and a
footstep manifested so I place
my left foot on the purity of the
white floor and another footstep
became evident.

At each step I take, I see a
noticeable stairway fully
manifest; and as I gracefully
skip up the stairway, I realize
this is no child's play.

For in the sight of God,
I see this is my first lesson
of the test of faith.

Here, I clearly see to believe
in what I do not realize, for this
is what faith brings to those
who wish to clearly perceive.

In this holy instant, He fully and
swiftly but gently brought to my
awareness that all the loveliness
I do not see is real and receiving
the test of faith will bathe away
the surreal.

For faith leads to the truth of
the reality of eternity of my
holy relationship with God
and Heaven.

Peace fell upon me, for in certainty,
I knew of His true reality and the
rest is history.

And so the test of faith is a lesson
given of the true reality of our
Father in Heaven.

It is written in *Hebrews 11:1, (NIV)*: "Faith is being sure of what we hoped for and certain of what we do not see." Martin Luther King, Jr., translated this into the world of action when he stated: "Faith is taking the first step even when you don't see the whole staircase." (To Heaven and Back, Mary C. Neal, MD)

The Illusionist

The illusionist conjures up
deceitfulness, we gaze in
amusement at the occasion.

We see before our very eyes
the magic of its surprise. We
walk away in admiration without
any question of its replication.

We are told it is but an illusion
of entertainment, and we
instinctively know not to believe
the effects of its show.

The life we live on this world is no
different, for everything we
experience through physical eyes
is a bittersweet illusion.

This is why when we are in the
midst of a tragic event, we say
too often, "It seemed so surreal,"
and so it is a dream.

Faith calls us to believe in the
lovely things we do not see, for her
proclaim is a declaration to truth
to wipe out all the guilt of the
tragedies we encounter and feel.

For everything you face and physically
perceive is but a dream of self-deceit you can

defeat through stillness, calmness, and
forgiveness not permitting the deception
to overtake the lovely power in you.

It's like if you were on the hot sands
of the Sahara desert, and from a distance,
you see blue waters through the airflow
of the heat wave.

You are joyful and move quicker to
get closer to the liquid just to get a
drop of water on your dry and thirsty
tongue, but the closer you approach
what you think is water, the more you
begin to realize it's a mirage because
the nearer you get to it, you begin to
grasp that it's an overflow of scorching
sand.

For the blue waters you think you see
from a distance is only the reflection of
the blue sky on the boiling sand, then
you remember that the sun is an
illusionist, after all.

This is the declaration of the ego of
our own making. We must be willing to
forgive it and let it go to see beyond the
falseness of our own cruelness to begin
the healing process of your brothers'
mind and your own.

This is hard to believe, because too often
we prefer to trust in all the things we see
through physical eyes we believe are true,
so we remain in the vicious cycle of sickness,

which is the illusional world that blinds us to
the reality of divinity.

If we recognize and accept not to believe
the magic of an illusionist or the mirage of
the baking sun, we can identify as we mesmerize
at the illusions of the malicious experiences of
revolving dreams.

For everything seen through physical eyes
is but an illusion that will one day come to its
conclusion and this is an explosion of true
reality and *I love to burst the bubble you
think is actuality.*

Call upon the Holy Spirit to show you what
is and isn't true, for it is the golden road of
Heaven He leads you to where you behold the
Golden Throne of God.

Faith is alongside of God waiting for your
willingness to accept her, for she patiently
waits to show you all things unseen that is
the loveliness of true life.

For she is valuable and leads you to the
treasures of what you will cherish as perfect
and faithful.

For what we experience and see through
physical perception is an illusion of the dream,
but the creation of all beautification unseen
are factual.

Heaven is no deception it is the Kingdom of
complete order and perfection, and Faith will

take you beyond false impressions and into the Kingdom of realism.

Here, your mind is restored to the remembrance of the true reality of whom you are and where you come from.

Now, you see the beautification of God's Throne where you are absolutely from and utterly adored.

Believe you are treasured and cherished from the grandeur of Heaven and this is no illusion.

The illusionist is the perfect example of all things seen through physical sight just as the world we see was made to be identical to Heaven, only Heaven is order and we made this world to be in complete disorder.

And so the illusionist is you; therefore, you have the ability to see all things untrue, but Heaven is actuality we see clearly once we've come to our divine sensibility.

III. The Altar of God

3. The acceptance of the Atonement by everyone is only a matter of time. This may appear to contradict free will because of the inevitability of the final decision, but this is not so. You can temporize and you are capable of enormous procrastination, but you cannot depart entirely from your Creator, Who set the limits on your ability to miscreate. An imprisoned will engenders a situation which, in the extreme, becomes altogether intolerable. Tolerance for pain may be high, but it is not without limit. Eventually everyone begins to recognize, however dimly, that there *must* be a better way. As this recognition becomes more firmly established, it becomes a turning point. This ultimately reawakens spiritual vision, simultaneously weakening the investment in physical sight. The alternating investment in the two levels of perception is usually experienced as conflict, which can become very acute. But the outcome is as certain as God. (Chapter 2, *ACIM*)

Criminal, Unusual, and Believable

We never remember what the
day will bring us, for we do not
recall what we appointed to befall
at the time of its arrival.

It does not matter whether we
encounter a killer, an alien, or
bigfoot because we bind the killer,
we fear the alien, and we want to
kill bigfoot.

When we criminalize a killer, we
corrupt ourselves; when we fear
an alien, we become frightened of
the illusion we created; and when
we want to kill bigfoot, we become
the criminal to try and kill off what
we ourselves made.

For we wrote and agreed to experience
fearsome things, we do not remember
until we are willing to call upon the
Sender Who shows you all things real
and all things deceitful.

If you remembered the time and day
the killer to face, you would chuckle
and say, "Oh, so my mirage of a nightmare
has arrived."

And you would not fear it because you
recognize you made it and so you release
the killer from his sick intent and yourself
from the experience you agreed to.

If you remembered the time and day
of the alien encounter you would say,
"Ah, the alien dream I've written to
experience is here."

And you would be at peace with what
is to develop and move on in certainty
it will vanish because of your recognition
of your own illusion.

To recall the day of the bigfoot arrival,
you would say, "Howdy there bigfoot. I
been waiting for this day."

And you would be at peace with what is to
occur but doesn't because you do not let fear
consume you and so you both perceive the
dream and you walk away in peace.

The killer might be shocked at your reaction
and walk away thinking you are crazy, and so
it's cruel you both are, but you give it no
power by being at peace with each other.

The alien may well be amused at your
response and disappear back into the
darkness of your own illusional making
because it sees no fun in the truth of
your recognition, it is false.

And bigfoot could very well be pleasantly

surprised at your reply and he might say
Howdy back to you in his language and
befriend you.

However, all too often, you think of these
encounters as criminal, unusual, and believable
so you take it too serious and react as if you
are being persecuted.

To label one a criminal, you criminalize
yourself, to brand an incident unusual
is really illusional, and to tag an experience
believable is because you are not willing
to see your own self-deceit in it.

For every fearsome thing you perceive
through physical eyes and experience in
the dream is your own miscreation you
wrote to befall, yet you do not recall when
all the props will arrive at the appointed
time you asked it to appear.

We wrote a bittersweet screenplay
and then asked to live it. This is the trip
and the twist to our own life script.

And so the criminal, unusual, and believable
is what you elect to make of it, and to see the
swift truth in this is to take a quantum leap into
faith of the truth in what you have forgotten and,
therefore, will behold the true from the false in all
its simplicity.

I. Bringing Fantasy to Truth

5. Think you that you can bring truth to fantasy, and learn what truth means from the perspective of illusions? Truth *has* no meaning in illusion. The frame of reference for its meaning must be itself. When you try to bring truth to illusions, you are trying to make illusions real, and keep them by justifying your belief in them. But to give illusions to truth is to enable truth to teach that the illusions are unreal, and thus enable you to escape from them. Reserve not one idea aside from truth, or you establish orders of reality that must imprison you. There is no order in reality, because everything there is true. (Chapter 17, *ACIM*)

Don't Laugh

Sometimes when I laugh,
I get a cramp in my calf.

There came a time through my
learning of the remembrance of
truth, the Lord said, "Don't laugh."
"Laugh about what?" I reply.

He replied in silence as I
understood to be compliant.

At the time, I did not understand
why He had said this to me; but
then one day, I found myself
laughing as I listened to a story
of tragedy.

Immediately, I recalled when the
Lord said, "Don't laugh"; and in this
holy instant, I understood fully what
He meant by that.

So you see, when we perceive through
spiritual vision and knowledge of true
reality, we tend to laugh at the meaningless
and senseless deeds that bring us to a
place of sadness and madness.

Understand, it is not the tragedy we laugh
at; it is the stupidity of darkness and fear
we chuckle at, for we simply see clearly the
unrealistic events of cause and effect.

An illusion where there could be no
effect unless we give up our divine
power to it making *cause* realistic.

Christ said, "Don't laugh," because He
knew the remembrance of this through
willingness to listen to the teachings
of God's Holy Spirit would prevail.

And He also knows people would
perceive the *laughter* as if we were
laughing at their devastation, but
this is not so.

It is better not to pass judgment at
this poetic confession, for the day
will come when you yourself will
remember the truth enabling you
to see the humor in the chaotic and
ridiculousness of the fear and darkness
we created to experience.

There is no difference between you
and me when we finally come to see
we are as one in guiltlessness, holiness,
peacefulness, and sinlessness, for here,
we see the deception of our own
creation.

So it is better not to giggle when another
is at a sniffle. It is better to uphold consideration
as the reaction to their desolation.

I am reminded not to laugh at what
I truly see and I thank God for that
because I prefer not to bring any

discomfort to another's distress,
and I don't have to deal with the
cramp in my calf at these moments
I aspire to laugh.

And so don't laugh when another is
in pain, for it is most important to
maintain compassion and faith in
times of grief for it ignites hope and
peace, lifting the relationship holy
complete and sweet.

I. The Present Memory

9. What *you* remember never was. It came from causelessness which you confused with cause. It can deserve but laughter, when you learn you have remembered consequences that were causeless and could never be effects. The miracle reminds you of a Cause forever present, perfectly untouched by time and interference. Never changed from what It is. And you are Its Effect, as changeless and as perfect as Itself. Its memory does not lie in the past, nor waits the future. It is not revealed in miracles. They but remind you that It has not gone. When you forgive It for your sins, It will no longer be denied. (Chapter 28, *ACIM*)

Never Lose Your Compassion

During the time of my studies
of truth, I was extremely blue;
and in my own sorrows, the
Lord said, "Never lose your
compassion." "Why would I
lose my compassion?" I reply.

He replied in silence, as I
understood to be compliant.

Then, the day came when I fully
appreciated the Lord's direction,
for the day arrived when I listened
to another's depression, I found
I showed no compassion.

I swiftly remembered that depression
derived at the separation from God,
but I also recognized it was not the
sadness I showed no compassion for
it was the blindness of another I had
no support for.

I utterly wanted the person to see
what she is facing is an unreal event
that will pass, for I wanted her to
know it is only but a dream she must
choose to wake from in order to see
the pettiness of it all.

Then, I remembered we are not at
the same place of spiritual vision and

knowledge of true reality yet, and the
most important thing is to remain
patient and in understanding and
compassion at another's devastation.

It is better not to pass judgment upon
my poetic confession, for one day you
will find the truth of reality and in your
spiritual vision and knowledge for a
split second will leave you without
compassion when you have always
been full of compassion.

Compassion is important to assist
one another to get through the
distress of a disastrous occurrence,
for it will help ease the heartbreak,
bellyache, and headache.

Most of all, uphold faith it will all be
OK, for every distress we encounter
always works out for the good in
the end of each dreamer because
it really never was.

Meanwhile, it is better too never lose
your compassion, but this does not
mean to join in the pain of another,
for it simply means to bless love, peace,
and wellness upon each other, for this
will sustain the holy relationship between
one another.

And so never lose your compassion
and remain in peace and patience, for
the day will come when we all will be

at the same place of spiritual vision and knowledge and we will simultaneously giggle at what was but really wasn't.

The States of Dreams

We all want pleasant dreams
to never be shattered, for we
all imagine dreams unbroken.

We call them the:
American dream,
Nevada dream,
Canada dream,
Alaskan dream,
Chinese dream,
Japanese dream,
and goes on and on.

We can call it whatever states
of dreams we wish. We can even
label it the national or international
dreams.

In some places on the world, there
are only shattered dreams, for there
are no lovely dreams only dreams of
guilt and devastation of battles and
wars struggling each day to survive
such gores.

No matter how pleasant the states
of dreams we live in, for dreams always
come crashing down no matter where we
are in the world because of the weak
foundation of guilt and change we built
it on.

For the illusion of darkness is so pathetic,
we run scattered in a panic when the lovely
dream we lived is fragmented making your
life disastrous.

Change causes chaos, love shattered,
peace tattered, joy hammered, faith
avoided, hope eluded.

Dreams unstabled, order stabled, let's
sit at the round table and brainstorm the
lovely cause of parables on the foundation
of love and light where there are no dreams
to come crashing down because love and light
are the strength of reality that holds everything
lovely and perfectly together.

Here, we implement order of calmness
love triumphs, light rejoices, joy prevails,
peace victorious, guilt shattered, and safety
enormous.

Now, faith succeeds, hope we see and
in unification we spree in all the loveliness,
holiness, guiltlessness, and peacefulness;
relationships restored to perfection obliterating
all deception of dreams made under the cover
of dark gravity.

So to honor redemption of all the states of
shattered dreams gives the opportunity for
all to live fruitfully, happily, comfortably, safely,
guiltless, and free in the loveliness of togetherness
from one side of the world to the next. Let this be
the effect.

And so the states of dreams are but a theme. A theme we can alter from fantasies of fear and darkness to certainties of love and light embracing joy, peace, innocence, freedom, unity, and safety for all of us alike and we are all the same within.

III. The Decision for Guiltlessness

5. The miracle teaches you that you have chosen guiltlessness, freedom and joy. It is not a cause, but an effect. It is the natural result of choosing right, attesting to your happiness that comes from choosing to be free of guilt. Everyone you offer healing to returns it. Everyone you attack keeps it and cherishes it by holding it against you. Whether he does this or does it not will make no difference; you will think he does. It is impossible to offer what you do not want without this penalty. The cost of giving *is* receiving. Either it is a penalty from which you suffer, or the happy purchase of a treasure to hold dear. (Chapter 14, *ACIM*)

I. Bringing Fantasy to Truth

3. When you maintain that there must be an order of difficulty in miracles, all you mean is that there are some things you would withhold from truth. You believe truth cannot deal with them only because you would keep them from truth. Very simply, your lack of faith in the power that heals all pain arises from your wish to retain some aspects of reality for fantasy. If you but realized what this must do to your appreciation of the whole! What you reserve for yourself, you take away from Him Who would release you. Unless you give it back, it is inevitable that your perspective on reality be warped and uncorrected. (Chapter 17, *ACIM*)

Through the Eyes of Knowledge

The Holy Spirit's Voice I follow,
for here, no longer am I frighten
of the creation of my own fears
and sorrows.

Wisdom and understanding
are ever so outstanding, for
here, they gracefully interlace
with spiritual vision as they
unravel all the confusion.

Their light fully beams out the
darkness. Here, I see the silliness
of everything I made.

I clearly see the artificial world
full of fictional tales. The only
testimony true is the testament
to all the loveliness of Christ and
Heaven everything else is false.

When you face tragedy, you see
the superficial world through your
very own words such as, "This is not
happening," "This feels like a dream,"
or "This is so surreal."

However, the moment you feel pain
and sorrow, you recant the realization
of its illusion. This is insane, for even
through the pain, it is an artificial
experience.

Choose to see through the eyes
of knowledge and you see past
all the synthetic pains and sorrows.

God will lift you from the battleground,
and in recognition of all the discomfort
you left behind, you gaze upon Heavenly
comfort of true reality.

When you see the realism of the world
you are from you look upon the stream
knowing it washed away the dreadful
dream.

Here, it is better to maintain focus on
the Holy Spirit's Voice, for this is the
wisest choice.

For you are now in true reality where
you are most loved and looking through
the eyes of knowledge brings you true
vision from Heaven above.

Here, you are side by side with Christ
looking through His eyes at the fabrication
you forgot you begot.

And so through the eyes of knowledge your
faith will be lifted because spiritual vision
brings everything true into focus dimming
out all the falseness.

The Drama of the Universe

All the props we planted in
the vastness of the universe
will emerge from the depths
of darkness in its time.

As we remember how to
create more and more probes
to be able to see deeper and
deeper into the vastness of the
darkness of space, we divulge
all the props we had placed.

Our brilliant astronomical minds
will study them in awe not
remembering this is no flaw.

There are no accidents in all
that we see, for we were free
to miscreate as we pleased.

We are shocked and surprised
at the drama of the universe,
but this has been prewritten
by our own imagination.

It is better not to be disappointed
at the props we selected to discover
and uncover at the time appointed.

The drama of the universe was
created by thoughts of the ego
who designs in darkness of

darkness, in chaos of chaos, and in
fear of fear; and so for a little
while, we ourselves unveil what
we forgot we begot.

Isn't this the ultimate twist of
the loveless, but brilliant script
we wrote to decrypt?

God creates in love of love and
in light of light, and there will come
the time we will return to design in
light of light in love of love.

Meanwhile, we are witness to the
devastation of what we made, like the
universal pebbles bombarding each other,
universal boulders blasting each other,
moons and worlds smashing into flaming
stars, meteors torpedoing into planets,
black holes swallowing up worlds, and suns
and galaxies fearlessly dancing with each
other only to devour one another.

We see fiery, icy, flaring, bursting, pulsing,
clashing, smashing, flashing, blasting, molding,
folding, flooding, heating, steaming, cooling,
creaming, bubbling, rumbling, stumbling, tumbling,
crumbling, grumbling, juggling, struggling, bustling,
fertilizing, stabilizing, rippling, guzzling; all most
puzzling.

It is incredible to watch the inevitable
unfold before our very eyes, but don't be
frazzled at the dazzle of your own making
of the drama of the universe, for one day

it will all be reversed in love of love in light
of light.

And so the drama of the universe won't
last forever. Have faith in this because
creating in loveliness, lightness, beautifulness,
peacefulness, joyfulness, and holiness, in the
end, reigns forever.

All the Possibilities

From one end of the world
to the other, from one life
to another, from one dimension
to the next, from one side of the
universe to the other, remember
all the possibilities already aligned
to transpire in its time.

We are shocked when the time
arrives to see what appears
before our very eyes.

We are stunned only because
we do not recall all the props
we had docked before time
began.

When the time arrives for all
the possibilities to come alive,
remember it is your illusion
you wrote to witness and
experience in its time.

When you hear yourself say,
"It is not possible," pause and look
at it for what it is not and recall
the illusion has arrived and
remember it too will pass and
move forward remembering the
next possibility you might have
anchored that will arrive at its
appointed time.

Keep in mind you might survive
all the possibilities, for there is
no such thing as impossibilities.

But, always remember, the only thing
that is impossible is the annihilation of
God and Heaven.

And so through all the possibilities,
stand in calmness and peacefulness
of our own creation and remember
it is an illusional recreation of the toys
we made to play with for a little while.

The Sun of the Universe

The universe is a world of darkness.
You could never have imagined the
sun of the universe, for it is a sphere
of blackness, cold, and sightless.

You would never see it unless you are
looking for it, but even when you find
it, you will wonder of it, because it
would be hard to believe a sun could
be black and cold a circle of silence.

Yet, it may appear to be silent; but
really, it's full of violence and you will
discover this as you study it, so keep an
open mind to all the possibilities the sun
of the universe holds.

For it will tell you the things you want
to know and you will know it if you
choose to take a quantum leap into
spiritual sight, for here, you will uncover
the mysteries of the sun of the universe.

And so the sun of the universe is what
helps to sustain all that the universe holds so
be bold in your search of it and you will behold it.

The Sphere of The Universe

The universe is soft like a fabric
of silk and its buoyance is bouncy
and is your friend if you permit
it to be.

It is skillfully pliable like a fabric
of elastic satin. It is as buoyant as
a tennis racket yet as strong as
flex steel.

All you must do is look around at
the roundness of other worlds in
the universe and you see spheres
of other planets, moons, and stars
to know the universe itself must be
a circle.

It is the same as looking at the various
life forms on your own planet to know
there is life everywhere throughout the
universe and in the universes of other
dimensions.

God thought it be better that we house
ourselves millions, billions, trillions, zillions,
kabillion, kajillion gajillion, and, in fact, godzillions
of solar light years apart from each other until
war and hate in our minds and hearts are purified,
cleansed, and abolished from the mind's world
we occupy and miscreation polished and truth
of love, joy, peace, safety, freedom, and unification
reestablished.

And this is where the universe becomes your friend because the energy of love, joy, peace, freedom, safety, and union you offer one to another goes to the fabric of the universe and it boomerangs it back to you the way God would have it be, a grandeur of blessings.

With that said, we agreed with God that we wouldn't bring hostility to other worlds that are in harmony so being godzillions away was our way of safeguarding their lovely world they learned to clean up in love, joy, peace, freedom, union, and safety.

So the life on other worlds have chosen and mastered the Atonement of Christ where they offered Him and crowned Him with the crown of white lilies. As a result, they no longer live in fear and darkness full of battles, wars, and gores.

Their world is illuminated with love, light, joy, peace, union, freedom, and safety, for they have learned wholeness and wholesomeness humbling themselves one to another radiating and combining their light where they are free to shine in the holiness of the vibrance of oneness.

For they have mastered the share of everything, freedom and unification, embracing love, joy, and peace, the essence of their holiness and sinlessness they clearly see in each other through the quantum leap of forgiveness and atonement.

This is the only thing that is meaningful because when we accept the Atonement of Christ, we are led out of fear and darkness of the ego's sinister prison.

Here, the Holy Spirit teaches you how not to fear your brother or to bring fear upon each other, and this, we must be willing to humbly, peacefully, and compassionately abolish.

In the light of atonement, no one can hurt your feelings because you clearly see the voice of the ego using their mouthpiece to say hurtful things.

And no one can destroy you or take your life because in the light of atonement, you clearly see you are the son of God, the immortality of His masterpiece.

In the midst of chaos, offer forgiveness, love, and completeness of your loving thoughts of God's truth, and light oozes from you where you bow and bless in humbleness and peacefulness.

This is the meaning of turning the other cheek.

This is the example Christ demonstrated in His era as a reminder to us in this day and age to honor one another in love, joy, peace, and union, the essence of your safety and freedom in all its glory of holiness, humbleness, and kindness.

Sharing all ideas of creation in unification and in goodness, for it strengthens the power of its fulfillment and this achievement is the only thing that is important.

Here, you no longer see the universe as flat and going on and on and on, for mastering the love, joy, peace, freedom, safety, and unification within takes you deeper into

spiritual vision where you see the sphere
of the universe in the truth of light in
harmony with Christ.

If you take a white background and place
the sphere of the universe on it, you will
see the sun of the universe hovering above
it, just as the sun hangs above the earth.

And so the sphere of the universe is just as
round as earth is and it is one of the most
beautiful sights you will ever see in time. All
you must be willing to do is accept the
Atonement of Christ and invite the Holy Spirit
to teach and guide you into the depths of love,
joy, peace, freedom, safety, and unification where
you will see all things you and the Sonship made,
but you will also behold all things lovely as cocreator
with God and you will know the true from the false.

IV. Teaching and Healing

1. What fear has hidden still is part of you. Joining the Atonement is the way out of fear. The Holy Spirit will help you reinterpret everything that you perceive as fearful, and teach you that only what is loving is true. Truth is beyond your ability to destroy, but entirely within your ability to accept. It belongs to you because, as an extension of God, you created it with Him. It is yours because it is part of you, just as you are part of God because He created you. Nothing that is good can be lost because it comes from the Holy Spirit, the Voice for creation. Nothing that is not good was ever created, and therefore cannot be protected. The Atonement is the guarantee of the safety of the Kingdom, and the union of the Sonship is its protection. The ego cannot prevail against the Kingdom because the Sonship is united. In the presence of those who hear the Holy Spirit's Call to be as one, the ego fades away and is undone.

4. I heard one Voice because I understood that I could not atone for myself alone. Listening to one Voice implies the decision to share It in order to hear It yourself. The Mind that was in me is still irresistibly drawn to every mind created by God, because God's Wholeness is the Wholeness of His Son. You cannot be hurt, and do not want to show your brother anything except your wholeness. Show him that he cannot hurt you and hold nothing against him, or you hold it against yourself. This is the meaning of "turning the other cheek." (Chapter 5, *ACIM*)

Universal Waters

We don't need to carry water into
the universe, for there is an abundant
of water all over the universe. We just
must be willing to learn to remember
how to harvest it.

Collecting water from other worlds
throughout the universe, just as the
aliens do that we created, is going to
be as complex as you make it to be or
as simple as you understand it to be
before you were even born.

If you elect the *complexity* of it,
then you blind yourself to the
simplicity of it.

To harvest water from other worlds
doesn't mean you need to dive, drill,
or land on it, for all you need is a
powerful, flawless beam of light, a
quantum leap into simplicity.

Light is so powerful it can obliterate, blind,
warm up, and lift up. This we already know,
the mechanism you want in the beam of light
to harvest is the *lift up*.

The strength of the light to lift needs to be
just right to be successful in lifting the universal
waters into the spaceship and you already know
how to test it and purify it, if need be.

However, you will figure out how to
create a purification mechanism that
will automatically purify the water as
you lift it up through the light.

Light can power the spaceship just as well,
and one day, you will figure out how to do
this, if you haven't already.

Harvesting universal waters is simple if you remove
the complexity of it, and one way you can remove
the challenge of it is by removing the planning of
stocking water for space travel, a quantum leap into
simplicity; and if you do this through spiritual vision,
then it becomes even easier.

And no need to plan to gather or harvest
gas, an ancient marketing, for you would
have already gone past that by the brilliant
creations of the power of light that will
ignite your spaceship.

And so universal waters is easy to harvest
if you take a quantum leap into spiritual
vision where you clearly see how to remove
complexity and work under the intellect of
simplicity. This is how God creates. He always
removes *complexity* first, and so too can
you.

Stardust

Scientist say, "Stardust is the aftermath
of a colossal star bust dispersing its
elements of creation," what our
brilliant scientific minds call,

The building blocks of life.

They say, "We are made of stardust
and it made us," according to their
physics.

And the Bible does tell us in Genesis
that God created Adam from dust, yet
creation is more sophisticated than this.

It goes beyond the physics we know,
it goes beyond the dust we blow, for
it takes a quantum leap of the quantum
system, we not yet learned how to
remember the function of its truth.

Stars, moons, and planets among all the
other things in the universe is what we
created, for stardust did not create us,
we created it, and this is the twist.

Through the eyes of illusional physics, it
looks like the stars is our maker; but
through quantum dynamics and the eyes
of spiritual vision, we can clearly see we
are its maker.

It's true we are connected to the universe
and everything in it, but it doesn't mean
stardust made us.

I am not a physicist. I am a spiritual
visionist. This means I call upon God's
Holy Spirit to teach and show me what
we forgot, we begot.

He never fails to show me the answer
of what I ask to see, for I choose to be
connected mind to mind, spirit to spirit.

If we all elect to do the same, we would
teach as a spiritual visionist because we
would be able to see beyond the illusional
physics as we leap into the science of the
spiritual quantum mechanics.

I have heard scientists say, "Physics is
fundamental to quantum principles," of
where their magnificent scientific minds
aim to go,

but it really isn't because they have had it
in them all this time; and to be willing to utilize
it through spiritual vision, they will certainly
bypass illusional physics and this is the brilliance
of quantum leap.

The incredible scientific minds would be able
to unravel the mysteries of the universe if they
elect to take a quantum leap into quantum
physics as a spiritual visionist where they gain
true knowledge as they gaze through illusion
and see the dream from reality.

It is true the deeper we boldly go into the universe, it does become a spiritual traverse where we immerse deeper into the illusional reality trying to unravel who we are and where we came from and other civilizations.

Discovering beyond what they can see, for it is what they don't see, is the key to a quantum leap into the invisible bringing it into light and making it visible in their sight where they see the true from the false.

The first greatest scientific mind that choses to use spiritual vision and spiritual knowledge to show the quantum hidden will make history of true reality of the universe, the world we made, and the truth of eternity, what God is and so too are we.

Einstein, Newton, and other beautiful, scientific minds, long ago, planted the seed for this to be, but illusional knowledge has flourished since. (But I'm not doing any research on it!)

However, the spiritual visionist will gain true knowledge of the universe if they choose to take a quantum leap as a spiritual visionist, not as an illusional physicist, and they will get past illusion much more swiftly through the quantum system because spiritual sight and quantum leap work in unison.

The further you travel into the universe through spiritual vision, which is the guidance of the Holy Spirit, you see in all clarity it is a reflection of what we ourselves made, who we are, and where we come from; and we are not alone, for we are the makers as cocreators of the universe and everything in it.

So who will be the first scientific mind to make the breakthrough that stardust did not make us, we made it?

And so if I were in this field, it would be me, but I am a poet not a scientist so I will pass the spiritual torch of glory to the brilliant scientific minds to discover quantum leap through spiritual vision that will show them we are the makers of everything made of stardust.

Teaching for Truth

Introduction

1. Yes, you are blessed indeed. Yet in this world you do not know it. But you have the means for learning it and seeing it quite clearly. The Holy Spirit uses logic as easily and as well as does the ego, except that His conclusions are not insane. They take a direction exactly opposite, pointing as clearly to Heaven as the ego points to darkness and to death. We have followed much of the ego's logic, and have seen its logical conclusions. And having seen them, we have realized that they cannot be seen except in illusions, for there alone their seeming clearness seems to be clearly seen. Let us now turn away from them, and follow the simple logic by which the Holy Spirit teaches the simple conclusions that speak for truth, and only truth. (Chapter 14, *ACIM*)

Total Solar Eclipse

Part of the world will be an eyewitness to the
total solar eclipse, and other parts of the world
will be a witness to a partial solar eclipse on
August 21, 2017, which will be one hundred
years to the day generations before us
witnessed this remarkable event,
according to NASA.

The moon will merge between the Earth and the sun
at midmorning and this event becomes evident, for
she grows large enough to completely cover the sunlight
darkening the morning daylight and the memory
becomes airtight until she passes; and once again,
the skies grow bright under the morning light.

At the precise moment, the moon blankets the
sun, her sphere shadows upon the Earth,
morning skies become twilight, and the sun
shines a graceful halo upon the silhouette
crown of the moon where sun rays fan a glow
behind her so spectacular you remember
God Almighty.

The excitement to be a witness to the bigness of
what seems greater than us, yet we are greater than
it because we created it before we were even born
and this is why in fearlessness we are eyewitness.

For subconsciously, we know it is our own creation
as an honor reminder to God and Heaven and how
brilliant we truly are, for everything we see through
physical eyes, we designed and brought to life.

And so the total solar eclipse is another stunning episode
of our life script; we forgot we prewrote to observe in the hopes
to become alert to the realization of our very own creation.
We appointed this breathtaking event to flourish in its time for the
chance to be a witness to our spectacular design, but it's a shame we
forgot we made it because to remember we asked the moon to
outshine the sun and merge twilight unto daylight would be a real
cause for celebration.

The Darkness of the Moon

The dark side of the moon faced the
earth and the bright side of the moon
faced the universe.

There came the time it was reversed
and the dark side of the moon now
faces the universe.

The moon orbited the earth and arrived
at a certain point where the sun entered
behind and above the moon.

The sun was once extremely bright it
lit up the dark side of the moon and
gave it an intense glow of white, but
the other side of the moon stayed
blackened and so the earth remained
in darkness and the seas stood still.

For an instant, the moon was so bright
but now dark and it darkened the world,
for the dark side of the moon for a time
faced the earth.

There was a time the entire moon was
darkened and the seas brought to stillness
and the darkness of the fog over the seas
slowly evaporated showing only patches of
dark clouds inches from above the sea.

The darkness of the moon emerged as the
blackness of the fog faded out, yet the skies

above the moon was so bright it was white
with an accent of a golden glisten.

Yet, the brightness of the golden white sky
did not reflect upon the moon and the seas
because the radiance of the sky shrouded
the mirage of the sun and only in illusions
is there reflections.

There were no blue skies in this period of
time only the blackened moon that reflected
its darkness upon the seas, because it too is
an illusion.

In this day and age, we see the reflection of
the blue sky from the fantasy of the sun
mirroring the blueness of the heavens upon
the seas, because illusion has fully entered
from out of the brightness of the sun.

The illumination of reality did not shine
its light rays through the fog of darkness
because God respected and honored what
we asked to experience.

And the reflection of the world had not
yet entered because the light of reality
cloaked the sunlight that we now
believe sustains illusional life.

The moon has been since time began
it was obscured from the thick clouds
of black fog of darkness over the seas
on the world.

When the darkness of the clouds began
to disperse the dark moon emerged from
out of the thickness of its clouds.

And we were witness to the brightness
of God's light, yet the moon so dark as it
hovers what seems like inches from above
the sea.

So large it looked as God's light so bright
above it honoring the show of the dark
moon that hovers over the houses on
the world.

This is what we wanted to witness and so
for a time we most certainly did and you
can remember this era through the guidance
of the Holy Spirit into spiritual vision.

And so the darkness of the moon was once
completely pitch-black until God fully retrieved
His light to allow the sun to shine upon the
moon and the seas on the world, the point
where illusion and reflections entered the
dreams of the world.

The Show of Love

Showing and showering
so much love is enormously
heartwarming.

My heart leaps in cheer to
watch love pour most dear
flowing heart to heart one to
another like a domino effect.

Such a beautiful emotion to
guard, a given at the timing of
the clock.

The heart tingles in warm
fuzzies and it is not in the
category of lucky, for the
spirit remembers God's love.

It is a blessing from above
to open your heart and let the
show of love shower upon your
brother through the current of the
air where you reach to receive the
warm drizzle of love and embrace
the lovely tingle of heavenly love
faultless, flawless, and spotless.

And so the show of love shines from
Heaven above, upon you and through
you; the glistening golden love of our
Father in Heaven.

I See the Stupidity

I see it, I see it, I see it, Lord!

I see the stupidity in all the
useless, senseless things we do
one to another all over the world.

The drama of all the karma in everything
we think, in everything we say, in
everything we do, and in everywhere we go,
for choosing to be born split minded
is certainly senseless!

We are all the same, for each and
every one of us needs to tame the
wickedness of the sickness.

We created in fear of fear in darkness of darkness
the design of the ego living in the split mind,
in which I now see the foolishness in it.

Here, we all fall like an unstabled pyramid
that comes tumbling down because
of the wavering of our thinking.

For feeding the ego makes us unstable,
it is better to get our minds settled by
the summon of the Holy Spirit Who wishes
to lead us to create in love of love just
as God created us to do just as He does.

I see clearly we are entering the era of
reuniting with the love, innocence,

holiness, and peacefulness already in us
and has always been.

We've gone too long nurturing the ego.
The time has arrived to serve in love,
peace, and holy without any guilt to bring
upon one another, for the miracle of Your love
has arrived to flourish in who we truly are.

And so I see the stupidity of all the insanity.

It's Not God We Are Angry at . . .

We walk on the world angered
because our minds are so twisted
and mangled.

Some of us walk around on this
world for a lifetime wondering
how to unravel what we made to
entangle.

We grow so tired at the angle of
where we are most fragile so we
blame God for the entire sob because
we don't remember it is not God we
are angry at, it is ourselves we are
enraged at.

We make all the wrong choices
because we listen to unholy voices.
As a result, from one end of the world
to the next, we are distorted cases
that go through all the prewritten
phases as we were smitten to step
out of the light of love and into the
darkness of fear.

Here, we express anger in a world
of danger only to accuse God for the
darkness of the fog.

We do not recall that we chose to
befall out of lightness and into
darkness, out of love and into fear.

Here, we are no longer under the safety
of God's cover, yet we are not alone in
the place of doom to the ego and body, safety
to the mind and soul.

It is not God who puts us in danger nor
is He the stranger, for it is the ego that
is deranged. This is what is strange.

Next time you feel fear and anger,
remember it is the stranger, for it is
love you chose to leave, yet it is love
you shall return to, for this is who you
are and all you've ever known before
you elected to transpire into fear and
darkness.

It is better you take responsibility of what
you do not remember and be most grateful
and thankful for the day you and the Sonship
will see this in clarity and forever uphold love
and light ever so dearly.

For it is not God we are angry at, it is
yourself you are enraged at, but God is
merciful because He pulls you out of the
dreadful phases of fear and darkness and
into the love and safety of His golden love
of lightness.

And so it is not God you are angry at, it is
yourself you are enraged at, but at your
arrival time you will learn to forgive God,
yourself, and your brothers for being so
wrathful against God, yourself, and
each other.

Why Don't Go Back Where You Came From?

From the time we are born, we
are destined to go through various
phases of life.

We cause pain at the birthing stage,
we cause sadness at the teething phase,
we cause trouble at the "terrible two's"
stage, we cause frustration at the
adolescent phase.

Finally, when we reach adulthood, we
look back and try to analyze what
happened that molded us into what
we've become.

For even in the chapter of our
adulthood, we cause pain, sadness,
trouble, and frustration.

There was a time in my adulthood
I caused trouble and frustration upon
another. Then, one day, she said to me,
"Why don't you go back where you
came from?"

I stopped still in my tracks, and in my
mind's eye, I went all over the world
trying to discover where I came from.

I could not find a single place on this
world where I originated from. Then,
I remembered when I was in Heaven
the only Kingdom I ever felt at home.

I prayed and asked God to show me
where I come from, for even though
I instinctively know Heaven is my
home, I did not recall that is where
I was actually rebirthed from.

"Why don't you go back where you came from?"

This question did a rewind to the day I
was born into the world then a forward
wind through every phase of my life all
the way to the day I died twice and went
to Heaven where I faithfully planted myself
to continue moving forward in my walk with
Christ.

Now I remember, it is Heaven where I came
from and it is Heaven I shall return to.

Jesus Christ tells me that my return to
Heaven is inevitable and I invite you to
join me in this belief, for it is Heaven we
all started from.

The next time someone says, "Why don't
you go back where you came from?"
Remember, it is Heaven where you
originated from.

Paradise is where you will return to because
Heaven is your home and where you belong,

for the Sonship Willed it with God before we
were born into the phases of the illusional
life we see through physical eyes.

And to be willing to be awakened and
released from the dream is pure bliss
and freedom.

Why don't you go back where you came from?
is the question that snapped me out of the
dream and got me back to thinking sending
me on the journey of seeking the answer,
which brought me to cling onto the memory
of Christ and Heaven.

And so the answer to her question is that
in certainty, I came from Heaven, and so
Heaven too is your home and one day we
all will go back where we came from.

Heaven or Hell

In a whirl wind of decisions,
we clash like a head on
collision.

Not knowing which way to
twirl, we spin in a chaotic
swirl.

We are constantly led to
the road to hell and for
a little while we take a
hellish ride until we
finally grow tired of the
hellish tide.

We are in dire need to
feed our desire to acquire
wellness over madness.

The mind must choose
Heaven or hell, for Heaven
is peace and freedom, and hell is
conflict and restriction.

Hell, the world where a speck
of God's light shines, but He
patiently waits for your willingness
to let Him unbind the agonies of
the mind with the fullness of His
light.

O' you tired, weary minds call
upon the name of Christ and
be a witness to God's Holy Spirit's
advice.

In the name of truth, embrace
His love. I promise He will free
you like the lovely white dove
you are.

Forgive all that is hellish and
invite the light of God to embellish
and you will see you and your
brother flourish under the cover of
His love, joy, and peace in the
Kingdom of Heaven.

Heaven is yours to explore. Here,
you are free, alive, and well under
the cover of His safety, for you will
always be His adorable baby.

For the Christ in you is the light you
bring and the guidance of the Holy Spirit
leads you out of the dream of turmoil full
of the fear and darkness you made to
experience and witness.

Be willing to behold a world so different
you instinctively know you have nowhere
else to go but to consider the truth of it.

And so the time will arrive when you
learn the world you choose is literally
Heaven or hell.

II. Your Brother's Sinlessness

7. Forsake not now your brother. For you who are the same will not decide alone nor differently. Either you give each other life or death; either you are each other's savior or his judge, offering him sanctuary or condemnation. This course will be believed entirely or not at all. For it is wholly true or wholly false, and cannot be but partially believed. And you will either escape from misery entirely or not at all. Reason will tell you that there is no middle ground where you can pause uncertainly, waiting to choose between the joy of Heaven and the misery of hell. Until you choose Heaven, you *are* in hell and misery.

8. There is no part of Heaven you can take and weave into illusions. Nor is there one illusion you can enter Heaven with. A savior cannot be a judge, nor mercy condemnation. And vision cannot damn, but only bless. Whose function is to save, will save. *How* He will do it is beyond your understanding, but *when* must be your choice. For time you made, and time you can command. You are no more a slave to time than to the world you made. (Chapter 22, *ACIM*)

IV. The Light You Bring

3. You maker of a world that is not so, take rest and comfort in another world where peace abides. This world you bring with you to all the weary eyes and tired hearts that look on sin and beat its sad refrain. From you can come their rest. From you can rise a world they will rejoice to look upon, and where their hearts are glad. In you there is a vision that extends to all of them, and covers them in gentleness and light. And in this widening world of light the darkness that they thought was there is pushed away, until it is but distant shadows, far away, not long to be remembered as the sun shines them to nothingness. And all their "evil" thoughts and "sinful" hopes, their dreams of guilt and merciless revenge, and every wish to hurt and kill and die, will disappear before the sun you bring. (Chapter 25, *ACIM*)

The Glory of Innocence in You and Me

You ask, "How do I see the divinity in me?"

When we judge, it separates us.
To be angry at others, we cannot
know their true self.

To fear one another, we cannot
love each other. To envy others,
hatred brews for one another.
When we covet what others
hold, we steal ever so bold.

These are the ego's negative
forces that create abundance
of relational divorces, which blinds
us to the glory of innocence in you
and me.

We let these energies consume us,
but it only brings us to the brink of
sickening believing and we plan how
to torment one another because
jealousy brews over.

There is an escape from nauseating
thinking if you are willing to adopt
healthy reflecting.

Through meditation, journey to the
golden altar; and in peace and humbleness,

lay down all the anguish of others you
harbor and place it upon the altar; and in
forgiveness, let divinity in to allow
purification to begin.

Here, you let judgement diminish and
you watch the guiltless in your brothers'
replenish, you let anger go to know your
brother, you let fear perish to love one
another, you let envy wither to not be so
bitter, and you let covet shrivel to be happy
for others.

For through forgiveness and acceptance
of your brothers, you see the futility on
the surface through the eyes of divinity
for the glory of innocence in you and me
is only when you can behold the holiness
within.

Invite the Holy Spirit to lead you to the
threshold of the purification process
where you have now entered the realm
of willingness to uphold a holy
relationship with the Sonship from
one side of the world to the other.

Hold up the spiritual torch and let go
of all negative influences and recite
this thought of God's and mine as follows:

"I wish to see the glory in me so I choose to let
go of all the harmful motives that will only bring
misery to myself and others. I am willing to allow
the Holy Spirit to be my guide through the purification
process, for I wish to bless the mess of my own thinking

to ensure I am no longer harmful to myself and others
to only see the glory of innocence in you and me."

This is how you see the divinity in
you and your brothers and where
healing begins and I assure you, you
will behold the glory of innocence in you
and them.

And so the glory of innocence in you
and me is the essence of our spirituality
of all the Sonship from one end of the
world to the other.

VI. The Justification
for Forgiveness

9. God's Son is perfect, or he cannot be God's Son. Nor will you know him, if you think he does not merit the escape from guilt in all its consequences and its forms. There is no way to think of him but this, if you would know the truth about yourself.

I thank You, Father, for Your perfect Son, and in his glory will I see my own. (Chapter 30, *ACIM*)

Let Faith Release You

While we are in the cloud of
madness, faith awaits the invitation
to salvation from the ego's thought
form.

For she is part of the Trinity to assist
the lead to infinity so find the sincerity
to see her in all clarity and let faith
release you from the fear of darkness.

Through the eyes of faith, you see
beyond all the hate, for she assists
in your perception to help
you in your redemption.

Be willing to receive deliverance
from the ego's grip of guilt, for
guilt is not of God and He Wills
you, not sob in sadness.

To see the innocence in you,
you perceive it in the Sonship,
for we are the reflection one
to another.

Do not put your faith in madness,
for it will only bond you to
hopelessness and unhappiness.

God Wills you be in happiness
and faith is all too pleased to see

you through all the hellish foolishness
where you behold the light of hopefulness.

Let faith release you to the
goodness in you, for you are a
blameless Son of God along with
all the Sonship.

And so we are, after all, a reflection
of each other. Let faith release you
to behold the holiness in you.

III. The Decision for Guiltlessness

8. God is the only Cause, and guilt is not of Him. Teach no one he has hurt you, for if you do, you teach yourself that what is not of God has power over you. *The causeless cannot be.* Do not attest to it, and do not foster belief in it in any mind. Remember always that mind is one, and cause is one. You will learn communication with this oneness only when you learn to deny the causeless, and accept the Cause of God as yours. The power that God has given to His Son *is* his, and nothing else can His Son see or choose to look upon without imposing on himself the penalty of guilt, in place of all the happy teaching the Holy Spirit would gladly offer him. (Chapter 14, *ACIM*)

III. The Borderland

5. Salvation stops just short of Heaven, for only perception needs salvation. Heaven was never lost, and so cannot be saved. Yet who can make a choice between the wish for Heaven and the wish for hell unless he recognizes they are not the same? This difference is the learning goal this course has set. It will not go beyond this aim. Its only purpose is to teach what is the same and what is different, leaving room to make the only choice that can be made. (Chapter 26, *ACIM*)

The Man I Love

I love him, but I can
never express my
physical love to him.

For he chooses to
remain bound to this
world listening to the
ego ways.

I lift him up in prayer and
I stand in faith he will one
day surrender the ego
thought structure and into
the Holy Spirit's perspective
to be healed and corrected.

For he is the perfection
of God's creation, but
he cannot see through
the eyes of knowledge
without the faith in
what he does not see.

When I see him, I give him
my undivided attention, but
I cannot speak of Christ
because he blocks the light.

I have learned not to force
God's Love upon another, but
it is never a bother to lift him
up in prayer.

I see past his flesh and bones
and I gaze upon the loveliness
of God's stroke of genius, for
he has a heart of gold and his
spirit glistens most bold.

If he ever so chooses to let the
Holy Spirit light up the dimness in
him, through his own salvation,
he would reclaim many to
the mind's revitalization.

He is the man I love who
I can never physically cove
while he remains bound
to the world of the ego
ways.

I Will to see him surrender
to Christ to brighten up his
handsome light.

And so if I never see it in my
lifetime, I look forward to uniting
with the man I love in Heaven,
for Heaven too is his home.

Dedicated to Paul in the Love of Christ.

The Faith of Madness

The ego is global and universal
in the sickness of its madness
rendering its guilt upon us only
to project it onto one another.

It enjoys passing judgment of
your faults in order to maintain
blame to ensure you never have
faith in the lovely things unseen.

It thrives on bringing fear upon
the Sonship from one side of the
world to the other in order to
maintain its existence, because
fear is what it rises on.

By doing so, it thinks it will hold
you down in the bondages of guilt,
judgment, and fear and it will if you
so choose to give it that power.

This is the core of the faith of madness,
for it thrives on drama, chaos, guilt,
judgment, fear, and death.

However, these seven seeds are
not worthy of you and the Sonship
because it is not real.

The ego is a false creation by our
own making and we must be willing
to find our way out of this darkness

of madness we made, but we cannot
do this alone.

Willingness is everything. Without it,
we have nothing, for God does not
force His love and truth upon us.

Be willing then to apply your faith
in the loveliness of the unseen, for
this is what is true.

The knowledge of God brings you
out of fear, darkness, madness, chaos,
guilt, judgment, and the belief in death
and brings you into the light of love, life,
joy, peace, unity, freedom, and safety.

These prerequisites show you who
you are if you allow yourself to look
within, for that is where the glory of
holiness lies.

Here, you see the Atonement of Christ
where the Holy Spirit shows you the real
meaning of who you are and where you
come from in the unification of the Sonship.

Value faith in this, for she will bring you out
of the nightmare of the faith of madness if
you are willing to redirect your faith in all
things unseen that are lovely and true.

Here, the Holy Spirit reminds you that you
are not alone and that separation must be
abolished restoring alliance.

And so this is where He will have you teach
as He does if you are willing to choose faith
of goodness to once and for all come out
of the faith of madness.

X. Release from Guilt

7. The Holy Spirit does not keep illusions in your mind to frighten you, and show them to you fearfully to demonstrate what He has saved you from. What He has saved you from is gone. Give no reality to guilt, and see no reason for it. The Holy Spirit does what God would have Him do, and has always done so. He has seen separation, but knows of union. He teaches healing, but He also knows of creation. He would have you see and teach as He does, and through Him. Yet what He knows you do not know, though it is yours. (Chapter 13, *ACIM*)

Let Peace Smooth out the Frown

In my second phase of looking at
true reality, I found myself in a
frown as I cried tears of earthly
disappointment.

A river of tears stream down my
face and so I close my eyes to
meditate.

Spiritual enlightenment of the truth
of knowledge might bring you to a
point feeling like you are carrying
the whole world on your shoulders.

It can be a rocky road but also a
smooth one depending on what
voice you choose to listen too.

Allow yourself to meditate. Let peace
be your chanting place if you must
contemplate and it is better to bring
the mind to a quiet and calm state.

Here, you heed to the Voice of the
Holy Spirit. Let His peace smooth out
the frown and let God honor you with the
crown of knowledge, the point where
faith fully enters.

As you spiritually bow to receive thy
crown of knowledge, the whole world
is lifted off your shoulders, for God carries

the burden to ensure you remain focused
on the impending tasks His knowledge
shows you led by faith.

Here, spiritual vision is fully given with
the reminder you do not have to reach
the whole Sonship from one side of the
world to the other in time, for even when
you are in Heaven you can complete your
mission.

At the vision of what He showed me,
I breathed a sigh of relief from the
ego's stronghold of trying to spear me
to the confinement of bereavement as
it tried to consume me in guilt by trying
to lay the whole world upon my shoulders.

God was swift to free me from this
burden the ego tried to load upon me,
for He honored my holy diligence and
vigilance with the Holy Spirit and placed
upon my head the crown of knowledge.

Here, I let peace smooth out the frown,
for only in stillness I heard the calmness
of His Voice, for I let this be my choice.

When the knowledge of the false and
true reality becomes overwhelming,
summon the Holy Spirit in the stillness
of the mind and ask Him to shower you
with His Holy bind so you don't lose
your mind.

Be sure to remain in silence and He will
merge with you in peace to ensure you
do not cease, for He will pluck away all
discomforts of the ego to safeguard
your comfort.

For once we are released to receive
the crown of knowledge of truth, He
always knows this is where we must
reboot and it's OK to take a break, for
He knows salvation is at stake.

Be calm in your investment to bring
the truth of knowledge to the Sonship,
for the only thing that is of value is to
persevere through the holy venue.

To be proclaimed to the full knowledge
of truth is the purity of liberty, and here,
you reach the beautification of virtue
merging as one with your Holy Father
in Heaven as you walk side by side
down the golden road of eternity.

And so let peace smooth out the
frown because God cannot enter
where there is a chaotic shutdown.

VIII. From Perception to Knowledge

8. When you have seen your brothers as yourself you will be released to knowledge, having learned to free yourself through Him Who knows of freedom. Unite with me under the holy banner of His teaching, and as we grow in strength the power of God's Son will move in us, and we will leave no one untouched and no one left alone. And suddenly time will be over, and we will all unite in the eternity of God the Father. The holy light you saw outside yourself, in every miracle you offered to your brothers, will be returned to you. And knowing that the light is in you, your creations will be there with you, as you are in your Father. (Chapter 13, *ACIM*)

I. The Irreconcilable Beliefs

1. The memory of God comes to the quiet mind. It cannot come where there is conflict, for a mind at war against itself remembers not eternal gentleness. The means of war are not the means of peace, and what the warlike would remember is not love. War is impossible unless belief in victory is cherished. Conflict within you must imply that you believe the ego has the power to be victorious. Why else would you identify with it? Surely you realize the ego is at war with God. Certain it is it has no enemy. Yet just as certain is its fixed belief it has an enemy that it must overcome and will succeed. (Chapter 23, *ACIM*)

In the Dark of Night

On the wings of metal, he took a
flight in the dark of night seeking
light, for the darkness He soars
from, he wishes to escape from.

Under the darkness of star lights,
he sees moonshines, but this is
not what he seeks because he
knows they are but artificial
moonbeams.

As he rises through the darkness,
he contemplates true lightness.
Eager to find it, he maneuvers
through the blackness.

He knows all he has to do is
find the natural light to escape
the artificial light, for once he
finds it, he knows he can transform
it.

The wings of metal he travels in,
he can transform to the wings of
holy chariot if he can only find the
natural light of Heaven.

For he has grown tired of the wings
of metal because it runs out of fuel,
clonks and settles.

So now, he seeks the light of God not
remembering His light is in him, for it
is too dim for him to see he is the
darkness he can alter to the lightness
he so desperately searches.

He doesn't need wings of metal to fly
in the darkness of night because at any
given time he chooses, he can manifest
the wings of metal to holy wings of light
and rise from artificial light out of the
darkness of night and into the natural
light of the Kingdom of Heaven within
because he is the light.

For in the dark of night through God's
natural light within will bring the
remembrance of the white wings of
elegance that fly ever so bright in the
never ending gift of light and life.

And so in the dark of night, you can
transform to the open eternal light
within because you are the natural
light and you have always been.

The Many Faces in Reflections

In all the images on the world we
perceive, we can see the many
faces in reflections, if we so elect
to observe it.

In the many faces of reflections is
the past that came and went. If we
so choose to see all the paintings of
the insanity to realize its illusion,
unraveling its confusion.

The loveliest reflection to see of the
many faces that echo is the face of
Jesus Christ.

For He too walked the world in
His era of time so divine is His
face like a gentle ringing of
wind chimes jingling, "You are
innocent and holy my brother
and friend who I love and cherish
most dearly."

As to help you unwind all the
confusion you might see in the
many faces in reflections.

When you see the many faces
in reflections, remember they
are illusions of the past, spirits
who were born into deception
to experience the fear and

darkness we are now facing in
the present.

For we are in agreement with
them just as we are in treaty
with each other from one side
of the world to the next, even
if we never met or briefly meet
in passing for a season.

The past has come and gone,
the reality we are blind to still
condemning one another to
the bondages of its illusions.

For even when I look at you and
you at me, we are looking at the
reflection of the past rather than
in the present of your holy and
sinless spirit.

For every rebirth is a reflection
echoing the evidence of all the
impressions of every image that
came and went.

Next time you see the reflections
of the world, take a good look and
you behold yourself just as well.

Remember the most important
reflection to cherish dear is the
face of Jesus Christ, for He is the
true way to be free from all the
many faces in reflections.

Here, we are truly released from
all the deceptions of the many
faces in reflections that have come
to pass.

And so the many faces in reflections
are but dreams of the past, present
and future, for there is nothing new
under the sun of illusion, and to
recognize your own reflection tells
you *you* are an illusion, just as well.

The thing that hath been, it *is that* which shall be; and that which is
done is that which shall be done: and *there is* no new *thing* under the
sun. (Ecclesiastes 1:9, Holy Bible, *KJV*)

IX. The Reflection of Holiness

5. In this world you can become a spotless mirror, in which the Holiness of your Creator shines forth from you to all around you. You can reflect Heaven here. Yet no reflections of the images of other gods must dim the mirror that would hold God's reflection in it. Earth can reflect Heaven or hell; God or the ego. You need but leave the mirror clean and clear of all the images of hidden darkness you have drawn upon it. God will shine upon it of Himself. Only the clear reflection of Himself can be perceived upon it. (Chapter 14, *ACIM*)

The Ultimate Remembrance
of True Love

As of now, we are deep in the abyss
of darkness roaming among minds
of sickness where there is quickness
in placing blame even though you
and I are the same.

We are so blind we do not see the
likeness in you and me, for we are
too busy listening to the ego's
structured ideas of what it thinks
is real; therefore, we cannot recognize
the truth of guiltlessness in you and me.

We are excessively active in looking
at what we see and obsessively
pursue what is untrue mercilessly.

This is the greatest distraction to keep
us from the ultimate remembrance of
the true love we have for God and His
true love for us.

This disruption will not last forever
for what is not real must come to its
end and we are in the era where this
will manifest ever so quickly.

Time has gone by slowly for what
seems like eternity, but we have

approached the point of the end
of time now ever so swiftly.

There is nothing to fear in this
because everyone will come to
their divine senses as time quenches.

The ultimate remembrance of your
true love for God and His true love
for you supersedes the illusion of what
we made and we will be all too happy
to return to the Kingdom of Heaven, the
very Empire we came from.

Here, all of Heaven rejoices where
trumpets blow, drums flow, cymbals
ring, and angels sing, to welcome us
back home.

And so the ultimate remembrance of
true love is the true love of God for you
and the true love you have for Him for
all eternity.

And the holy banquet is another story!

X. Release from Guilt

9. You who have been unmerciful to yourself do not remember your Father's Love. And looking without mercy upon your brothers, you do not remember how much you love Him. Yet it is forever true. In shining peace within you is the perfect purity in which you were created. Fear not to look upon the lovely truth in you. Look through the cloud of guilt that dims your vision, and look past darkness to the holy place where you will see the light. The altar to your Father is as pure as He Who raised it to Himself. Nothing can keep from you what Christ would have you see. His Will is like His Father's, and He offers mercy to every child of God, as He would have you do. (Chapter 13, *ACIM*)

The Welcome of Your Homecoming

To put your faith in righteousness is to
master the kindness within, for we cannot
see the energy of empathy until we
demonstrate goodness consistently.

Faith of blamelessness is the ultimate
lesson to learn to free the Sonship
from all guiltiness and judgment and
so you too will be free from your own
through love and forgiveness.

This is a step we must be willing to
receive in order to gain the return to the
Kingdom of Heaven where God awaits
the welcome of your homecoming.

Not only will the angels sing, cymbals
ring, drums flow, and trumpets blow,
but all of the Sonship that has already
returned home will be there to greet
you and escort you to the holy banquet
room as you walk ahead alongside of
Christ.

The first thing you see in the ceremonial
area is a fabulous long table draped with a
pearly white satin tablecloth and upon the
table is the most delightful food that will
eagerly welcome your arrival just as well.

Christ will gesture you to the food asking
you to take in their aroma and your hunger
shall be quenched.

And so this is just a peek of God's lavishness
of His acknowledgment of the welcome of your
homecoming.

And so at His Throne is another story!

III. The Agreement to Join

9. This is a feast unlike indeed to those the dreaming of the world has shown. For here, the more that anyone receives, the more is left for all the rest to share. The Guests have brought unlimited supply with Them. And no one is deprived or can deprive. Here is a feast the Father lays before His Son, and shares it equally with him. And in Their sharing there can be no gap in which abundance falters and grows thin. Here can the lean years enter not, for time waits not upon this feast, which has no end. For love has set its table in the space that seemed to keep your Guests apart from you. (Chapter 28, *ACIM*)

At God's Throne

Faith is the heart of all things
unseen in all its holy goodness
that are true.

In order to gain the golden
crown of eternity, you must
be willing to embrace faith
of all the goodness of God
you have forgotten.

For to revert your faith from
all the ugliness you see to the
loveliness you do not see is the
ultimate gift of God's Love He
promised to each and every one
of us.

When you are willing to accept
His invitation to receive His Faith
is a blessing on a grandeur scale.

Faith gives the remembrance of who
God is, who you are, who your brothers
are, and where your home is.

Love is the only reality there is and love
is where you will return to through your
willingness to behold the unseen of all things
delightful and true.

You do not remember, but you are
cocreator with God of all things created
in the light of loveliness. But when we
agreed to make a loveless father of fear,
darkness and ugliness all the beauty became
invisible to our spiritual sight only to be witness
to the viciousness we made to witness and
experience.

There is no such thing as the opposite of love.
It had to be created in order for it to exist, but
then really doesn't.

Because we created it in fear of fear and in
darkness of darkness, it is nothing more
but an illusion and fantasy, which was
God's master plan because He would
never permit fear and darkness to be
real and true, let alone exist forever.

We elected to create in the fashion in fear
of fear in order to make a loveless father
who is vicious and thrives on guilt and terror,
and to banish the loveless father forever from
our thought system, we must be willing to
recognize it as a false god because this
is what it is.

Through all the stages of healing of the
minds that created it, which is the whole
Sonship, faith shows you all the beauty
you left behind as a reminder you are
cocreator with God of all things in the
love of light.

In order to permit faith to bring to your
remembrance of the beauty of God,
Heaven, you, and the Sonship, you must
be willing to choose to expel the darkness
to receive your lovely inheritance beyond
what you can imagine.

Here, you finally return to the Kingdom of
the healed and wholeness of the mind where
you behold the golden road back home and
the golden infinity where you receive the
golden crown of eternity at God's Throne.

God's Spirit is golden. This is why the road
to righteousness is gold and so too is
timelessness and the crown of eternity
and even you can glisten golden if you so
wish to do so.

Here, you have inherited your golden crown
of eternity where Christ Himself escorts you
to the Throne of God where God Himself
crown's you as His Grandeur Thank You for
choosing to return home where you belong
and will be forever.

The Throne of God is a magnificent site to
visit where you will glance upon glorious
pearls and brilliant diamonds that glisten
brighter than any shining star in the universe,
and you will be witness to the stunning rubies
that shine various colors you have never seen
on earth and His throne sparkles golden, pearly
whites, purples, and much more, a spectacular
scene beyond anything you could ever imagine!

And so at God's Throne, you humbly and happily
kneel at His golden feet; and God respectfully,
humbly, and joyously stands to honor you with
the golden crown of eternity as His final welcoming
that you have decisively returned home.

VIII. The Attraction
of Love for Love

3. When you made visible what is not true, what *is* true became invisible to you. Yet it cannot be invisible in itself, for the Holy Spirit sees it with perfect clarity. It is invisible to you because you are looking at something else. Yet it is no more up to you to decide what is visible and what is invisible, than it is up to you to decide what reality is. What can be seen is what the Holy Spirit sees. The definition of reality is God's, not yours. He created it, and He knows what it is. You who knew have forgotten, and unless He had given you a way to remember you would have condemned yourself to oblivion.

4. Because of your Father's Love you can never forget Him, for no one can forget what God Himself placed in his memory. You can deny it, but you cannot lose it. A Voice will answer every question you ask, and a vision will correct the perception of everything you see. For what you have made invisible is the only truth, and what you have not heard is the only Answer. God would reunite you with yourself, and did not abandon you in your distress. You are waiting only for Him, and do not know it. Yet His memory shines in your mind and cannot be obliterated. It is no more past than future, being forever always. (Chapter 12, *ACIM*)

Holy Cake

In this world, we say, "You
can't have your cake and
eat it too," and we see to it
this is true.

In the eternal world of
Heaven, you can have your
cake and eat it too.

Holy cake, the best cake you
will ever have, for in Heaven
you are in His holy presence
where you never have to desire
to acquire His holy essence.

For you are as holy as God is
and He is the holy cake, He
hands to you where you can
have your cake and eat it too.

Through the aroma of His sweet
scent, have your holy cake and
breathe it in.

Just to breathe in the aroma of His
holy cake is a hallowed quencher,
leaving you full and satisfied, the
very cover you once denied.

God doesn't hold this against you,
for He forgave you the instant He
seen the black speck of the heart.

In the twinkling of an eye, He forgave
you before the dark manifestation of
the heart began and flourished.

He asks we too forgive all circumstances
before they even emerge from the dark
drawings we ourselves matured.

For in this dark world of fear and terror,
those who think they can serve two
masters and have their cake and eat it
too is but a deception of their insane
distortion because fear, greed and guilt will
never let you have your cake and eat
it too.

There is only one true God Who gives
His true love, giving freely everything,
angels singing, thanking Him for all He
gives, even the offering of the aroma of His
holy cake.

As you breathe in the sweet scent of His
holy essence, you know never again will
you desert Him Who gives everything freely
realizing no need to ever again get greedy,
for this is the eternal holy treaty.

And so enter Heaven and breathe in His
lovely essence and have His holy cake
and breathe it in because this is how we
eat in Heaven.

The Golden Cherry

The golden cherry is golden
delicious full of juicy silver
berries with a burst of holy
pearly tonic.

The walls of the inside of the
golden cherry are pearly silver
with a spurt of scrumptious
golden, silver chocolaty berry
flavors.

It is heavenly tasty beyond
anything you ever ate on
earth.

The golden cherry with a golden
stem and three golden leaves at
its stem is seedless glistening
golden on the surface.

Yum is not the word, but give
its zests a sevenfold multiplied
by nine multiplied by three and
you have a fit for a king of one
hundred and eighty-nine thousand
silver, golden, and chocolaty cherry
berry flavors you breathe in and savor.

It's like a silky burst of a gold and silver
rainbow where you find a multicolored
chocolate tree full of chocolaty gold and
silver berries most delightful.

In Heaven, no need to plant a golden seed to grow a golden cherry tree, for all you do is manifest it through your lovely and holy thoughts of creation.

The concept of the golden cherry is beyond anything you could ever imagine.

You will see them at the homecoming feast, and its aroma is the loveliness of every holy deed complete and sweet.

For the three leaf golden cherry is the holy, wholeness and wholesomeness of the Trinity upholding every divine deed the Sonship ever created.

In contrast, the seed of an earthly cherry tree must be planted in the soil of the earth in order to grow a cherry tree.

The tree branches red leaves and cherries and a seed develops in each cherry, which is the opposite of a seedless golden cherry made with golden pearly silvery berries so chocolaty and savory.

There are silver and golden grapes, strawberries, berries, bananas, melons, oranges, and apples.

Every fruit you can think of and not yet know of you can create flavorsome spices from a multitude of colors.

Colors in Heaven are divinely, exquisitely,
beautifully, and delightfully delicious and
their aroma is ever so hunger quenching.

Just take your pick of the fruit you wish
to flavor and breathtakingly savor the
loveliness of your creation and mine.

The golden cherry is the creation we
share with one another in Heaven and
I am all too happy to bring to your
remembrance its holy fascination of
the golden cheery you and I created.

And so the golden cherry ever so
chocolaty lovely full of pearly silver
berries is most delicious and ever so
nutritious.

Colors

What color would you like to be?
Take your pick because you see
colors are fabulously flavorsome
and lovely.

We can manifest colors to hot,
cold, warm, form, sweet, sour,
fruity, and juicy flavors beyond
anything you could ever imagine
because they come from Heaven.

Here, colors are not deceiving
for they are purely pleasing
because they are part of the
royalty of God's loyalty to all
the Sonship.

It is ever so delightful to see
the colors of His beauty never
ceasing ever so complete and
sweet.

Do not let anything the world
offers to bring you deceit of colors,
for every color is a sinless spirit that
glistens rays of shimmery colors of
gold, silver, and all the colors of the
rainbow you can mend together and
they give you an abundance of
delightful colors.

Here, you can fix, mix, flick, flip, spin, split, and dip to create the most Heavenly structures, flavorful colors your puny memory has forgotten.

In Heaven, we can divide and blend colors into extraordinary flavors. Take in their lovely aroma and you can fall into a coma.

This is probably what we did to fall into a deep sleep. We just don't recall the formula of the colors we divided and combined to sleep and dream dull, earthly colors.

Colors are most fascinating. It is better to remember to respect and appreciate them, for the spirit is beautifully colorful in Heaven glistening golden.

I have been taken to the remembrance my spirit oozes a glow of silver such a lovely honor to the admiration of spirit.

You too can remember the color you've chosen for your beautiful spirit while you were still in Heaven.

Spirit is fully matured and complete so neat to recall the lovely Kingdom where spirit had befallen.

I appreciate and am thankful my fallen spirit is a temporary occurrence, for spirit

will return to the glistening beautiful colors
at its Heavenly homecoming.

And so colors are magnificent a beautification
of Heavens glistening spirit, flavors and aromas.

The Detective

Even the detectives in this world are
blind to the truth of the bondages they
seek on a daily basis of those who break
the laws of man, yet they themselves
break man's law, but this is not what's
important.

For we all break the laws of God, which
is the ultimate sin of the ego ways, to
recognize this is what's important in
order to see in clarity the truth of this.

From the beginning of time, Christ
has asked us not to threaten and confine
one another to the captivities of the
world.

Yet we turn a blind eye to His direction
of this knowledge and squash peace and
patience to those who scream out for love,
healing, and help no matter the form.

We turn a blind eye because we don't
remember that we agreed to every wicked
deed including the detectives, judges, juries,
executioners, perpetrators, victims, and witnesses,
all of us, even if we are not a party to a tragic
event.

When the detective uses God's name and
false laws to bind another to man's law, he
chooses not to listen to the way of the Holy

Spirit chaining himself to each and every
person he seeks to trap into a wicked and
false deed the offender never committed.

If the detective realized the knowledge of
God and his own, nothing would surprise
him as a witness to the illusional crimes on
this world and the same is true if he remembered
the agreement between him and the offender
before they were even born.

To understand the laws of God, the detective
would have to be willing to see what Christ
means when He asks us to forgive the ancient
crimes of man one to another through all the
devastations one life to another that really
never was.

If the detective remembered his agreement
with the offender, he would overlook the
ancient crimes of the past and see the illusional
truth of what is not true of those who break
the laws of man.

Yet it is better to honor the laws of man so the
ego thinking detectives don't devour you, shackle
you, and cage you because they don't remember
they too agreed to wicked deeds.

But the day will come when we all will learn
and remember the dream of the primal crimes
we all agreed too and now want to be freed from.

Here, the detective will understand to make no
one guilty and do not bring fear or threat upon

another, for everyone is innocent no matter the
form of the obsolete crime.

Here, the detective would see it is better not to
bondage anyone to time of an antiquated crime
that never occurred because he would see he
shackles himself to those he binds in their dreams
of crime and his own.

The detective would embrace forgiveness knowing
we must all set each other free from the chains and
shackles of fake offenses.

For as long as we are blind to the prehistoric crimes,
and deaf to the call of remembrance of the agreement,
we continue to threaten and confine each other to the laws
of man recycling misbehavior after misbehavior.

Here, we are rebirthed to reenact all over again the
bondages of ancient crimes until we elect to see
the illusion of its reflection coming to the
understanding of God's laws of redemption.

The detective would see the importance
of reclamation and guide the offender to
the act of his past that never happened
breaking his chains of bondage and his own.

Here, you are on your way to your eternal
home, for you have chosen to free yourself
and your brother from ancient crimes that
never was.

One day, the detective will have eyes to see
the illusional crimes of ancient history blessing
love, healing, and help upon the sick and wicked

minded freeing them and himself from the bondages of fear and darkness.

And so this is true not just for the detective but for all the Sonship because we are all in agreement to every evil and wicked deed that occurs all over the world and it is your duty to learn and remember this treaty to bring forgiveness and release from bondage into motion.

Abraham Lincoln once said, "Those who deny freedom to others deserve it not for themselves."

I. The Judgment of the Holy Spirit

3. There is but one interpretation of motivation that makes any sense. And because it is the Holy Spirit's judgment it requires no effort at all on your part. Every loving thought is true. Everything else is an appeal for healing and help, regardless of the form it takes. Can anyone be justified in responding with anger to a brother's plea for help? No response can be appropriate except the willingness to give it to him, for this and only this is what he is asking for. Offer him anything else, and you are assuming the right to attack his reality by interpreting it as you see fit. Perhaps the danger of this to your own mind is not yet fully apparent. If you believe that an appeal for help is something else you will react to something else. Your response will therefore be inappropriate to reality as it is, but not to your perception of it.

4. There is nothing to prevent you from recognizing all calls for help as exactly what they are except your own imagined need to attack. It is only this that makes you willing to engage in endless "battles" with reality, in which you deny the reality of the need for healing by making it unreal. You would not do this except for your unwillingness to accept reality as it is, and which you therefore withhold from yourself. (Chapter 12, *ACIM*)

VII. Looking Within

13. Remember, then, that whenever you look without and react unfavorably to what you see, you have judged yourself unworthy and have condemned yourself to death. The death penalty is the ego's ultimate goal, for it fully believes that you are a criminal, as deserving of death as God knows you are deserving of life. The death penalty never leaves the ego's mind, for that is what it always reserves for you in the end. Wanting to kill you as the final expression of its feeling for you, it lets you live but to await death. It will torment you while you live, but its hatred is not satisfied until you die. For your destruction is the one end toward which it works, and the only end with which it will be satisfied. (Chapter 12, *ACIM*)

The Sorrow on My Brow

Hold me Father, hold Your child,
embrace Your loving arms around
me, for I am weary and in misery;
see the sorrow on my brow for I am
witness on a world where many brawl.

Through eternity You've always loved
me and my mind You offer salvation,
yet I continue in contemplation because
I am not so brave to be saved.

Hold me Father, hold your child, wrap
Your loving arms around me, for I am
broken feeling hopeless.

See the sorrow on my brow, let me lay
my head upon Your chest, and help me
remember You are the best love I have
ever known.

Hold me Father, hold Your child, for I feel
so lonely and all alone. I plea the release
of my soul and I ask You please take me
home.

I no longer wish to be friendless and on
my own, for to know the truth of You can
be a very lonely place to be on a world,
many do not see the truth of You.

Send me those who see the truth of You
so they would know of me and I would
know of them.

Hold me Father, hold me close, let me lay
my head upon your chest, for I am cold as
my light seems to fade through the sadness
of this day.

See the sorrow on my brow, for through
eternity You've always loved me and my
life you offer redemption, yet I linger in
deflation.

Give me courage to clasp Your hand, for
I ache to stand at Your side to abide with
You in Heaven, for I am tired and dejected.

Deep inside my heart, my only desire is to
return home where I belong, for I no longer
belong on a world where I am rejected by
many because they have not yet detected
the loveliness and truthfulness of You.

Hold me Father, hold Your child, let me sense
the welcome of Your loving arms where I
never feel alarmed.

For I am lonesome not knowing anyone who
knows the truth of You as deep as the Holy
Spirit and I do even though there are many
on the world who do.

Hold me Father and wisp me up swiftly, for
through eternity You've always loved me
where life is sweet, and divinely sunny.

For it is only in eternity where I want to be
under the cover of Your warm and loving light
of joy, peace, and safety.

Hold me Father, hold Your child to never
again let me go. Let me shine bright under
the cover of Your light.

I lay my head upon Your chest so warm and
cozy feeling comfy, loved, and accepted and
not ever rejected.

And so the sorrow on my brow is but a temporary
brawl I have with myself until the arrival time I lay
my head upon Your chest and never again leave
You as lonely as what I experienced on a world I
don't belong.

Dedicated to God in the Love of Christ.

The Fragments of His Broken Heart

There are godzillions of scattered
fragments of His broken heart of
sadness dispersed all over this world
because the broken picture of the
Sonship is symbolic to God's shattered
heart of sadness.

For the instant we decided to leave
Heaven, God was not mad. He was
extremely sad, for He knew the
separation would result in sickness of
the mind and affliction of the body by
all the danger made of anger. Despite
that we became angry, spoiled brats
He permitted us to complete the quirky
tasks we asked for.

So here we are dwelling in the guilt of
specialness because we lost our holiness,
thank God this is not permanent.

I so yearn to return to Heaven, and one day,
you too will grow tired and weary and
scream out for God's mercy hungering for
His clergy you threw away because you didn't
get your way.

We are all the same in this way. This is why it is
better we pick up the pieces of the shattered
picture to help mend the fragments of His

broken heart together.

We can join with the Holy Spirit to help Him
put broken parts of God's family picture back
in its place, for every case we link to bless, the
Holy Spirit picks up the broken fragments and
tenderly and happily places the pieces to the
broken family picture God sadly cried over.

Everything that shatters is symbolic to every
soul scattered, but one day, the broken family
picture will be fully put together and God will
once again look upon it with adoration as He
always did.

It's like spending so much time and dedication
putting together a puzzle, and when you complete
the whole puzzle, you frame it and admire the
beautiful picture you put together and are torn
when someone shatters it.

For it feels like shattered pieces of your broken
heart because you put the love of your heart
into it.

When we create something out of love that took
so long to finish and the lovely result of the picture
is broken, it can be heart shattering.

So the fragments of His broken heart is symbolic
to His shattered heart as He watched His lovely souls
depart and scatter under the umbrella of sin, guilt,
judgment, specialness, unholiness, fear, and darkness.

Here, we dream we are angry, bitter murderous
thieves and believe we are guilty for these deeds

because we asked for special treatment, which
put the separation into motion.

And so the fragments of His broken heart tore
apart the family of God's holy creation, but the
miracle of His love sees to it this is not everlasting.

III. The Agreement to Join

7. Count, then, the silver miracles and golden dreams of happiness as all the treasures you would keep within the storehouse of the world. The door is open, not to thieves, but to your starving brothers, who mistook for gold the shining of a pebble, and who stored a heap of snow that shone like silver. They have nothing left behind the open door. What is the world except a little gap perceived to tear eternity apart, and break it into days and months and years? And what are you who live within the world except a picture of the Son of God in broken pieces, each concealed within a separate and uncertain bit of clay? (Chapter 28, *ACIM*)

IV. The Greater Joining

8. The Holy Spirit's function is to take the broken picture of the Son of God and put the pieces into place again. This holy picture, healed entirely, does He hold out to every separate piece that thinks it is a picture in itself. To each He offers his Identity, which the whole picture represents, instead of just a little, broken bit that he insisted was himself. And when he sees this picture he will recognize himself. If you share not your brother's evil dream, this is the picture that the miracle will place within the little gap, left clean of all the seeds of sickness and of sin. And here the Father will receive His Son, because His Son was gracious to himself. (Chapter 28, *ACIM*)

The Hate of the Heart

We fear everything because
everything we made hates us,
for this is the adverse result
of our hate for God.

For everything we made we
designed to turn against us,
it's a lesson to ourselves to
ensure we never again turn
against our Father in Heaven,
yourself, and each other.

God did not create hate, but
He permitted us to hate our-
selves and each other only
to hunger for His holy love, light,
peace, safety, and life, not death.

To hate is sickness and stress
eventually wearing ourselves
down and we wonder why we
wear a permanent frown.

The frown can be lifted if we
let go of all the hate of fear the
ego holds that God never gifted.

He will swiftly but tenderly begin
the cleansing and purification
process of the hate of the heart.

Here, you will remember the love
you always had for God and all the
figures in the dream. Happiness and
peacefulness will be restored into
the heart God simply adores.

Here, mind healed with His Holy
seal and love, light, and life being
a forever done deal.

The hate of the heart will no more
exist, for you turned the key to its
exodus and peacefully walked passed
its threshold and quietly closed the
door behind you.

Here, you see in front of you all the
lovely treasures that brings you utter
pleasure.

For to see the golden chest of gifts is
a reminder of the golden eternity of
Heaven where your creations of divine
treasures never wither, rust or turn to dust.

No more are you a fibber because
you can see the golden road leading
to the Kingdom of Heaven, the world
you are elated to reach to never again
breach the love of God's heart.

Teach your brothers of your
deliverance from the hate of the
heart so they too learn to release
from all the destruction, fear of
hate and death the ego brings.

Let them know the moment
they clasp the hand of God's
outstretched hand that in this
holy instant, His love washes
away the hate of the heart.

No need to fear because God
is always here to ensure you
get the miracle of His love.

And so the hate of the heart is
but the ego's manifestation of
the fear of death and dark, but
thank God for the love and light
of His heart and your own.

II. Reversing Effect and Cause

8. The separation started with the dream the Father was deprived of His Effects, and powerless to keep them since He was no longer their Creator. In the dream, the dreamer made himself. But what he made has turned against him, taking on the role of its creator, as the dreamer had. And as he hated his Creator, so the figures in the dream have hated him. His body is their slave, which they abuse because the motives he has given it have they adopted as their own. And hate it for the vengeance it would offer them. It is their vengeance on the body which appears to prove the dreamer could not be the maker of the dream. Effect and cause are first split off, and then reversed, so that effect becomes a cause; the cause, effect. (Chapter 28, *ACIM*)

Film Within a Film

Have faith you will fulfill
your role in this world. Focus
your faith on Heaven and let
the Holy Spirit lead you to
unravel the role-play of
self-deception.

We can change the prewritten
life script and this you want to
do when you find yourself in the
temptation of evil.

Just as actors in a film might
change the prewritten script
they are given to act out.

This is the perfect example to
show we too can change our
own prewritten life script if we
wish to do so.

We are after all watching a
film within a film. The little
television screen and the
theater screen is the actors
stage, but earth is your stage.

Have faith in your role-play
through the perception of
the Holy Spirit, and you will
give a show of love and
righteousness, which is the

best deed you can ever display
on a world of fear and
devastation.

God knows the screenplay is
in desperate need of a loving
replay.

In the film within a film, we
can rewrite every fear to love,
a delightful character of Christ
and our own if we just give it
all our might.

Let faith show you the way of
love and as you walk the golden
road, glance up to see the flying
holy white dove.

You instinctively know the Holy
Spirit is on the golden road you
and faith travel to ensure the evil
verses of your script are unraveled.

Remember their kind gesture to
know you never have to fester
in fear when you can choose love
as you are in the dream of a
film within a film.

And so a film within a film is just that.

The Greatest Healing

We are roaming in a dream where
we see everything around us getting
violently creamed.

This is no joke for faith has been
increasingly cloaked through all
things seeing, for the blindness of
what we see is nothing but a deceit
doggedly trying to defeat the truth
of faith.

So much animosity in an upside-
down backward walk forgetting
to move about cautiously to
remember to walk vertically.

The greatest healing to upside-
down thinking is to be willing,
above all else, to set aside the
naughtily and unlawfully actions
of every infraction.

God hands you faith on a golden
platter because she is more
valuable than anything the
world offers.

She is the solution to the greatest
healing of the dream we made
where you can choose not to stay.

You don't have to transition from
this world to the next to make this
possible, for all you must be willing
to do is bless the mess of all the wicked
figures in your dream and your own that
want to see you defeated and dead.

Blessing every figure in the dream
with faith of love not fear, sanity
not insanity, joy not sadness, peace
not conflict, and freedom not bondage
enables you and them to escape the
doggedly dog world of dreams.

Even the word "dog" is a clue to
flee the dream. Just spell it in reverse
and you get "God" as a daily reminder to
you of our Father in Heaven.

We have been forgetful of faith, but
there is God always handing her to us
as she waits in patience and peace for
you to trust she is the reality of all lovely
things unseen that are true.

For she is the greatest healing from
blindness of all we see to alertness
of the beautification of spiritual sight
that is pure delight and you won't close
your eyes because there is not a speck
of fright to see.

You will be most pleased to learn and
remember you can choose not to join
in the feature of another's nightmare.

When you are a witness to an image
trying to inflict harm upon you or others,
you can say, "Don't put me or them as
a figure in your frightful dream."

Bless them faith shows them they can
alter the upside-down script to right side
up and giddy up in love, sanity, safety,
joy, peace, unity and freedom.

For she is the greatest healing through
all the tangled and mangled dealings
the figures on the world hand over to
try and cover up the love, sanity, joy
peace, unity, safety, and freedom
God offers.

And so love is the greatest healing you
can receive and give in a world of time
mangled in danger where we worship
the evil stranger.

Talia

Talia, the princess of God's dew
so clear, pure, and bright full of
Heavenly light.

In the reflection of her dream, you
can see she was a bright shining star
in her time, for she embraced the light
of God and her own, not in separation
but in unification.

She is the dew of God and Heaven and the
sparkly dew of the heart and this she
knew, for she saw clearly the divine
dew of the beautiful treasure of your
friendship if you will receive it.

She is the beautiful dew inside of you
that sticks together like a light of
golden glistening glue.

For through spiritual vision you see
clearly, she is the dew of no division,
for the dew of Talia is flexible and
sensible the same as the dew in you.

She is the dew of love, but you never
need to cove, because she shows you
the divine dew of love in you.

You are the blessed ones for she shows
you the important parts of life that are
true and never again will you be blue.

She is accountable to the grandeur faith
she has in God so you can count on her,
for she honors the most valuable
possession, the spirit in you.

And so Talia is the divine dew of
Heaven and she shares the golden glistening
soft liquid of God's heart and this makes
you the blessed ones.

The Whistle

I was preparing for bed and walked
into the restroom, and as I was looking
in the mirror getting ready to brush my teeth,
I suddenly heard a long soft whistle.

I leaned my head passed the threshold
and lent an ear so I could clearly hear
the whistle that sounded as if it were
coming from the window.

I went to look, but it was at night and
I couldn't see a person in sight. Then,
I thought, 'I must be hearing things.'

Then, the chimes began to ring, and so I
listened for the sound of the whistle, but
all I heard were the leaves fluttering in the
gentle breeze.

Then, I noticed the chimes had stopped
humming and I heard some rustling at
the front door, but I decided against
taking a second look.

So I laid in bed to relax and sleep. My eyes
were very heavy, my body so fatigued, but
the words in my mind wouldn't stop flowing.

So I picked up my journal and began to
write about the whistle waiting to hear
it one more instant, but it never arrived
the second time.

And so the story of the whistle left as
swiftly as it arrived so I dismissed it as
part of my waking dream and went right to
sleep after writing this episode of my illusion.

Nothing in This World
Is Greater Than . . .

The world and the universe seem
measureless and so it is in this
reality, but we are blind to this.
This is why we seek endlessly to
measure it.

It has always been said that
numbers never end. This is the
clue Heaven is boundless.

Only through spiritual vision
can you grasp this cognition
because the ego mind is so
puny it can never understand
that nothing in this world is
greater than God.

As massive as the universe is, it
too is not greater than God, for
it is part of God who created it;
and for a time, He just retrieved
His light from it.

Everything in the universe we made;
therefore, will one day fade into oblivion
because of its destruction, it cannot be
permanent.

We are the author of all things made
in fear of fear in darkness of darkness,

but God is the contrast of all things
made in love of love in light of light.

All things made of fear is not greater
than God, but the ego likes to believe
it is, for this is how arrogant it is.

For a time, God let us create a loveless
and arrogant father that thinks it is
greater than Him.

Here, we have lost the brilliant power
in us that creates lovely and delightful
treasures that are forever resilient because
nothing destructive can ever touch it.

Nothing in this world is greater than
God because everything the ego makes
is so weak and hostile it can never sustain
itself but only for a little while.

And so nothing in this world is greater
than God, have faith in this, and the fear
the world offers will fade into its mirage
of the nothingness it is, for it can never
be greater than the loveliness of God's
true reality of Love, Light, Life, Heaven,
and Eternity.

The World of Broken Promises and Shattered Dreams

The various life on this world is made
of broken promises and shattered
dreams from one side of the world
to the other.

For we see human against human,
animal against animal, mammal against
mammal, insect against insect, plants
against plants, weather against weather,
and so on and so on.

We betray them and they betray us, for
everyone and everything is mad listening
to the insane thoughts of the ego.

There is no serenity and safety to every
life on this planet, for the danger seems
to come out of nowhere, yet the time has
arrived to act out what you wrote to
experience and agreed to, one to another.

Even if it is human, animal, mammal, insect,
plant, or weather disaster that attacked you,
harmed you, or killed you, yet no one or
anything can take your life.

No matter if the threat is a person murdering
you, bear attacking you, lion clawing you, snake
coiled around you, a lethal spider bite, a plant
poisoning, or a tornado, for the form of the

figures and images in your dream does not
matter because it is all acting out the life
script you asked to experience.

What matters most is to recognize it for
what it is, forgive it, learn and remember
it is but a dream you won't wake up from,
yet you are asleep dreaming you are awake.

The illusional effect can be painful, tearful,
and fearful, but it's still a dream that feels
you can't wake up from, yet you can wake
up from it if you are willing to see it through
the eyes of the Holy Spirit Who shows you the
false of the dream and the truth of divine reality.

Here, He comforts you and ensures your peace
is not disturbed as He walks alongside of you as
an example to walk alongside of your brothers in
calmness and love to help them see the truth of
what you learned and remembered of what you
behold in your own spiritual awakening.

Those who refuse to believe and flee, let them go
and stay focused on those who hunger to know the
false from the true and walk in peace to never again
fear the illusional effects of every frightful encounter,
for it has no control over you unless you give up your
divine power to it by cowering before it and declaring its
reality is real.

For every unpleasant combat is made out of
fearsome thoughts of fear and darkness to ensure
a world of broken promises and shattered dreams
and this is what we all wanted so here we are
experiencing it.

Remember this, the broken promises are symbolic to the unbroken promises God relishes and the shattered dreams are metaphoric, a contrast to the world where there are no dreams, only all things true where His light holds everything together like a holy golden glistening glue that never separates or breaks.

And so the world of broken promises and shattered dreams is so weak it can never sustain itself forever and be happy for this, for when you wake you will finally see you wouldn't want it to be eternal because the pure love you now see you receive with adoring ease that there is a world so pleasing you wouldn't want it to ever cease.

III. The Fear of Redemption

4. You have built your whole insane belief system because you think you would be helpless in God's Presence, and you would save yourself from His Love because you think it would crush you into nothingness. You are afraid it would keep you away from yourself and make you little, because you believe that magnitude lies in defiance, and that attack is grandeur. You think you have made a world God would destroy; and by loving Him, which you do, you would throw this world away, which you *would*. Therefore, you have used the world to cover your love, and the deeper you go into the blackness of the ego's foundation, the closer you come to the Love that is hidden there. *And it is this that frightens you.* (Chapter 13, *ACIM*)

The Calmness of Spirit in You

There is a calmness inside of you
that calls upon you on a daily basis,
but it is your choice to hear the voice.

All the drama of the world is a distraction
that will keep you blind and deaf if you so
choose to let it bind you to the ways of
its deception.

The laws of man are very different from the
laws of God, for we write laws according to
our distorted perception and so this is the
blindness you want to escape from.

Through the eyes of blindness, we see ugliness
and we run scared and frightened through the
chaos of destruction because we have not yet
learned to maintain calmness in the midst of
devastation.

We bring guilt upon others who maintain
composure in the midst of trouble because
we are so blind; we want to see others fall
apart when loss and frightening situations
and circumstances arise.

The calmness of spirit in you is so tranquil
it waits in the background in quietness and
peacefulness for you to recognize the serenity
and stillness in you, especially in the middle of
madness, for this is the natural.

But we are so blind we think and believe it is normal to get all ruffled at bad news, and when one is calm, we think there is something wrong with them and we accuse them of being guilty as the perpetrator of a bad situation just because they are unruffled.

Yet when we make a frantic 911 call, the first thing the dispatcher says is, "I need you to stay calm" or "Calm down."

And so release the blinders and admire the coolness and learn about the calmness of spirit in you.

II. The Way to Remember God

5. Let us not save nightmares, for they are not fitting offerings for Christ, and so they are not fit gifts for you. Take off the covers and look at what you are afraid of. Only the anticipation will frighten you, for the reality of nothingness cannot be frightening. Let us not delay this, for your dream of hatred will not leave you without help, and Help is here. Learn to be quiet in the midst of turmoil, for quietness is the end of strife and this is the journey to peace. Look straight at every image that rises to delay you, for the goal is inevitable because it is eternal. The goal of love is but your right, and it belongs to you despite your dreams. (Chapter 12, *ACIM*)

The Sons of God

In the soft misty whirl winds
of shimmering, pearly white
comes a glistening of a golden
light.

He is Spirit and His nature is
true love so peaceful He is the
purity of joy.

He is the King of Royalty, the
Majesty of Holiness, and the
Grandeur of Creation and
Magnificently Sinless.

He only knows to create in
loveliness and beauty so
wholesome and steady.

He saw He was alone and
made a decision to clone and
through His thoughts came the
Son of God He calls Jesus Christ.

He saw that it was good and
created His Holy Spirit and
adored what He created and
shared His royalty with Them
to create with Him and like Him.

Together, they created the Sons
of God they call the Sonship. They
became as One with God in the

holiness of His family He glorifies
and loves.

It was a meticulous process of spiritual
cloning from one creation to the next to
ensure love, light, holy, wholly, eternity,
unity, innocence, joy, peace, safety, truth
and freedom are never lost.

God showered the Sons of God, man and
woman with His royalty and Willed we
live freely in the Kingdom of Heaven as
His imperial family for all eternity.

Here, we create as He creates in
loveliness of loveliness, in
beautification of beautification
just as He created us to create.

The treasures we value dear to
the heart is the lovely creations
we share with Him in Heaven.

They wait the return home of
the Sonship when time has ended
and we no longer roam a world of
gloom, for we are the Sons of God
He loves dearly and endlessly.

He cloned us to be like Him pure
love, light, wholesome, holy, and
sinless in the safety of eternity of
endless joyfulness and boundless
peacefulness, the true nature of
Heaven's essence.

We can achieve this in time through
forgiveness and atonement, let the
the Holy Spirit in to let the cleansing
and purification processes begin.

For God Himself will gently guide you
through the process as each and every
dreadful dream is forgiven in your
mind and heart.

And so the Sonship are the Sons of God
and you have every right to learn and
remember this is true for all of you if
you so cheerfully and peacefully elect
to receive His love and accept the fact
that you are holy, sinless, and royalty
and forever God's family.

VI. The Bridge to the Real World

2. Love is freedom. To look for it by placing yourself in bondage is to separate yourself from it. For the Love of God, no longer seek for union in separation, nor for freedom in bondage! As you release, so will you be released. Forget this not, or Love will be unable to find you and comfort you. (Chapter 16, *ACIM*)

VII. The End of Illusions

9. There is nothing you can hold against reality. All that must be forgiven are the illusions you have held against your brothers. Their reality has no past, and only illusions can be forgiven. God holds nothing against anyone, for He is incapable of illusions of any kind. Release your brothers from the slavery of their illusions by forgiving them for the illusions you perceive in them. Thus will you learn that you have been forgiven, for it is you who offered them illusions. In the holy instant this is done for you in time, to bring you the true condition of Heaven. (Chapter 16, *ACIM*)

The Ultimate Separation

We come from a world where
there is no such thing as
separation, but because of the
manifestation of specialness
and guilt, we have fallen into
a deep sleep.

First, Adam fell asleep and then he
dreamed the gift of Eve. Their
dream combined and now
confined into a deep sleep to
dream of specialness and guilt
and everything destructive that
follows from thoughts ever so
hollow.

Cain, the first born from the
womb of Eve and into Adam's
dream and his own.

Then came his brother, Abel,
and now the stage is set to
demonstrate in their own
dream the destruction of what
specialness and guilt brings.

The thoughts of specialness and
guilt spread from one end of the
world to the next, for everyone is
birthed from Heaven and out of
the womb and into Adam's dream

where we too dream our own
thoughts of specialness and guilt.

Here, our minds are so warped we
consistently try to join illusion to
reality, earth to Heaven, time to
timelessness, and false to true.

This is the ultimate deception of
the separation and we must be
willing to learn to identify the true
from the false to come out of
confinement of a deep sleep and
be awakened to the lovely truth
in you and me.

Here, we remember specialness
separates us, holiness unites us,
guilt consumes us, innocence
restores us, fear weakens us,
love heals us, sadness is insanity,
joy is sanity and lifts us, battle
declines us, but peace advances
us.

To be awakened is to see through
the illusion and into true reality,
wake from the dream to get a
glimpse of Heaven, and remember
the truth from the false.

This is the ultimate separation
from illusion, the false, and into
the reality of Heaven, the true.

Child of God, come, be willing to
be awakened from Adam's dream
and your own and be free as the
Love of God Willed you to be.

This has been done a godzillion times
over, for there is no new thing under
the sun. And every new generation
birthed into illusional worlds at the
beginning of every new time cycle
didn't necessarily always begin with
Adam and Eve. But this story is in
another edition.

And so the ultimate separation started
in Heaven and now we are dreaming to
learn to unravel the final separation from
the dreams of bondage, fear, guilt, and
judgment where we learn and remember
the false from the true, for the truth of
love, joy, peace, innocence, and forgiveness
unites us and will set us free.

VI. The Bridge to the Real World

3. There is a way in which the Holy Spirit asks your help, if you would have His. The holy instant is His most helpful aid in protecting you from the attraction of guilt, the real lure in the special relationship. You do not recognize that this is its real appeal, for the ego has taught you that freedom lies in it. Yet the closer you look at the special relationship, the more apparent it becomes that it must foster guilt and therefore must imprison. (Chapter 16, *ACIM*)

VI. The Bridge to the Real World

8. Fear not that you will be abruptly lifted up and hurled into reality. Time is kind, and if you use it on behalf of reality, it will keep gentle pace with you in your transition, the urgency is only in dislodging your mind from its fixed position here. This will not leave you homeless and without a frame of reference. The period of disorientation, which precedes the actual transition, is far shorter than the time it took to fix your mind so firmly on illusions. Delay will hurt you now more than before, only because you realize it *is* delay, and that escape from pain is really possible. Find hope and comfort, rather than despair, in this: You could not long find even the illusion of love in any special relationship here. For you are no longer wholly insane, and you would soon recognize the guilt of self-betrayal for what it is. (Chapter 16, *ACIM*)

Where Faith Meets Hope

To awake from the dream in
time and escape it is pure
joyfulness, peacefulness, and
relief to see and remember it
is true that this reality is but
a dream of self-deceit.

You will be extremely elated to
see the exodus of the illusion you
created and thought you were
imprisoned in forever.

Where faith meets hope, you
fully see the lovely Kingdom she
has taken you to and where you
meet hope and realize she does
not release the tender grip of your
heart of all the hope your mind
and heart embraces in the world
of time.

Because there is hope after all
to break free from the pains of
self-deceit you thought was real,
but now, you see how fake it truly
is where you behold the waterfall of
the golden lake you insanely
forsaken for a little while.

Here, you are so excited to return
to the illusion to boast of Christ

atonement and salvation, for He
is not a travesty after all.

For He is God's call to every mind
who receives His atonement to wake
from the world of devastating dreams
we can gently cream through the beam
of His light of atonement to be lifted up
into the realm of salvation.

Where faith meets hope, the pains of
destruction dissolve and hope gently
releases her grip on your heart
because you now see that the Trinity,
Faith, and Hope never left you even
during the times you left them for
a little while.

God does not hold this against you
because He loves you and He will
never forsake the Sonship no matter
how long it takes to bring us all back
to our divine senses in oneness.

For His Will and yours is to see all
relationships entirely restored through
forgiveness of all the madness.

For He brings you out of the maze of
fear to love, sadness to happiness,
wretchedness to righteousness,
specialness to genuineness, guiltiness
to guiltlessness, sinfulness to holiness,
insanity to sanity, hatefulness to
pleasantness, bondage to freedom,

danger to safety, and separation to
unification.

Here, love reinstated, joy reestablished,
peace restored, holiness recreated,
innocence returned, goodness reloaded,
wellness replenished, pleasantness,
filled, peacefulness renewed, freedom
certain, safety a given, and unity agreed,
all in one, an overflow of your holy cup
as a congratulatory salute that you made
it through the maze of illusion to the
amazement of the reality of Heaven.

Here, you will return to the Kingdom
of Heaven where you spree freely
acknowledging its eternal beauty.

And so embrace where faith meets hope, for
they bring you all these lovely gifts to help
you cope as a mortal to the remembrance
of your immortality.

VI. The Bridge to the Real World

10. Be glad you have escaped the mockery of salvation the ego offered you, and look not back with longing on the travesty it made of your relationships. Now no one need suffer, for you have come too far to yield to the illusion of the beauty and holiness of guilt. Only the wholly insane could look on death and suffering, sickness and despair, and see it thus. What guilt has wrought is ugly, fearful and very dangerous. See no illusion of truth and beauty there. And be you thankful that there *is* a place where truth and beauty wait for you. Go on to meet them gladly, and learn how much awaits you for the simple willingness to give up nothing *because* it is nothing. (Chapter 16, *ACIM*)

Turning on Yourself

In the dream, you turn on
yourself because of the
self-deceit you are blind to,
in fact, because of this every-
thing eventually turns on itself.

If we elect to stick to the insane
ideas of sickness, we fall into its
ferocious cycle of cruelness.

The nature of the ego is vicious
to every ambitious mind who
seeks to leave its thoughts of
maliciousness.

It turns on you so it's like turning
on yourself and you wonder what
happened when it's all over when
really it never happened because
it is an illusion of the ego.

The ego is suspicious of everyone
who seeks to leave its unambitious
ways to get to the golden circle of
uprightness.

For it thrives on drowning you
in the guilt of the past always
making sure you blame yourself
for its critical bombshell.

It's a sadistic circle, you can't
seem to get out of and you can't
if you elect to listen to the lies of
it, for the outcome of heeding to
its voice is wicked behavior we
blame on the devil and say, "The
devil made me do it."

The "devil" is the same as the "ego"
and it can't make you do anything
you really don't want to do, for you
have a choice to listen to the righteous
Voice Who is the Holy Spirit always
with you.

He waits in patience and peace for
your invitation to your holy cognition
where He enters and lets you see the
loveliness in you through His perception.

To see through His eyes brings you gently
out of the vicious circle of constantly turning
on yourself lashing out the guilt of it inward
and onto others.

Don't underestimate the power of the Holy
Spirit, for His peace is not weakness because
He is very capable of taking you to the fullest
length of the beauty in you.

He is the master of relational restoration that
for a time is shattered into oblivion.

You get huffy and puffy with others not realizing
you are just turning on yourself each time you get
grumpy and inflated.

The Holy Spirit can deflate it if you allow Him to
teach you how to let go of all the hate and anger
to look past all its animosity and danger.

Beyond this, you see the wonder of the beauty
up yonder the Kingdom of Heaven you always
pondered.

And so turning on yourself is everything
you think, say, and do out of fear, hate,
and anger.

VII. The End of Illusions

3. Do not underestimate the intensity of the ego's drive for vengeance on the past. It is completely savage and completely insane. For the ego remembers everything you have done that has offended it, and seeks retribution of you. The fantasies it brings to its chosen relationships in which to act out its hate are fantasies of your destruction. For the ego holds the past against you, and in your escape from the past it sees itself deprived of the vengeance it believes you so justly merit. Yet without your alliance in your own destruction, the ego could not hold you to the past. In the special relationship you are allowing your destruction to be. That this is insane is obvious. But what is less obvious is that the present is useless to you while you pursue the ego's goal as its ally. (Chapter 16, *ACIM*)

The Golden Circle

The world is round, the sun
is round, the moon is round,
the stars are round, in fact,
even the universe is round.

The only reason we can't see
the roundness of the universe
is because we cannot reach
above its atmosphere to be
able to see the nature of its
figure.

Yet there are an abundant
of clues to show us it's round,
and one day, our brilliant minds
who study the universe will
clearly see the evidence of the
circle of the universe.

The circle is perfect for it is the
evidence of completion and it
is a wonder of sensation to
everything on it that it holds.

When we seek to find who we
are and where we come from,
we travel in a circle; and when
we complete the circle, we end
up at the same place where we
started, but now we see things
differently.

For through the travels of the circle, we learn of spiritual vision and knowledge where we find our answers and the answer you will always find through the Holy Spirit is the connection to God at the finish line.

Because when you circle the path of which you seek of you and everything, you will always find God at the completion of the circle.

For God is complete and sweet and you will bow to His golden feet confessing His holiness, loyalty, royalty, and yours as you, once again, join as one.

This is where you enter the golden circle, which completes your journey to the face of Christ where you are joined most tender and sweet at the golden circle of life eternal where you see it is true God is your Creator and you are just as holy and sinless as He is.

For the golden circle holds your salvation of mind from fear to love the holiness of the Son of God, you and the Sonship, and this is the ultimate connection.

And so the golden circle completes
the things you seek through God's
spiritual vision and knowledge the
Holy Spirit gifts you through your
mission to find the answers to
everything.

Salvation and the Holy Relationship

Introduction

4. Think what a holy relationship can teach! Here is belief in differences undone. Here is the faith in differences shifted to sameness. And here is sight of differences transformed to vision. Reason now can lead you and your brother to the logical conclusion of your union. It must extend, as you extended when you and he joined. It must reach out beyond itself, as you reached out beyond the body, to let you and your brother be joined. And now the sameness that you saw extends and finally removes all sense of differences, so that the sameness that lies beneath them all becomes apparent. Here is the golden circle where you recognize the Son of God. For what is born into a holy relationship can never end. (Chapter 22, *ACIM*)

The Illusion of Differences

Time and time again, I hear
people try to explain how
different we all are and go
as far as declaring others
to be "special."

The truth is we are the same,
for you are no different from
me and I am no different from
you.

If you look within and see your
lovely spirit and then look passed
my flesh and bones, you will
see we are the same.

It is only on the outside we
look diverse and this triggers
what we label "special
relationships."

But this too was prewritten
to be an inevitable occurrence
for everyone to experience the
illusion of differences.

Now, we must be willing to
learn and remember we are
all holy and sinless because
we are all spirit and the body
is its armor that gets inflicted.

When God looks upon us, He
looks past flesh and bones and
sees the specialness of spirit.

This is where we are all special
through His eyes, for He loves
us dearly always joining His
love equally upon all of us.

We all get an even share of
His true love we crushed to
follow the rebellious thoughts
of Lucifer.

God does not hold this against
us because He truly loves us
and His love for us will never
cease and for this I am ever so
pleased.

And I invite you to join me in
this delightful truth of God's
call to you for the remembrance
of His endless Love for you and
your never-ending love for Him.

For it is the illusion of differences
on the surface that distracts us from
Him, but we no longer have to be
sidetrack, for we are in the era of
a powerful holy comeback.

No longer let the illusion of differences
be a distraction that blinds you from the
equality of who we are, for we must be

willing to look past flesh and bones just as God does.

And so the truth is, the Sonship is just as part of the Trinity as God, Christ, and the Holy Spirit is because God created us to be as one with Him for all eternity; therefore, despite the illusion of differences, we are all the same and special in the eyes and heart of God and we are never alone.

IV. The Two Pictures

2. In this world it is impossible to create. Yet it *is* possible to make happy. I have said repeatedly that the Holy Spirit would not deprive you of your special relationships, but would transform them. And all that is meant by that is that He will restore to them the function given them by God. The function you have given them is clearly not to make happy. But the holy relationship shares God's purpose, rather than aiming to make a substitute for it. Every special relationship you have made is a substitute for God's Will, and glorifies yours instead of His because of the illusion that they are different. (Chapter 17, *ACIM*)

His Voice Always Speaks to You Twenty-Four Seven

Twenty-four seven we are
spoken to, for the Holy Spirit
is always speaking to the
memory of God.

The mind is so cluttered
with the noise of the world
we ignore His peaceful Voice
so soft, yet most great.

His Voice always speaks to
you and your day will come
when you will hear Him and
listen to Him.

You will be amazed to learn
how to get through the maze
of a jumbled world full of
mumbled and senseless noise
you one day won't care to
listen to anymore.

This is inevitable, and this
time ensures, for that is what
time is for to help you hear
the call of God's Voice.

Through His Holy Spirit Who
stands by in patience and peace
for your arrival time to finally be

willing to hear His Voice that
always speaks to you on a daily
basis will come through.

This is factual to every case
birthed on earth and you will
heed to His Voice that always
speaks to you twenty-four seven.

For He knows the day and time
of your arrival to hear and listen
to the attention to the call of
God's truth is inevitable.

The sooner your willingness to
hear and listen, the sooner you
will know the truth of everything
curtailing your wandering and
suffering.

And so be willing then to listen
to His Voice that always speaks
to you twenty-four seven.

IV. The Two Pictures

3. You have made very real relationships even in this world. Yet you do not recognize them because you have raised their substitutes to such predominance that, when truth calls to you, as it does constantly, you answer with a substitute. Every special relationship you have made has, as its fundamental purpose, the aim of occupying your mind so completely that you will not hear the call of truth. (Chapter 17, *ACIM*)

The Insanity of Your Thinking

When you realize there is no
safety in a world you were born
into, you are in constant awareness
of danger; but this is no stranger, yet
it is the stranger, for you just forgot
you propped it to popup in its time.

This is the insanity of your own
thinking, but in deep denial of its
sneaky, trickery ways you made.

It is better to be willing to remember
you are the author of the insanity of
your thinking and peacefully admit to it.

This will enable you to be free from its
stealthy surprise as it tries to dictate the
fear of your demise.

Rather than living in constant fear, live
your life in awareness that anything can
happen at any moment.

To learn and remember the insanity
of your thinking is your own making
will help you to be happy and at peace
in the moments of your life when things
are sane, calm, and pleasant.

Even in the midst of tragic storms or
fearful forms, you will be in serenity
as you remember this is all your own

making of insanity, you asked to be
born into and experience.

*How can you be afraid of what you
you yourself realize you made?*

Fear might be the initial reaction when
unpleasant events arrive, but if you bring
the awareness of your insane creation to
the forefront to no longer take the brunt
of its surprise, you won't let it dictate
your demise.

Through calmness and peace, don't
give it the power and it will cower
into oblivion, for the insanity of
your thinking is nothing but an
illusion.

It's all a dream, a mistake of fake
events you planted to arrive at its
appointed time; and if you remember
this, you will no longer become
fearful and sick at its frightful flick.

Because to recall the insanity you
made takes the fear out of the fun
you thought it would be and all the
fake occurrences you experience
and see all around you will be
meaningless deeds, indeed.

And so the insanity of your thinking
is but an act of faking all that we
fantasized to experience and be
glad it's all fake, for God sake.

IV. The Two Pictures

5. The ego is always alert to threat, and the part of your mind into which the ego was accepted is very anxious to preserve its reason, as it sees it. It does not realize that it is totally insane. And you must realize just what this means if you would be restored to sanity. The insane protect their thought systems, but they do so insanely. And all their defenses are as insane as what they are supposed to protect. The separation has nothing in it, no part, no "reason," and no attribute that is not insane. And its "protection" is part of it, as insane as the whole. The special relationship, which is its chief defense, must therefore be insane. (Chapter 17, *ACIM*)

The Rewarding Feeling
Feeds the Ego

God doesn't need praise of
how great He is nor does He
need anyone to cry on His
shoulder to feel rewarded
as your Savior.

For the rewarding feeling
feeds the ego and God has
no ego, for He is pure love
that only asks you love Him
back.

Be genuine in your love for
Him because He knows when
you fake it to make it through
a world so tainted and painted
with the illusion of an ancient
ego.

The rewarding feeling feeds
the ego even when you are
clapping to show you are
happy at another's skill and
talent.

It feels rewarding to the
successor who worked long
and hard to feed the ego.

Your praise to every success
of the ego swells its head and
puffs out its chest who faked
the way through the challenges
of the illusion of its life script.

You chose to clap at another's
success while you fall down at
every step, and they don't even
know you exist to help you up
in the times of rift.

Even if they know you exist,
they would pass you up with
their nose lifted and not a
blessing gifted because you
already gave them the
rewarding feeling that feeds
the ego.

They listen to this puny god
and shove you aside because
they don't care for your
own victory, well-being,
and demise.

Just look at the evidence of
starvation and homelessness
all over the world, for the ego
does not seek to bring salvation,
only damnation.

For the ego is so swelled it wants
the world all to itself, this is the
result of the rewarding feeling
that feeds the ego.

To worship God in authentic
love, appreciation, and thanks,
He blesses you with the desires
of your heart, whereas the ego
gives you nothing for your praise
of its accomplishments.

For it is selfish and greedy and
does not care for those who are
selfless and needy.

Give God appreciation and
thanks and lift the ego to His
golden feet and pray deliverance
from its selfish and greedy feats.

Forgive its behavior, step aside,
and let the Savior do His part
to ensure they depart from the
ego's thought system and into
the embracement of God's bosom.

Have faith in your thoughtful
prayers, for God collects them
and honors them.

You will be OK because your
loving prayers are successors and
this makes you a holy achiever and
this is the only thing that matters.

And so the rewarding feeling feeds
the ego, but worshipping God in true
love, thanking Him for His blessings of

ego deliverance in appreciation of His
genuine Love, is a magnificent blessing
to Him He will return to you in abundance
and you will behold His miracles.

The Cover of the Ego

Every protection is a
deception and every
resistance is a scream
for love and help.

For every relationship
you claim to be special
was derived from jealousy
and retaliation.

This is a weak foundation
that will eventually come
crumbling down like a
house of cards over any
little slipup your fingers
touch anywhere around it
and even at its base.

The cover of the ego is very
deceiving for its frame is
the ultimate betrayal most
weak and misleading.

Its frame is full of glistening
emeralds and sparkly teardrop
diamonds most enticing, but look
closer at its picture and you will
see the gift of conflict it offers.

You do not want the cover of
the ego, for to discover its betrayal
can be grievously devastating.

A heartbreaking realization that
the world you picked is fake, but
to learn and remember it is of your
your own making brings a chuckle
rather than a fearful buckle.

And so the cover of the ego is a
deception of destruction mixed in
with shattered pleasures.

IV. The Two Pictures

7. It is essential to realize that all defenses *do* what they would defend. The underlying basis for their effectiveness is that they offer what they defend. What they defend is placed in them for safe-keeping, and as they operate they bring it to you. Every defense operates by giving gifts, and the gift is always a miniature of the thought system the defense protects, set in a golden frame. The frame is very elaborate, all set with jewels, and deeply carved and polished. Its purpose is to be of value *in itself,* and to divert your attention from what it encloses. But the frame without the picture you cannot have. Defenses operate to make you think you can. (Chapter 17, *ACIM*)

The Ego's Offering

As you stroll through the
shadows of darkness from afar,
you see sparkles of diamonds
that can be luring and enticing.

At the corner of your eye, you
catch a signal of a shimmery light
closer to you, but the sparkly
flickers in the distance of its
dimness seem more inviting.

As you approach near, you see
deep red rubies and teardrop
diamonds placed neatly in the
golden carvings of the structure
of the ego's offering.

You are so mesmerized by
the beauty of the frame you
cannot see it's the ego's trap
that will never give you the
gift of remembrance of who
you truly are and where you
come from.

You cove the frame but then
realize the frame is not the
offering, for it is the picture
it proffers.

You gaze your eyes upon the
picture and see all the beauty
its world offers.

Blinded by the charm it shows,
you cannot see the conflict
mixed up in it.

For the ego's offering is deceiving
and its picture pitches thieving,
killing, and grieving; but if you
choose not to see this, it can be
dreadfully misleading.

And you will be hurdled into its
web of all its discomforts taking
you through phases of pains and
slains of pleasures and sorrows.

You think back and remember
the deep red rubies as you
become a witness to all the
bloodshed of the picturesque
you find yourself in.

You recall the shape of the teardrop
diamonds realizing it's a symbol to
the fears and tears you see all over
the charming world of beauty of the
ego's offering.

The ego's frame has shattered
annihilating all the beauty its
picture gifted, for it's a dream
of attraction most devastating.

Now you wonder what the
shimmery frame of light was
that was closer to you, eager
to get your attention to the
realism of the world you forgot.

It's never too late to take a better
look at what the glistening frame
closer to you presented as opposed
to the ego's offering you first
accepted.

And so the ego's offering is charming
intertwined with desolation, but it
is never too late to choose again.

IV. The Two Pictures

8. The special relationship has the most imposing and deceptive frame of all the defenses the ego uses. Its thought system is offered here, surrounded by a frame so heavy and so elaborate that the picture is almost obliterated by its imposing structure. Into the frame are woven all sorts of fanciful and fragmented illusions of love, set with dreams of sacrifice and self-aggrandizement, and interlaced with gilded threads of self-destruction. The glitter of blood shines like rubies, and the tears are faceted like diamonds and gleam in the dim light in which the offering is made.

9. Look at the *picture*. Do not let the frame distract you. This gift is given you for your damnation, and if you take it you will believe that you *are* damned. You cannot have the frame without the picture. What you value is the frame, for there you see no conflict. Yet the frame is only the wrapping for the gift of conflict. The frame is not the gift. Be not deceived by the most superficial aspects of this thought system, for these aspects enclose the whole, complete in every aspect. Death lies in this glittering gift. Let not your gaze dwell on the hypnotic gleaming of the frame. Look at the picture, and realize that death is offered you.

14. The other picture is lightly framed, for time cannot contain eternity. There is no distraction here. The picture of Heaven and eternity grows more convincing as you look at it. And now, by real comparison, a transformation of both pictures can at last occur. And each is given its rightful place when both are seen in relation to each other. The dark picture, brought to light, is not perceived as fearful, but the fact that it is just a picture is brought home at last. And what you see there you will recognize as what it is; a picture of what you thought was real, and nothing more. For beyond this picture you will see nothing. (Chapter 17, *ACIM*)

The Glistening Gateway
of Heaven

As you glide through the shadows
of darkness, you see a shimmery
frame under a glistening of light;
and as you get closer, you see the
beauty of its picture.

As you enter, the frame becomes
the picture and you realize it was
never a frame. It was the entrance
to the loveliness of the glistening
gateway of Heaven.

Everything is breathtaking beyond
anything you ever seen, and from
the brightness of light, you are
greeted by Jesus Christ and He
welcomes you to the reminder
of who you are and where you
are from.

You are surprised and timid
because of a world so different
you just escaped from, but you
instinctively know the glistening
gateway of Heaven is your real
home.

You turn to Christ and grip His
arms at His elbows and as He
lovingly looks upon you, your

eyes fill with tears to have
made it out of a world that
brought you much conflict
of fears and tears.

Christ wipes the tears from
your face, wraps His arms
around you, holds you tender
and dear, and telepathically
thanks you for choosing to
enter the glistening gateway
of Heaven you saw in the
picture.

He reassures you fear and
darkness cannot enter the
Kingdom of Heaven, ever.

You are appreciative and
enthusiastic to the love, joy,
and peace Christ embraced
you with and at the glistening
gateway of Heaven His picture
showed you this.

You know it's true because what
looked like a frame merged with
the world as you entered because
it never shatters, it joins.

And you instinctively know nothing
there ever splinters nor can anything
ever obliterate the world of Heaven
because the power of Heaven is infinite
and nothing can ever destroy it, because
light is the gravity of Heaven, the power

that holds everything together.

God is generous to let a fictitious world
borrow part of eternity to make up a
temporary world of infidelity.

And so the glistening gateway of Heaven
is your reality if you will graciously have it,
and I don't see how you would deny it
because God is divinely Good. Amen!

IV. The Two Pictures

15. The picture of light, in clear-cut and unmistakable contrast, is transformed into what lies beyond the picture. As you look on this, you realize that it is not a picture, but a reality. This is no figured representation of a thought system, but the Thought itself. What it represents is there. The frame fades gently and God rises to your remembrance, offering you the whole of creation in exchange for your little picture, wholly without value and entirely deprived of meaning. (Chapter 17, *ACIM*)

Father and Brother Always Knows Best

Sitting in my living room
contemplating what to
make for dinner.

But then I remembered I had
no food, only one slice of turkey
pastrami, one slice of bread, a
handful of linguine, one piece
of salmon, parmesan cheese, and
the ingredients to make a peanut
butter sesame sauce.

So I stood up to make a sandwich
with the one slice of turkey pastrami
and one slice of bread I had, but I was
so unsatisfied with this thought, I was
thinking of just not eating.

So I sat back down on the couch
wondering if I should have a glass
of wine when I heard the Holy Spirit's
Voice say, "You have a carrot. Shred
it and mix it."

I was so inspired by His reminder of
the carrot. I forgot I had. So I got back
up from the couch, opened a bottle of
wine, and prepared my dinner.

As I was preparing and bringing water
to a boil, I poured a glass of wine and
sang, *"Thank you Father Lord in Heaven
for the reminder of the carrot. Father
and Brother always knows best because
You always remind me not to worry of
what I don't have and make good with
what I do have."*

So the water came to a boil and I put
in the linguine, shredded the carrot,
and made the peanut butter sesame
sauce.

While I waited for the linguine to be
done and soft, I added the seasonings
to the sauce including garlic.

I baked the salmon for thirty minutes
because it was hard and frozen just
out of the freezer.

When the linguine was fully cooked, I
mixed the shredded carrot in it while
it was still steaming hot and I mixed it
up with the peanut butter sesame sauce.

When the salmon was cooked, I diced it in
cube like squares and mixed it in with the
linguine and the shredded carrot already
mixed in the sauce.

I sprinkled parmesan cheese and mixed
it all up and topped it with another sprinkle
of parmesan cheese just to touch it up.

In the end, I had a wonderful and tasteful dinner because Father and Brother always knows best, and so my dinner was fabulous after all even leaving another dish for one more night of a delightful dinner.

And just to let you know, I used two table spoons of Sriracha hot chili sauce and three sprinkles of Cayenne pepper to the peanut butter sesame sauce just to give it a kick of zest, which turned out to be very nice if you like a pizazz of spice.

The linguine, carrot, salmon, peanut butter Sesame sauce dinner topped with parmesan cheese was wonderfully delicious and I shared a portion of it with my neighbor because she appreciates my cooking.

But I must give credit where credit is due and I thank Father and Brother Who always knows best for reminding me of the carrot I could shred and mix it all up in the linguine and peanut butter sesame sauce to make it enjoyably delicious and nutritious.

And so when the Holy Spirit speaks to you, always remember to have faith that Father and Brother always knows best.

Unbroken Sleep

May the craving and asking for
unbroken sleep always be a
blessing upon you.

Unbroken sleep finally arrived
and I suddenly realize I had
never been deprived.

Sleep deprivation had gone on
for so long, I forgot what it was
like to sleep through the night.

I understand this is not God
doing this. It is I who did it to
myself because I programmed
the ego's dictate to interfere
with the very sleep I struggled
to keep.

When we make choices by
listening to its voices, we
prolong our own suffering
not realizing its cunning
dictates.

I dreamed I fell into a deep
sleep that overflowed into
my sleep permitting the
snooze to be unbroken.

It turned out to be a blessing
because I recognize all those

years, I let the ego come a
trespassing upon the pattern
of my sleep.

God told me once to be as
persistent as it is, and today,
I see clearly how insistent I
had been to get my sleep
even if it broke every fifteen
minutes or hour upon hour.

Today, I feel released from the
bondages of broken sleep, for
I slept for seven hours straight
without any interruptions to
erupt unbroken sleep.

An unbroken sleep is a blessing
in a world where the ego intrudes
upon it through life's experiences
and fearful dreams.

For in the unnatural world, we
need a good night's sleep in order
to function in a world where every-
thing malfunctions when you don't
get the best rest of sleep.

And so an unbroken sleep is a blessing,
whereas a broken sleep is upsetting.

The Test of Fear

In a calm winters night the
inner peace ever so still and
bright.

The night brings a slight of
moonlight reflecting upon the
dark sea, a cold breeze passes
through me, yet there is no plea
for safety, for there is not even
a speck of fright in me.

For I embrace the stillness in me
and let it be what it will be, for
the enjoyment of its dormant is
so divinely potent.

In this moment, the smile has
spoken, for the atonement of
His light is not a postponement
but an enthronement ever so
devoutly Heavenly.

As I simmer in this divine cloud
I surrendered and bowed to the
relaxation of its sleepiness.

My eyes grow heavy, my yawn
enormous and I am all too happy
to fall into its temptation of its
drowsy influence.

I lay my head all too happy to
go to bed and swiftly I fall into
a deep sleep.

All hours of the night, I am
awakened, I open my eyes to
see a figure at the foot of the
bed.

His broaden shoulders, his
forehead and only his eyes
I see, he bends his arms, elbows
wing placing his palms on the
foot of the bed.

He rises himself with his flatten
palms, his fingers ever so slender
and long, fingernails dark, lengthy
and pointy.

He rises tall and I gaze upon his
dirty gown and wondered why
his hair color is darker than the
universe, thin, stringy and long.

Instinctively I knew he was nine
feet tall, but in no way did I feel
a speck of small.

Nor did I feel frightened when he
glided to hover over me and brought
his face eye to eye ever so close to
me.

I gazed into his big blackened eyes
and he gave a sinister grin showing

off the rolls of his sharpened teeth,
hoping to defeat.

I intuitively knew this was the test of
fear and I am all too happy to share
that I did not fall into the temptation
of what could have been a frightening
experience.

For I did not cower to it and this gave no
power to its manifestation, for I simply
humbled myself to it, closed my eyes
and prayed it into the light.

Then, I tenderly open my eyes to see fear
in its face, its sinister grin slowly fades,
and poof, it was swiftly gone as suddenly
as it appeared.

In that calm winters night, I passed
the test of fear, for not even a speck
of fright stirred in my heart and my
mind ever so calm and my tummy
remained still.

And so the test of fear was an event
of my awakened dream where I remained
in the realm of the power of love, light and
peace where fear and darkness cannot touch
you or me when we keep our divine power
of love, light and peace in harmony
with Christ.

Bless the Night

Do not fear the night because
it is an illusion you wished to
experience that has no power
over you unless you cower it
and announce its strength.

To overcome the fears of it,
bless the night with your
lovely light, for your light
outshines all the fears of
its darkness.

Close your eyes and bow your head
to all the toils and snares that want
to see you tremble in fear and dead.

In this holy instant, remember
no one can take your life, for
the body is the shield to the
spirit and spirit is life.

When the hostile of darkness
comes a trespassing, remember
it's the illusion you chose to
experience.

Do not cower to it because you
don't want to give up your holy
power to it.

Bless the night and humble yourself
to it in calmness to remain under the

Atonement of Christ light in love and
peace.

In this holy instant, He will pluck
your spirit and gently hurdle you
through the cosmos and unto the
safety of His bosom.

No matter what the darkness brings,
remain peaceful through its turmoil,
for in this hallowed second, God lights
up your light to give you the strength
to bless the night.

Blessings are powerful, whereas
fighting back is powerless, for it
only brings on sickness and
weakness.

The moment He turned His back,
remember the stone that was
thrown at Christ. He turned and
looked and blessed them with love
and peace in His mind and heart.

They peacefully walked away
their opposite ways, which
speared the heart of Christ.

For He was setting the example
of forgiveness to bless the night
within to outshine the darkness
inside the mind and heart they
did not yet see within.

Remember it this way, the night
sky is symbolic to the dimness we
all live within ourselves.

Night after night, we see the night
sky overhead as a reminder to us
to see the darkness in us instead.

When you lash out for justice to
kill and punish the minds and hands
of darkness, you are demonstrating
the night in your own mind and heart;
therefore, you too can have blood on your hands
when you elect to execute and devastate.

This is not a sacred instant. It is a
chain and shackle moment where
you cage yourself to the very persons
you take justice and vengeance on
only to sooth your pain of loss
and devastation.

But you realize the hurt does not
go away and this is because only
forgiveness can wipe the slate of
your misery and pain you thought
justice and punishment would wash
away.

You must be willing to bless the night
to turn on the light in them and you,
for this is the holy instant theirs and
your chains and shackles drop off.

Here, all of Heaven rejoices to the
freedom you've given to yourself

and others from the sorrows of the
heart and the sickness of the mind.

This is what it means to bless the
night and your light and theirs
shines most bright annihilating
all the hostile and bitter fight.

And so bless the night within and
forgive what really has never been.

Conjoined Twin

To be born into a bittersweet world
of time means to be born out of the
delightful and pleasurable world of
timelessness.

At the open gate of Heaven, I see the
light in me so bright, there is never
anything to fright because Heaven is
an open sunlit that embraces the
adorn spirit.

To be born out of timelessness is to
disconnect from righteousness, which
is a lonely place to be.

But, we hurdle ourselves deep into the
dream of darkness where we eventually
feel the effects of fearfulness and
hopelessness.

The trials and tribulations of the dream
do not define who you are, for they are
only lessons to learn and remember the
divinity in you.

This is where I've come to clearly see the
carelessness of my agreement to separate
from the Divine of Oneness.

But, I am not alone in this because we are
all in it together regardless whether you do
not remember it or do not believe it is

beside the point, because you are part of
the holy Trinity in certainty and indefinitely,
and one day you will undeniably admit to this.

There is a sense of deep passion of fear and hate
in a bittersweet world, yet through the passion of
a tender whirlwind love and light dwell's within
waiting for your conjoined twin to be embraced
and rejoiced.

At the center of the passion of love and light, I
can no longer ignore the attraction of the Divine
in you and me because we are delightful in His
eyes and it is time to be mindful of this.

For I see my conjoined twin in me and so I behold
the lovely twin within the Sonship and so I ache
for your friendship!

Looking past flesh and bones, I see clearly the
kingship of our Heavenly home, for you are a
god of greatness because you were created by
the God of Majesty Who is the passion of love
and light Who loves you with all His might.

We don't recall the passion of the love and light
within, but when you do remember, you will
definitely feel the passion of love and light from
the center of your mind and heart where you
clearly see your conjoined twin within.

When you behold the glow in you, spiritual vision
fully enters and you see your brothers' gleam
all perfect and clean.

And when you look behind you it is the wave
of the dream you see and when you look again
in front of you to gaze upon the clear and shiny
world, you instinctively remember the home that
glows golden is where you most certainly belong.

This is such a profound fact that must be told
because it will help you become joyously bold,
so no longer be cruel and cold to all your immortal
brothers, for we are here together to learn and care
for one another and to remember the importance
and power in sharing everything without expecting
anything in return.

This is the divine charity of giving from the heart!

Half of what is in us is ruthless and the other half
within is righteous and this is why we are given
freedom of choice by the Divine from above.

Please choose wisely so you shine most brightly!

Be willing not to take this mildly or lightly because
the most important quality in you is ever so patiently
and peacefully waiting for your invitation to lead
you to the golden path of Heaven.

Here, He gently leads you ensuring you are not
harmed as He tenderly lifts you to decompress
from the miserable depressed state of mind you
desperately want to escape from.

Eventually, we all grow tired and weary of all the
dreary, eerie, and despicable criminal and clinical
nonsense of battles, wars and gores.

Merge with the Holy Spirit within and travel the golden road to eternity where you remember your delightful conjoined twin of immortality.

And through the glistening petals of white lilies you will learn to offer, is where your suffering ends and through quantum leap into spiritual vision and knowledge is where you come out of misery ever so swiftly to never again feel filthy and guilty about anything.

For the purification into spiritual vision is where you grow and glow fresh, pure and clean where you learn to no longer be so glum, filthy, dirty and mean.

To take the journey from time to timelessness with God's Holy Spirit is to gently go through quantum leap where you will smile, not weep.

Because when you behold the golden world of Heaven where there are no tears to dry up and no mess to clean up, you can't help but to smile.

Everything in timelessness is in perfect order and you will be all too happy to be released from the dream world of complete disorder.

You will be overjoyed to reunite with your conjoined twin within and it too will be all too happy to be released from the imprisonment of the body it no longer wishes to embody.

Here, the mind restored from the egos sinister prison of insanity to sanity a transformation from a horizontal axis to a vertical axis where you return to wholeness and wholesomeness.

This is the essence of your true existence of your immortality where your mind is no longer split minded, for it returns to holy wholeness.

Thinking on a vertical axis brings the passion of love and light to the sweet power of immortality of sinlessness and holiness the core of your divinity and innocence.

Here, you shine so bright you are all knowing and all seeing of every beautification of the wholesome sanctifications you left behind.

Yet you are destined to return to everything lovely hallowed by your name because your conjoined twin is the Son of God, the light in you that shines ever so bright in its healthy state of mind where darkness completely abolished and lightness fully reinstated.

And so fear and darkness can never reign forever because this is what your conjoined twin is not so be happy the kingship of your immortality is the love and light in you that glistens for all eternity.

Divinely Lovely

The God of true reality so
divinely lovely, for there
are no other true gods but
God.

He is the first and will always
be the first and I thank Him
for being a divinely lovely
God of love, light, life,
true, and peace.

There is no beginning and no
ending to Him because only
love, light, life and truth has
always been.

If you let your mind grasp the
true concept of His creation, you
would see clearly the truth of
His nature and your own.

His Holy Spirit is always with you
to assist you in your faith to get
through all the fake of the world
you perceive so you may see the
other world fresh, new and true.

For the God of true reality is
divinely lovely, you wouldn't
want to overlook the loyalty
He has for you.

This is a fact so immense you
can see it through His love most
tenderly intense.

He softly surrenders His love to
you and I guarantee you will
remember the great love you
have for Him.

You can deny this all you want,
but if you are reading this poem,
it is a sign your time has arrived
to no longer defy yourself from the
truth of love, light and life in
Him and you.

For He created you in His
thoughtfulness to forever live
in love, light, life and truth in
togetherness.

The day will come when you
transition from time to
timelessness where the golden
eternity prospers forever and
you along with it.

For lovely and beautiful creation
is endless and you are splendidly
adorable and delightful because
you are God's creation.

And so in God's eyes, you are always
divinely lovely because He created
you perfect.

IV. Your Function in the Atonement

1. When you accept a brother's guiltlessness you will see the Atonement in him. For by proclaiming it in him you make it yours, and you will see what you sought. You will not see the symbol of your brother's guiltlessness shining within him while you still believe it is not there. His guiltlessness is *your* Atonement. Grant it to him, and you will see the truth of what you have acknowledged. Yet truth is offered first to be received, even as God gave it first to His Son. The first in time means nothing, but the First in eternity is God the Father, Who is both First and One. Beyond the First there is no other, for there is no order, no second or third, and nothing but the First. (Chapter 14, *ACIM*)

Fallen in Love All Over Again

In the world of fake, I finally see
who I had forsaken, for He hands
me the real world on a daily basis,
but I continue on the world of
ugly phases.

There are traces of beauty on a
world so ugly. I eventually realize
the world He hands is of endless
beauty.

He is lovely especially when He
asks me to hold Him dearly, for
it grabbed my attention because
I was ready to come out of
self-deception.

I had to ask Him to repeat to me
again and again to hold Him dearly,
and so He did, absolutely.

I found it most endearing and I
remembered that I loved Him
before and found I had fallen
in love all over again with the
only God I ever truly loved.

He is Jesus Christ Who helped
me remember the true love of
my Father in Heaven I have
forgotten about for too long.

In asking me to hold Him dearly,
I remembered very clearly how
much I miss Him as I embraced
Him closely; and in doing so, I had
fallen in love all over again.

For He is my brother in Heaven
I always loved but could not
remember through the senseless
noise on a world so far from home,
yet ever so close.

I had forgotten what I had wanted
through the years of deception, for
He was vital at my own decision to
return to the heart Who loves me
dearly.

The Holy Spirit remembers for
me by releasing all the lovely
things of God darkness blocks.

Through the faith of the light
of Christ, I hold Him with all my
might because through His light,
I feel His love most faithfully.

Here, I had fallen in love all over
again with the King of Innocence,
Peace, Love, and Light. I hold close
and tight to never again let go of the
true love we both cherish most dear.

So to have fallen in love all over
again, my love is deeper for
Him, more than it ever has been.

I miss the Trinity of Heaven most
sweetly, and this I feel devotedly and
devoutly deeply, and I see it in His eyes
ever so naturally.

And so fallen in love all over again
brings me further into spiritual vision
where I see clearly His Love, yours, and
mine ever so pure and true.

Dedicated to Jesus Christ in the Love of God.

VII. Attainment of the Real World

16. In me you have already overcome every temptation that would hold you back. We walk together on the way to quietness that is the gift of God. Hold me dear, for what except your brothers can you need? We will restore to you the peace of mind that we must find together. The Holy Spirit will teach you to awaken unto us and to yourself. This is the only real need to be fulfilled in time. Salvation from the world lies only here. My peace I give you. Take it of me in glad exchange for all the world has offered but to take away. And we will spread it like a veil of light across the world's sad face, in which we hide our brothers from the world, and it from them. (Chapter 13, *ACIM*)

She Reads

Her soul glistens golden, for she
is most bolden, yet she thinks she
has no courage because she believes
she is a sinner.

Then she is given a divine poetic
book to read lo and behold she
flourishes in the knowledge of love,
light, joy, and peace because she
reads the poetic word of God.

It's like being stuck in a maze of a
tangled web she feels she cannot
escape from, but when she reads
this divine book, she looks up and
clearly see's the open glistening
gates of Heaven.

The rays of light shine through
outshining the darkness she was
blind too, but now she clearly see's
because she reads.

Where there was night there is now
light, for her willingness to receive the
divine blessings handed permits her
to see where Christ holds the door
wide open.

For He waits in patience and in peace
for her readiness to let Him fill her cup
of emptiness.

And because she reads and receives the
blessings of the goodness of love and light
she no longer lingers in the dark shadows
of empty meadows.

For she perceives she is not alone, for
her Father in Heaven beams aglow and
this she sees through spiritual vision
because she reads His divine word of
wisdom.

So when she offers the crown of white
lilies to Christ, she will look back and
wonder how she could have ever been
so silly to fear what has been given her
most dearly, sweetly, and freely.

And so now that she reads the divine
poetic word of God, her eyes are wide
open to the door Christ always held
open, and she crosses the threshold to
receive the goodness of God's blessings
for all eternity.

Dedicated to Tobitha Webb in the Love of Christ.

Toby, whenever fear and sorrow comes a trespassing upon your peace be willing to recite this scripture and forgive everyone and everything that bring distress upon your peace:

PSALM 23:1-6, THE Lord is my shepherd; I shall not want. He maketh me to lie down in green pastures: he leadeth me beside the still waters. He restoreth my soul: he leadeth me in the paths of righteousness for his name's sake. Yea, though I walk through the valley of the shadow of death, I will fear no evil: for thou art with me; thy rod and thy staff they comfort me. Thou preparest a table before me in the presence of mine enemies: thou anointest my head with oil; my cup runneth over. Surely goodness and mercy shall follow me all the days of my life: and I will dwell in the house of the Lord for ever. (Holy Bible, *KJV*).

The Slave She Was

When one chooses to pick up
the vacuum and dance around
while they vacuum, rejoice in
their achievement and clap
at their enjoyment of the task
of vacuuming.

Because this person treated
another like a slave turning her
into the slave she was.

She was a slave to her own
injury and needed to hear the
noise of the vacuum to tune out
the agony of her minds misery.

She had her servant she treated
as a slave ordering her to vacuum
so many days.

But one day, she asked her to sit
and rest for she is going to vacuum
on this day and she danced around
as she vacuumed, for she embraced
it and did the task in enjoyment.

All her servants were watching, for
they were shocked at her launching
the vacuuming.

They transformed it to a show and
the curtain rolled and they all

applauded at her achievement to
let go of the superior attitude and
for humbling herself in that moment.

She saw it was good and decided to
take the quantum leap and offered
all her servants white lilies and they
all bowed to one another and rejoiced
in the gift of humbleness, peace and purity.

This is what it means to wipe out
all the hate, fear, and sorrows of
darkness we harbor and become
a slave to it rather than the savior
of Christ, the Sonship, and our own.

All of Heaven rejoices in the
accomplishment in taking the
quantum leap to finally defeat
self-deceit and the denial we
hang onto for way too long,
but now it's gone.

All washed away and the goodness
of your innocence is right on its way
to being the purification from the
slavery of your own misery.

Here, you have chosen love and life,
holy, wholesome, joy, peace, and the
innocent light of your humbled spirit.

You have released your brothers and
yourself to the enjoyment of being free
from the slave she was and the slave you
were to self-deceit and self-destruction.

We move away from the crucifixion,
the act of death, and we rise in the
resurrection, the release of life and
into the realm of eternity where life
always flourishes in loveliness.

This is what's true, for you will never
be blue because joy rules in the world
of eternal life.

For in taking the quantum leap, you
squashed all the negative forces and
released yourself into the realm of
love, joy, and peace the eternity of life.

And so let go of the slave she was and your
own in love and faith and freedom reigns.

The Simplicity of Quantum Leap

A quantum leap is real simple.
All it means is to make a decision
from ruthlessness to righteousness
from choosing to move from backward
to forward and from choosing to take the
leap from out of darkness and into lightness.

There is nothing difficult about quantum
leap. It is when we bring complexity into it
that we are blind to the simplicity of it.

All you have to do is be willing to see
through spiritual vision and you get the
whole concept of what the mechanism
of what quantum leap really is.

And all it is *is* a decision to leap from
bitterness to sweetness, hostility to
serenity, ruthlessness to kindness,
sinfulness to holiness, guiltiness to innocence,
rejection to acceptance, judgment to embracement,
fear to love, sorrow to joy, and war to peace.

Choosing to jump from all the negative forces
and into the positive realm is taking a
quantum leap into the ultimate righteousness
of the essence of your immortality because this is
what you are, for you are life not death, light not dark,
love not fear, joy not sad, peace not war, innocent not guilty,
and holy not sinful.

Remember this and be willing to act upon it and when you do, you've taken a quantum leap from ruthlessness into the realm of righteousness where you discover the reign of life where there is no such thing as a loveless world of death and you will rejoice in this because righteousness is what you forgot you always were and want and so it's yours if you will have it.

And so the simplicity of quantum leap is to make the decision to embrace innocence and holiness freeing the mind from sickness and the heart from bitterness.

Let Your Innocence Flourish

They couldn't stand to be in
the same room with each other
because they refused to forgive
and accept one another.

You can have pleasant and
enjoyable relationships if you
are willing to forgive and accept
everyone's differences.

Let go of the entire fleet of
negative energies because
whatever you hate what you
think happened is the past of
ancient yesterday.

Jealousy, hostility, animosity,
hatred, enmity, bitterness,
resentment, horridness, badness,
unfriendliness, spitefulness, ugliness,
nastiness, offensiveness, trouble,
scandal, argument, quarrel, fear,
rejection, and conflict.

These are just a puny fleet of negative
energies that can do so much damage
upon damage if you hang onto it and
let it increase its darkness in you.

Push self-deceit and destruction aside
and look passed flesh and bones of the

Sonship to see the likeness of the light inside.

This does not make you special, the stem of separation. It makes you holy the root of unification.

When you look upon your brothers with loving and forgiving eyes, you see the holiness in them, a holy reflection of yourself shining upon your mind.

And when you recognize you are the same, you will come to embrace and not push away.

You will release the fleet of negative emotions you harbor and receive the entire positive passions that brings everyone together.

Love, light, holy, affection, adoration, devotion, unification, friendship, tenderness, fondness, kindness, goodness, guiltless, harmless, happiness, peacefulness, thankfulness, and gratefulness.

This is just a small fleet of positive energies. You could adopt, value, and cherish it for the rest of your duration in time, for this is the quantum leap into timelessness.

You do this, and it filters the harmful attitude cleansing the heart of darkness

and purifies the mind of shadows and
abolishes separation and completes
unification.

If you do this, you can accomplish
what you see is impossible when in
true reality is possible if you are so
willing to let go of all the bad feelings
and receive and embrace all the goodness
in you and the Sonship that has always
been in you since time began.

You can do this. Just think of the crown
of white lilies you will give to Jesus as
an offering to release Him from the
pains of the crown of thorns and the
spear of the nails, for here, you will
release yourself from the pains of
sorrow and the blame and judgment
this world offers.

Offering the crown of white lilies to
Christ and your brothers means you
have taken a quantum leap from release
of death to life, fear to love, sinful to
holy, sadness to joyfulness, aggression
to peace, cruelty to kindness, roughness
to tenderness, and guilt to innocence.

You can do this if you so choose to
release Christ, the Sonship, and
yourself from the fears of guilt and
the pains of thorns the world puts
upon one another.

When you adopt the forgiving stance
and let the innocence of your light
flourish, you will clearly see we are all
love, joy, peace, sinless, holy, and
innocent of everything we made,
after all.

And so let your innocence flourish,
for you can do this if you so choose
God's brilliance of His goodness in all
its magnificence of purity and serenity
in you and your brothers.

The Guiltlessness In You

Through the physical eyes you see
stories of crime, this is how blind you
are only because you are unwilling
to see through the eyes of God.

For through His eyes, He beholds the
sinless spirit in you and me awaiting
in patience and peace for your
willingness to behold the guiltlessness
in you.

In His time, Jesus Christ saw this
clearly, but He also knew God would
not intervene between Him and His
life script.

For Christ too agreed He would be
born into time to set the example of
the guiltlessness in you.

Christ was innocent, yet we screamed
out for His crucifixion, but this too is the
innocence in you, for you do not know
what you do or say until you forgive every
sad and frightful venture and speak the
truth of the guiltlessness in you and your
brothers'.

You can only speak the truth of reality
through spiritual vision, but to do this,
you must be willing to forgive and lay

down the physical sight to see the
guiltlessness in you and the Sonship.

For it is only through God's eyes can you
behold the innocence of Christ in you and the
Sonship and you see the dreamy mirage of
ancient crimes that never was.

For it is a projection of your thinking that has
you possessed in believing you are sinful and
guilty of dreams most senseless and silly.

And when we are a witness to brutal
crimes, we do say too often, "It was
a senseless crime," and it always is.

You are feeling the effects of dreams and
not of realism, for in true reality, darkness
and fear can never touch you because you
are a child of God.

Just look at skin to skin under the
microscope and you are a witness to
the skin never touching each other.

This is the evidence that fear and
darkness can never touch you unless
you give up your divine power to do so.

Christ was never crucified. Only in your
insane, delusional thinking do you see
a crown of thorns placed on His head,
imprisoned, beaten, scourged, and nails
hammered into His hands and feet onto
a cross.

So this is the crime you believe to see in one
another for millennia until you choose to remove
the crown of thorns from His injured and bloody
head and honor Him with the crown of white lilies
where you are witness to the transformation of His
innocence and beauty, and your own.

Here, you see Him rise to help you rekindle the
brotherly friendship you always had, for this is
the quantum leap into union, spiritual vision, and
knowledge, and this is the simplicity of it.

Now is the time to be willing to remove the
blinders and be utterly kinder one to another
and recognize the dream is everything you
made up to experience and now must be
willing to clean up to transition into Heaven.

Not through physical sight where you see
and seek to judge, kill, torcher, destroy, and
confine, but through spiritual vision where
you are a witness to the dream within your
mind always seeking to be free from the cruel
world in which you spree.

Let the Holy Spirit lead you to the golden
light where you see clearly and in certainty
the example Christ set in motion, the
guiltlessness in you.

For it does not matter what you do or go
through because it is all a dream you made
up to experience something else other than
what you have always known.

Love, light, life, truth, joy, peace, safety, unity,
royalty and freedom are all you've ever known;
and in time, this is what you spend a lifetime seeking
in the tangled maze of your dream until you
finally understand you can awaken through
spiritual vision where you see the rays of light
shining through the door that has always been
wide open.

You are no longer blind when you see
this, for here, you make your way past
the threshold where you behold the
loveliness of your Heavenly home.

Here, you remember Heaven is what
you always known and you witness the
pureness and freshness of it compare
to the blurry mirage of the false world
you see behind you and you instinctively
know everything you believed, in the dream,
is all but just a dream after all.

And so the innocence you see in Christ is
the guiltlessness in you, be willing then, to
take the quantum leap where you remove
complexity and learn of the simplicity of the
safe journey into paradise where you remember
who you are and where you come from. For
in the land of Heaven's Kingdom is where you
remember all the gifts of purity and immortality.

I. The Message of the Crucifixion

12. The crucifixion cannot be shared because it is the symbol of projection, but the resurrection is the symbol of sharing because the reawakening of every Son of God is necessary to enable the Sonship to know its Wholeness. Only this is knowledge.

13. The message of the crucifixion is perfectly clear:

Teach only love, for that is what you are.

14. If you interpret the crucifixion in any other way, you are using it as a weapon for assault rather than as the call for peace for which it was intended. The Apostles often misunderstood it, and for the same reason that anyone misunderstands it. Their own imperfect love made them vulnerable to projection, and out of their own fear they spoke of the "wrath of God" as His retaliatory weapon. Nor could they speak of the crucifixion entirely without anger, because their sense of guilt had made them angry. (Chapter 6, *ACIM*)

Toss the Crown of Thorns

Be willing to accept and celebrate
Palm Sunday as freedom to life not
death, for Easter is a time of happiness
not sadness.

In this holy season and each day that
comes, offer love not fear and be happy
the resurrection is a representation of
life not death.

Toss the crown of thorns and lift the
crown of white lilies unto the Heavens
and be a witness to the conversion of
Christ from sadness to happiness.

Here, you free Him from the pains of
suffering of the crown of thorns and so
you free yourself from the thorns of the
world and into the eternal beauty of
immortality.

The crucifixion is the act of death.
Ultimately, it is the example of love
not fear so throw away the nails and
no longer keep Him bound to the cross,
and you free yourself from the spears
of toils and snares.

For Christ is free, alive, and well to be
the loving Christ He is, the natural essence
of His existence and your own, but His pains

still linger as He patiently and peacefully awaits
your willingness to spiritually awake.

Be willing then to free yourself and the
Sonship from the belief in guilt and death
permitting love to spread and together your
light outshines all fear and darkness that tells
you, life is nothing but bleakness.

The resurrection is the evidence that there
is no such thing as guilt, sorrow, and death
because spirit is true life, whereas the body
is the act of death.

So throw away the crown of thorns, the slain
of scourge, and the spear of nails to obliterate
the act of death and embrace the resurrection,
the true reality of immortality.

Let your body release from bloody and spirit
to beauty, for ugliness is only on the surface
not remembering the adorableness within.

For only loveliness is eternal and true and
fierceness is temporary and false because no
one wants to live in fear and darkness forever.

Be willing then to toss the crown of thorns
and embrace the crown of white lilies, for
this is true victory of the lovely, holy, and
innocence in you and all the Sonship.

Remember to forgive God, yourself, and
the Sonship and hold the crown of white
lilies on the palm of your hands as an

offering of peace recognizing the innocence within must be released.

Toss the crown of thorns as you take the journey of time and offer your brother the crown of white lilies where you cherish the radiance of holiness and innocence of all the Sonship and you behold the imperial of their purity and your own.

Here, the Holy Spirit hands you the gift of joy for tossing the toy of guilt and judgment and for accepting their innocence and peace and your own.

And so toss the crown of thorns and embrace the crown of white lilies where you adore the innocence and peace in Christ, the Sonship and your own releasing Him, your brothers' and your own pains and sorrows from the thorns of the world.

I. Holy Week

1. This is Palm Sunday, the celebration of victory and the acceptance of the truth. Let us not spend this holy week brooding on the crucifixion of God's Son, but happily in the celebration of his release. For Easter is the sign of peace, not pain. A slain Christ has no meaning. But a risen Christ becomes the symbol of the Son of God's forgiveness on himself; the sign he looks upon himself as healed and whole. (Chapter 20, *ACIM*)

The Symbol of Peace

My Friend has risen from the
depths of fear and darkness
that never really was and so
silly to believe it was true.

He was born into the dream to
bring peace and to show we are
not alone in the circus of war.

The symbol of peace is Easter, the
holy week of the resurrection, for
in the dream we thrive on the
crucifixion and death remembering
the crown of thorns placed on His
head.

The crucifixion is an ancient fiction.
Now, let's refocus to the resurrection
to no longer wander into the
temptation of fear and death.

The resurrection has always been
the light of your innocence lighting
the way to redemption and freedom.

The symbol of peace is Easter. The
celebration of sins end so I throw
away the crown of thorns and hand
you white lilies to the redemption
of thoughts of fear so senseless and
silly.

Look through the shimmery veil of
its snow-white petals of the lilies
and be a witness to the lovely face
of Jesus Christ.

For He will smile beautifully upon
you as He gazes upon your mind to
remind you to let go of the crown
of thorns and receive the white lilies
as the symbol of innocence and peace.

Here, you see He is alive and well
and you see the dream of thorns
and nails disappear as you recall
He will never fail you, for His light
and yours combined is the power
of love and peace most divine.

The crucifixion is the act of death
and the resurrection is the symbol
of life, innocence, and peace for this
is what you are right alongside of
Christ Who loves you with all His
might.

And in the light of His Atonement,
you are redeemed and released as
you take a quantum leap from the
dream of fear and war if you would
only accept the gift of white lilies and
once and for all toss the crown of thorns,
the ancient war of hate.

Share this goodness with the Sonship
and you release the shackles of war's
bondage and together you walk side

by side into the light of redemption of
love, life, innocence, joy, peace, and
safety, your royal inheritance of union,
freedom, and immortality.

So the holy week of Easter is the
symbol of love and peace because
Christ is no longer on the cross and
the crown of thorns long ago tossed
to be honored with the gift of the crown
of white lilies where you are witness
to His golden blazing amazing smile.

For the genius of white lilies is the
brilliance of your innocence and
peace to all the Sonship from one
end of the world to the other.

Be willing to take a quantum leap
and teach the crown of thorns
and the crucifixion is the ancient
script that passed away long ago
and rejoice in the resurrection in
redemption of love, innocence, and
peace that will free you from the
hates and wars of self-deceit.

And so the symbol of peace is the
celebration of atonement, forgiveness and
innocence rejoicing in the resurrection
of Christ and yours embracing love not
fear, happiness not sadness, peace not
war, innocence not guilt, safety not
jeopardy, embracement not judgment,
union not separation, freedom not
bondage, and life not death.

I. Holy Week

4. Easter is not the celebration of the *cost* of sin, but of its *end*. If you see glimpses of the face of Christ behind the veil, looking between the snow-white petals of the lilies you have received and given as your gift, you will behold your brother's face and recognize it. I was a stranger and you took me in, not knowing who I was. Yet for your gift of lilies you will know. In your forgiveness of this stranger, alien to you and yet your ancient Friend, lies his release and your redemption with him. The time of Easter is a time of joy, and not of mourning. Look on your risen Friend, and celebrate his holiness along with me. For Easter is the time of your salvation, along with mine. (Chapter 20, *ACIM*)

The Ultimate Offering

In the Lord's honor, make an imperial
crown of white lilies so you return home
freely, swiftly, gently, safely, and in purity
and beauty.

For through spiritual vision you are a witness
to the loveliness of the transformation of
Christ from bloody to beauty where you see
Him rise with a golden blazing amazing smile
wearing the crown of white lilies.

Here, all the Sonship has a crown of white
lilies in the palm of their hands willing and
ready in togetherness and in unison to give
the ultimate offering and so we lift our eyes
and palms to the Heavens in love, forgiveness,
and peace, for we now see clearly the reality
of the innocence of Christ peace and beauty
and our own.

We behold the loveliness of the golden glow of
His light and in oneness our light combines,
for the ultimate offering of the crown of white
lilies frees Christ, you, and the Sonship from the
crown of death giving everyone a wave of breath,
like a domino effect.

This is the ultimate offering Christ ask we give
to Him and to one another to show we have
risen in the recognition of the resurrection of
love not fear, joy not sorrow, peace not war,
innocence not guilt, embracement not judgment,

safety not jeopardy, freedom not bondage
and life not death.

Here, we instinctively remember the love we
have for God we no longer need to fear, for
His love for us He has always held most dear.

So we gift to Christ the ultimate offering of the
crown of white lilies to show we are no longer
roaming senseless and silly in the midst of fear
and blindness, war and hate, blame and division,
judgment and confinement, selfishness and greed.

For the ultimate offering of the crown of white
lilies shatters the ancient bondages of these
negative forces freeing the Sonship to atone and
forgive so we may merge in loveliness, holiness,
togetherness, kindness, tenderness, joyfulness,
and peacefulness to forever dwell in the beauty
of love, light, safety, royalty, freedom, and innocence.

We offer this Atonement to Christ first to bring
us to our true senses of our true nature as we offer
in love and peace the final offering of the crown of
white lilies and be a witness to the transformation
from bloody to beauty, from frail to sovereignty,
which gently nurtures the bones of fracture.

Here, we too transform from split minded to
wholly wholesomeness in the glow of our
true loveliness.

For to offer the crown of white lilies is a blessing
that will transform you from fear, sorrow, war, sin,
guilt, judgment, separation, and imprisonment
to the essence of love, joy, peace, holiness,

togetherness, and innocence, for this is the release
of the naturalness of mind and spirit where it knows
of its safety and freedom.

And so your willingness to embrace the ultimate
offering of the crown of white lilies permits the
spirit of faith and forgiveness to follow you through
the offering of white lilies to everyone you meet
releasing you and them from the dreams of fear and
darkness and into the Kingdom of love and light and
this is a blessing on a grandeur scale where Christ showers
you with peace and the Holy Spirit hails joy upon you.

I. Holy Week

2. This week begins with palms and ends with lilies, the white and holy sign the Son of God is innocent. Let no dark sign of crucifixion intervene between the journey and its purpose; between the acceptance of the truth and its expression. This week we celebrate life, not death. And we honor the perfect purity of the Son of God, and not his sins. Offer your brother the gift of lilies, not the crown of thorns; the gift of love and not the "gift" of fear. You stand beside your brother, thorns in one hand and lilies in the other, uncertain which to give. Join now with me and throw away the thorns, offering the lilies to replace them. This Easter I would have the gift of your forgiveness offered by you to me, and returned by me to you. We cannot be united in crucifixion and in death. Nor can the resurrection be complete till your forgiveness rests on Christ, along with mine. (Chapter 20, *ACIM*)

The Crown of White Lilies

The white lily is of purity, for it is the flower
of innocence, a representation of the Son of
God's love, light, holiness, happiness, beautifulness,
forgiveness, and freedom from the sufferings of
Christ and your own where you atone and unify.

All this time, we favored fear, hate, sin, guilt,
judgment, punishment, bondage, separation, and war
because we kept Christ nailed to the cross wearing
the crown of thorns.

Yet He was taken off the cross and the crown of
thorns tossed, long ago, since then, we have dwelled
on the crucifixion and the crown of thorns rather than
the resurrection and life galore.

Now, it is time to release Him from the crown of thorns
and let go of the fear and sadness of the crucifixion, the
act of death, but also the symbol of love and peace, and
rejoice in the resurrection, the icon of release, transformation,
and transition.

Have faith in the forgiveness of Christ because of the
innocence in Him and you, and adopt His way and forgive
one to another as you toss the crown of thorns you hold
in one hand and humbly and lovingly offer the gift of white
lilies you hold in the other hand.

Correct the crown of thorns to a crown of white lilies
and place it on the head of Christ and be a witness to the
transformation from guilt to innocence, suffering to joy,

bloody to beauty, frail to sovereignty, gloom to light, separation to union, and from bondage to freedom.

And be a witness to His delightful smile as He gives a golden glow of delight that you have chosen to take the quantum leap to release Him, yourself, and the Sonship from the pains of suffering and from the fears of death and into the light of love, joy, and peace of your immortality ever so swiftly.

The crown of white lilies represents the release of love, innocence, and peace where you finally see there is no such thing as guilt, judgment, grief, and a deceased.

For even though we think Christ was crucified, we were unsuccessful in taking His life, and so, it is true, no one can take yours.

Offer the crown of white lilies to remember the light of the spirit within is innocent and in its time will resurrect, transform, and transition to eternal life, light, love, joy, peace, innocence, beauty, safety, royalty and freedom, just as Christ did.

For no matter what the body endures, just remember what Christ suffered, yet His life was preserved just as your life is forever conserved because God will never desert you and He knows no one can ever harm you and this He Wills for you.

Remember the offering of the crown of white lilies is the release of suffering from all the thorns in every corner of the world and the resurrection is the liberation from out of fear, darkness, and death and into the utter joy of love, light, freedom, peace, and safety of eternal life.

And so the quantum leap into the offering of the crown
of white lilies releases the King of Innocence and Peace,
you, and the Sonship ever so swiftly from the pains of suffering
and lets joy and wellness enter to spread the truth of what
atonement and forgiveness offers; sanity not insanity, love not fear,
happiness not sadness, peace not war, innocence not guilt,
embracement not judgment, union not separation, freedom
not bondage, royalty not poverty, safety not danger, and life
not death.

II. The Gift of Lilies

10. This is the way to Heaven and to the peace of Easter, in which we join in glad awareness that the Son of God is risen from the past, and has awakened to the present. Now is he free, unlimited in his communion with all that is within him. Now are the lilies of his innocence untouched by guilt, and perfectly protected from the cold chill of fear and withering blight of sin alike. Your gift has saved him from the thorns and nails, and his strong arm is free to guide you safely through them and beyond. Walk with him now rejoicing, for the savior from illusions has come to greet you, and lead you home with him.

11. Here is your savior and your friend, released from crucifixion through your vision, and free to lead you now where he would be. He will not leave you, nor forsake the savior in his pain. And gladly will you and your brother walk the way of innocence together, singing as you behold the open door of Heaven and recognize the home that called to you. Give joyously to your brother the freedom and the strength to lead you there. And come before his holy altar where the strength and freedom wait, to offer and receive the bright awareness that leads you home. The lamp is lit in you for your brother. And by the hands that gave it to him shall you be led past fear to love. (Chapter 20, *ACIM*)

King of Innocence and Peace

King of Innocence and Peace
is not deceased, for He is alive
and well in the realm of the
Kingdom of Heaven your eternal
home.

He is King of Kings and Lord of Lords
for He is King of love, King of joy, and
King of innocence and peace.

He defended His love for you by
permitting you to miscreate in fear
of fear in darkness of darkness.

He proved His love for you by agreeing to
the greatest act of death by writing in His
life script the brutal afflictions He would
endure through the act of the crucifixion.

He proved His joy is true by exhibiting
the resurrection showing you that you
are immortal and life is eternal.

He demonstrated His innocence by
His compliance to carry out His life
script to prove your own guiltlessness.

He showed His peace by not accepting
and reacting to the snares of those who
hated Him and screamed out for His
crucifixion.

King of Innocence and Peace is alive and
well and He displayed this at the time of
the resurrection.

King of Innocence and Peace is not a
departed for He has always been with
you and has now clearly returned to
once again show you He is in you and
you in Him as the essence of His
immortality and your own.

His life script was to act out as if there
were such a thing as death because
this is what we asked for; therefore,
we receive what we ask.

We were born to dream it because
there is no such thing as death and
be happy for this and bow to the
immortality in you that exist and
forever reigns.

King of Innocence and Peace
demonstrated this at the
resurrection and so this shows
we were unsuccessful in killing Him.

This means no one can be victorious
in killing you, for this is the way it is
as an immortal and this is the gift of
life.

For when the body is wiped out, the
spirit rises up into eternal life where
you thrive as an immortal because
spirit is life not death and this is God's

ultimate gift to the Sonship.

Be willing then to release the King of
Innocence and Peace from the crown
of thorns and you release yourself and
your brothers' from sufferings galore.

Free the King of Innocence and Peace
from the spearing of nails and you free
yourself from the bondages of toils and
snares.

King of Innocence and Peace is not
deceased, for He lives because He is
the Spirit of love and light and can
never die and so neither can you.

And so the King of Innocence and
Peace is the royal innocence and
peace of Christ in you.

VII. Looking Within

15. When you are tempted to yield to the desire for death, *remember that I did not die.* You will realize that this is true when you look within and *see* me. Would I have overcome death for myself alone? And would eternal life have been given me of the Father unless He had also given it to you? When you learn to make me manifest, you will never see death. For you will have looked upon the deathless in yourself, and you will see only the eternal as you look out upon a world that cannot die. (Chapter 12, *ACIM*)

Artist and Author

Upon completion of the portrait of
Christ wearing the crown of white lilies,
artist and author took the portrait
to Staples for printing.

We were explained the basics of their
standard procedure of how they can
show a sample of how His portrait
would look on glossy paper compared
to the usual paper.

We agreed to see both samples and they
began the printing process when an irate
women walks in and begins demanding they
move quickly with her printing orders because
she was in a rush.

So the focus was turned away from us and we
stood there in patience and in peace waiting for
the staff to return to us, and in silence, I prayed
calmness and peace befall the irate customer.

Through her angered mind, it seemed every
demand she gave did not go her way when,
in fact, it was going her way, but she was blind
to this because she was too busy in her senseless
frustrations to see and receive the calmness and
peace that was offered her.

Had she been willing to receive it she would
have calmed her mind and would have been
able to clearly see that everything is going her

way, but left an unsatisfied customer in her
irate state of mind because of her own refusal
to forgive herself for such nonsense behavior
and would had appreciated the staffs' efforts
to meet her every request including loading
her stacks of prints in her car.

When the staff returned to complete the
service, we were there for they were apologetic;
and when the first glossy sample of Christ portrait
was complete, the artist, Jenna, said, "OMG!"
and the author, Lorenza, said, "Oh how beautiful."

The staff were surprised to see our reaction and
asked, "Would you still like to see the sample on
the other paper?"

Author looked at artist and said, "What do
you think?" Artist said, "It's amazing!" So
this was my answer and we opted not to bother
with the process of the other sample that
would be printed on standard paper.

We met the staff at the register ready to
pay for their service, and the staff who cut
the portrait to a 9x12 size said, "Oh no it's
OK. We are done here. Thank you for your
patience." I said, "You mean it's free." She
said, "Yes."

This was a holy instant of the evidence
that she was so moved, not by our patience
and peace, ultimately, as witness to see
Christ wearing a crown of white lilies and
not a crown of thorns.

I know this brought her great joy because Christ tells me this is what would happen to anyone who is willing to release the suffering from Him to be free from their own suffering from any circumstance or situation they are in and they would offer miracles, and not charging for their service is a miracle.

The Holy Spirit was with us when we went to Staples and His blessings poured upon everyone present in the printing department including the irate woman who will eventually receive what has already been given her.

And so the artist and author are in it together alongside Christ and the Holy Spirit and we are all too thrilled to share how to release Christ from the sufferings of the crown of thorns and release yourself from your own sufferings, a quantum leap into forgiveness, atonement, patience, joy, peace, and miracles.

Reject

She happily received the offering
of a brochure that speaks of the
word of God from a Christian
woman.

Yet, in return, when she offered the
Christian woman the opportunity to
be featured in her blazing amazing
smiles video representing the release
of The King of Innocence and Peace from
the crown of thorns and honor Him with
the crown of white lilies to release Him
from His sufferings and our own from every
thorn propped all over the world, the Christian
woman rejected this divine invitation.

The ambassador of Christ kindly and respectfully
received her brochure as the way she understands
the truth of reality as the way she remembers it
before we were even born and was shocked
when the other representative of Christ rejected
the divine gift to release Christ from the crown of
thorns and our own.

Yet, she instinctively knew the Christian woman's
answer would be "no" because through the whole
insight of this divine offering to release Christ from
His sufferings and our own, the Christian woman
refused to smile, her lips even quivered as to ensure
she didn't gleam ablaze.

Nevertheless, the ambassador was stunned only because she did not recall that on this very day and in that very moment this episode would take place in agreement with each other before they were even born.

Then, she realized that if they remembered the agreement at the occurrence of their screenplay there would be no lessons to learn through rejection from all over the world.

The ambassador swiftly remembered that the variety of life, beliefs and understanding would get very boring not permitting any kind of earthly glory.

For if we remembered what is to happen at every moment of each day, we would immediately recall the Atonement of Christ putting a swift end on what we agreed to learn through our experiences of every rejection of the compilation of every single episode of our synthetic demise.

And so we must be willing to accept and not reject through respect and thoughtfulness of everyone's beliefs before wisdom and understanding can ever enter to tenderly correct and enlightened us with the truth within regardless of how we judge ourselves to be in our beliefs.

You Are Not a Thorn in My Side

You are the light of God's eye no
need to cry out or sigh, for He knows
your every need and desire because
He knows exactly how you are wired.

For He is your Creator and so it is you
I value and admire because everyone
and everything God creates I appreciate.

So no matter what you do or say
that might bring harm to my body
or tears to my eyes, you are not a
thorn in my side.

So I offer you a bouquet of white
lilies and you will know this is not
silly because I offer you lilies in
honor of innocence and peace the
holiness of Christ in you and me.

For you are the altar of our Father
in Heaven and this makes you a glow
of purity, glistening alongside the
glimmering bouquet of white lilies
I offer you.

For I look upon you through spiritual
vision and value the spirit in you
because God created spirit in love of
love in light of light the immortality
of freshness and loveliness most
flawless.

When I see you, I see our home and
my only goal is to bring you back home
to Heaven where you are forever loved
and safe.

I am a host of God working alongside
the Holy Spirit and His duty is to
see you return back to God safely and
I am all too happy to assist Him through
this journey.

And so no matter what you do or say,
you are not a thorn in my side, for I
offer you a bouquet of white lilies
most tenderly and sweetly as a royal
salute of your peace, innocence, and
my own.

I. Holy Week

3. A week is short, and yet this holy week is the symbol of the whole journey the Son of God has undertaken. He started with the sign of victory, the promise of the resurrection, already given him. Let him not wander into the temptation of crucifixion, and delay him there. Help him to go in peace beyond it, with the light of his own innocence lighting his way to his redemption and release. Hold him not back with thorns and nails when his redemption is so near. But let the whiteness of your shining gift of lilies speed him on his way to resurrection. (Chapter 20, *ACIM*)

VIII. The Vision of Sinlessness

4. The Holy Spirit guarantees that what God willed and gave you shall be yours. This is your purpose now, and the vision that makes it yours is ready to be given. You have the vision that enables you to see the body not. And as you look upon your brother, you will see an altar to your Father, holy as Heaven, glowing with radiant purity and sparkling with the shining lilies you laid upon it. What can you value more than this? Why do you think the body is a better home, a safer shelter for God's Son? Why would you rather look on it than on the truth? How can the engine of destruction be preferred, and chosen to replace the holy home the Holy Spirit offers, where He will dwell with you? (Chapter 20, *ACIM*)

The Core of the Play

The world is a stage a hallucination
of the roles we play trying to mold
our fake thoughts to the reality of
what we dream.

Like a pottery artist molding the
clay to the manifestation of her
imagination, but when the art
piece she is trying to make does
not express what she envisions,
she judges it harshly and smashes
the clay and begins molding it again
to her liking.

For she does not realize, to let the
clay form as it will be and love it
as to not pass judgment upon it
so she can see its purpose of the
way it molded.

It's like trying to make someone
whom they are not, trying to mold
them to our liking and when it
doesn't work, we try to break
them down to recreate them to
what we think they should be.

This is loveless and judgment
where we look upon another
through physical eyes looking
at the body and not past it.

For to look past the body is to
see through spiritual vision where
we behold each other's perfection.

To look upon one another with
love and without judgment is pure
love, for love does not judge.

Judgment is the core of the play
on the stage of the world, for we
judge harshly the body, behavior,
popularity, financial status, and
lifestyle.

We do not recognize that we are
so blind we do not see that all
these things are but an illusion,
a hallucination of the dream.

Judge the body, character, financial
status, and the personality and you
are blind and loveless, but look past
flesh and bones with love in your
heart and you see sinlessness and
holiness and this makes your mind
and heart the loveable soul you are.

Here, you see the reflection of yourself
and when you achieve this vision you
will want nothing more but to toss the
core of the play right in the middle of
the stage.

God is always thrilled every time His
Holy Spirit is given the opportunity to

fulfill His duty and bless you with God's peace and joy.

For only through tossing the toy of judgment against the Sonship can peace and joy enter where you release one another from the bondages of illusional fantasies of destruction.

And so toss the core of the play and let the clay form as it may and love it anyway.

VI. The Holy Instant
and the Laws of God

1. It is impossible to use one relationship at the expense of another and not to suffer guilt. And it is equally impossible to condemn part of a relationship and find peace within it. Under the Holy Spirit's teaching all relationships are seen as total commitments, yet they do not conflict with one another in any way. Perfect faith in each one, for its ability to satisfy you completely, arises only from perfect faith in yourself. And this you cannot have while guilt remains. And there will be guilt as long as you accept the possibility, and cherish it, that you can make a brother into what he is not, because you would have him so. (Chapter 15, *ACIM*)

VIII. The Vision of Sinlessness

3. Your brother's sinlessness is given you in shining light, to look on with the Holy spirit's vision and to rejoice in along with Him. For peace will come to all who ask for it with real desire and sincerity of purpose, shared with the Holy Spirit and at one with Him on what salvation is. Be willing, then, to see your brother sinless, that Christ may rise before your vision and give you joy. And place no value on your brother's body, which holds him to illusions of what he is. It is his desire to see his sinlessness, as it is yours. And bless the Son of God in your relationship, nor see in him what you have made of him. (Chapter 20, *ACIM*)

The Holy Way or Unholy Way

As long as you perceive yourself
as a body, you are choosing to look
at everything you see as outside of
you being true.

This is an unholy way of thinking
because there is nothing outside
of you and this is why you are the
dreamer.

To recognize everything is in you is
to see the illusion of the dreamer
and the Holy Spirit teaches you and
reminds you what is true and what
is false.

The holy way of thinking is to recognize
you are mind and spirit and you see the
the holiness of Christ in you.

The unholy way of thinking is to deny
the holiness of Christ in you and believe
the body and everything that happens to
you is true.

The holy way or unholy way of thinking
is certainly your choice, but remember,
the holy way is the Godly truth in you and
the unholy way is the ugly false in you.

The holy way leads you to the reality of
Heaven and life eternal; the unholy way

leads you to the belief in hell and death.

And so the holy way or unholy way is
the one road you ultimately will choose
to take, so no longer forsake yourself by
believing the body and your nightmares
are true.

After all, why would you want to believe
in things that wither, rust and turn to dust,
and in fearful things that lead you to cry,
cower and thrust?

I. The Link to Truth

2. How can you manifest the Christ in you except to look on holiness and see Him there? Perception tells you *you* are manifest in what you see. Behold the body, and you will believe that you are there. And every body that you look upon reminds you of yourself; your sinfulness, your evil and, above all, your death. And would you not despise the one who tells you this, and seek his death instead? The message and the messenger are one. And you must see your brother as yourself. Framed in his body you will see your sinfulness, wherein you stand condemned. Set in his holiness, the Christ in him proclaims Himself as you. (Chapter 25, *ACIM*)

The Body Is the Frame

You are the lovely picture of God's
chef d'oeuvre, for the frame of you
is only the body, which is meaningless
because the prize inside is what is
beautiful and meaningful.

Don't be mindful to the mindless
because the holiness in you is what
is significant.

Embrace the Christ in you and the
Sonship and you enrich His existence
in you and the frame goes into oblivion,
but the picture of you and your brothers
stands under the open power of God's
light.

No need to fear the term "frame goes
into oblivion" because we all know we
are born into this world to live the
experiences we chose to encounter.

Well, eventually, you will know this;
and ultimately, the spirit transitions
back to Heaven eternally and this
you will also learn.

Here, the recognition that the body is the
frame that withers away is the ultimate
breakthrough from dark to light and you
see the holy truth in you and me.

The same is true of God. Initially, you
will see a frame of His picture; but when
you enter His holiness, the frame becomes
Him and all the beauty in Heaven because
everything of God is life.

For He is the fundamental picture where
everything lovely He holds dearly in eternity
waiting patiently and peacefully for your
return home.

Here, you see clearly now, the body is the
frame that annihilates once you recognize
you are the masterpiece of God's lovely
picture that does not ever shatter because
you are loved under the safety of His sparkly
golden light forever.

And so the body is the frame that is empty
until you see the lovely face of Christ within
beholding His holiness, the Sonship, and
your own.

II. The Savior from the Dark

8. Within the darkness see the savior *from* the dark, and understand your brother as his Father's Mind shows him to you. He will step forth from darkness as you look on him, and you will see the dark no more. The darkness touched him not, nor you who brought him forth for you to look upon. His sinlessness but pictures yours. His gentleness becomes your strength, and both will gladly look within, and see the holiness that must be there because of what you looked upon in him. He is the frame in which your holiness is set, and what God gave him must be given you. However much he overlooks the masterpiece in him and sees only a frame of darkness, it is still your only function to behold in him what he sees not. And in this seeing is the vision shared that looks on Christ instead of seeing death.

9. How could the Lord of Heaven not be glad if you appreciate His masterpiece? What could He do but offer thanks to you who love His Son as He does? Would He not make known to you His Love, if you but share His praise of what He loves? God cherishes creation as the perfect Father that He is. And so His joy is made complete when any part of Him joins in His praise, to share His joy. This brother is His perfect gift to you. And He is glad and thankful when you thank His perfect Son for being what he is. And all His thanks and gladness shine on you who would complete His joy, along with Him. And thus is yours completed. Not one ray of darkness can be seen by those who will to make their Father's happiness complete, and theirs along with His. The gratitude of God Himself is freely offered to everyone who shares His purpose. It is not His Will to be alone. And neither is it yours. (Chapter 25, *ACIM*)

He Who Understands

As we wander our way on a
world of dismay, we point
fingers calling each other
sinners.

We nitpick at each other's
faults whether big or small,
but it doesn't even matter
because every mind is
shattered alike.

We are so blind to self-awareness
we can't see our own reflection
in one another, but this is why we
are so bothered by others because
our faults are the same.

In blindness, we have no concept
of the true knowledge we threw
away to be born in a world of a
confused maze.

He who understands this comes
to self-awareness, emerging from the
depths of murkiness to the surface of
clarity where you rest in serenity.

Here, you are calm and still, patiently
waiting for the Holy Spirit to gradually
fill your cup with the knowledge of
truth until the blues come to its end.

He who understands will never again
recant the loveliness of God's nature
because you will be fully nurtured with
His love, light, and yours combined.

Once your mind is aligned with His, there
is no going back to the dream of attack,
for now, you are moving forward to never
again move backward.

He who understands the reality of
Heaven will never again be rebirthed
into a caveman or animal, for you can
even be retransformed into a fish
if you so wish.

He who understands this has the full
knowledge of all things possible
through creation, for creation is greater
than evolution because creation is the
fundamental foundation of the
transformation of completion.

He who understands this has his mind
tightly braided and combined with God's
to never again unravel into a frenzy of
crazy, hazy, senseless, and meaningless
miscreations.

For time is nearing to come out of fearing
and into the loving, lightening, brightening
wonders of Heavenly sightseeing where
the sun never grows dim and stars suspend
in the sky of Heaven where there are shiny,
sparkly diamonds hanging from shimmery
tree limbs.

For the starring diamonds are a representation
of the star you are, understand this and your
spirit skips in the joy of remembering who you
are as you see Heaven is not barred to he who
understands and receives God and Heaven as
their eternal home.

He who understands this will never again be
homeless in the vastness of darkness because
your light and God's outshine it.

And so understand this and you will let your love
and light shine like the diamond star you are.

Reestablished Relationships

When we say, "He/she is insane,"
we are speaking illusion, but we
are also claiming our own insanity
of illusion just as well.

We are all insane in the life of this
illusional game, for there is nothing in this
world we can tame as true.

But we can come to a state of
healing and correction by offering
and accepting the Atonement of
Christ as we are in the dream of
self-deception and self-destruction.

"Have faith in the things you do not
see," saith the Lord, for this will bring
us to admire Him in adoration, for He
knows there is no such thing as
damnation.

Maintain focus and concentration
in all that He offers and move it
forward to share with others.

We will not be bothered, for spirit
will remember the loveliness of faith
handed by the Sender, receive to no
longer be deceived.

Faith is a gift that will lift self-deceit,
for she is not a downfall, she is God's
up call.

Maintaining faith in all situations and
circumstances of relationships and events
is a certainty of God's sovereignty.

And so faith will free you from hopelessness
to hopefulness in certainty reestablishing
relationships in peacefulness, holiness,
guiltlessness, and sanity, for she is true.

Imprisonment of Time

I desperately want to be free from
the imprisonment of time, we want
everything swiftly and instantly, yet
we are in a world of time, therefore,
everything takes time.

This is why patience and faith is a holy
virtue, be willing to embrace them in
love, joy, peace, and forgiveness because
in time you will receive what you ask.

The reason we want everything instant
and swift is because it is our true nature,
for in spirit as an immortal anything we
want all we do is think of it and boom it's
there, that quick. This is divine power.

In a holy instant, through our thoughts
it manifests and it is there before us in a
holy instant and this is the natural.

And so Lordy, Lord, Lord, at the moment of my
transition from earth to Heaven, I am so ready
to be released from the imprisonment of time
to return to the freedom of timelessness where
everything lovely we want is in a holy instant.

The Diamond Stars

You've never seen anything
so lovely until you behold the
diamond stars most Heavenly.

They are so radiant that your human
eyes cannot look upon them, for its
beam of dazzling twinkles will leave
you sightless.

The diamond stars are complete
and sweet as a holy memoir to
your Creator and Savior of your
lost soul to be restored to the
Kingdom of Heaven.

The diamond tree hovers over the
skies of Heaven with diamonds
suspended from the shiny branches
of Loves elation.

The diamond tree sheens most
bright because God's light sustains
the brilliance of its diamond stars.

Each diamond has a name on it,
and when your time arrives for
you to shine, the diamond with
your name on it glistens its
brightness sending you messages
of your vibrance.

You are a super shining star that
God will never bar from Heaven
because Heaven is your home
and you will remember this at
your appointed time particularly
when it's time for you to transition
back home.

Time is here to be awakened from
the dream and this is the message
we must be willing to deem.

For it is time to remember the
diamond stars in Heaven to give
a boost to the radiance in you.

Remember it and embrace it
so the sparkly vibrance of it
lights up the brilliance of who
you are, for you are not dull,
sad, conflicted, creepy, wicked,
or evil.

You are bright, fun, exciting,
likeminded, soothing, gentle,
enjoyable, loving, peaceful, and
joyful forever in the playful
openness of Heaven where
anything dark cannot reach it.

Remember the diamond tree
and your diamond star lights up
the dream where you spree
gently awakening you to come
and be free in the loveliness of
the Kingdom of Heaven.

The diamond tree is spiritually
awaiting your willingness to be
awakened to the diamond star
with your name on it waiting to
gleam upon your memory the
diamond star you made in
Heaven.

So in God's honor, we made the
diamond stars before we were
born into a long journey of a dream
to ensure God never forgets us and
we never forget Him.

And so the diamond stars await the
awakening of your memory and the
resurrection of spirit to transition
from the dream world to the real
world.

III. Beyond All Idols

8. The Thoughts of God are far beyond all change, and shine forever. They await not birth. They wait for welcome and remembering. The Thought God holds of you is like a star, unchangeable in an eternal sky. So high in Heaven is it set that those outside of Heaven know not it is there. Yet still and white and lovely will it shine through all eternity. There was no time it was not there; no instant when its light grew dimmer or less perfect ever was. (Chapter 30, *ACIM*)

The Diamond Tree

We look around on this world
and see the lovely trees filled
with green leaves.

At every season, color changes
leaves tumble at the falling
season without any good
reason.

But this is the point of the dream
to show what disappears, clears,
and ceases in the season of dreams.

Minds imagine a "money tree" not
remembering the "diamond tree" we
created with God but can never see
until we are released and spirit lifted
to Heaven or you accept the Holy Spirit's
perception a quantum leap into spiritual
vision.

The diamond-filled tree can never cease
because it is a permanent creation of
loves elation.

The diamond tree is in the safety of the
Kingdom of Heaven where there are no
seasons to bring down the diamonds
and for a very good reason.

For each diamond represents the
glistening spirit of your holiness
where no sinful god or anything
frightful can tear you down from
the diamond tree safely in the
Kingdom of Heaven.

One day, you will see through
the eyes of spiritual vision the
diamond tree you helped create
in Heaven while God awaits every
lovely spirit to return home from
the kingdom of gloom where nothing
here sparkles greater than the
diamond tree filled with diamond
stars in Heaven.

For each diamond that hangs under
the open sun of Heaven represents
you where the diamond tree that
branches out above your head on a
world where you briefly spree.

Your diamond star patiently and
peacefully waits for your willingness
to take a quantum leap where it
assists you to be free.

I see it clearly through the perception
of the Holy Spirit and so this too you can
see if you choose to receive the beauty and
trustworthy miracles of God's lovely
spiritual vision.

And so the diamond tree is breathtakingly
spectacular and true.

III. Beyond All Idols

9. Who knows the Father knows this light, for He is the eternal sky that holds it safe, forever lifted up and anchored sure. Its perfect purity does not depend on whether it is seen on earth or not. The sky embraces it and softly holds it in its perfect place, which is as far from earth as earth from Heaven. It is not the distance nor the time that keeps this star invisible to earth. But those who seek for idols cannot know the star is there. (Chapter 30, *ACIM*)

Transition or Death

When the spirit leaves the
body, it is a resurrection to
transition to the gift of
immortal life.

For each body that utilizes
their time on this dream world,
the spirit resurrects to transition
from a dream world of sorrows
to the real world of happiness.

We have reached the era of
looking at it as a transition or
death, for the time has arrived
for you to recognize that death
is in your own mind where the
ego dwells and wants you to
believe in "death."

To gain the knowledge of "transition"
is to be willing to learn to take a
quantum leap into spiritual vision.

Here, when you experience loss,
you will no longer refer to anyone
as "dead" because you will clearly
see and know the spirit resurrects
and transitions from the dream
world to the real world.

Be happy you have the choice
to look at loss as a transition or

death because in the transition
phase you see clearly there is no
such thing as death.

But if you keep yourself imprisoned
in the dream, then you clearly remain
blind and you see death indeed.

In the realm of spiritual vision and
knowledge, you will speak of loss as
a transition not death.

And so transition or death is your
choice to learn and remember
there is no such thing as death,
for only in dreams is there death
and this you dream indeed.

The Truth Will Set You Free

Before time began, all of Heaven
stood in truth and silence because
we were about to leave Heaven to
be born into a world of lies and
violence.

We stood in love and peace, bowed
our heads, and blessed one another with
forgiveness because of the experiences
we agreed to endure one to another.

Everything we do upon each other is a
lie because it is the hallucination of the
dream we wrote to deem.

To admit what you do in this world is
real is untrue and to drag each other
into the lies of your dream is judgment
and loveless.

Everything we think, do, and say that
is the dictation of the ego is all a lie,
loveless, and only leads to judgment,
bondage, and the belief in guilt,
punishment and death.

Everything you confess from the ego's
perspective will not set you free because
it is not true, for only the truth will set
you free.

The truth will set you free is the spiritual
truth in you, not what you see what you
think is outside of you.

You think everything that happens to you
are happening outside of you when the truth
is it's all happening inside of your own mind
because you are dreaming it.

Never recant the dream just because you feel
the dreadful effects of it, for if you do, you
prolong your own suffering and the blindness
to the truth in you.

When the ego tells you to steal, kill, and destroy,
let God fill your heart with love, peace, and joy,
for this is the truth in you and only the truth
of this will set you free.

Forgive the lies of the ego and you will literally
be set free. Believe the lies of the ego and you
remain a prisoner of your own dream.

You have the power to not allow yourself to
be a figure in another's sick ideas of their dream
and your own. Swiftly forgive and you will be
lifted to spiritual freedom releasing you from the
savages of the bondages of guilt, punishment
and judgment.

The true meaning of "the truth will set you free"
has nothing to do with the ego because the ego
wants you to believe that if you admit to horrid
deeds, it will set you free, but the truth is it
will put you in bondage and this is savage.

Begin to free yourself from ego thinking by not admitting your life experiences are real because they are but an illusion of your dream, therefore false.

Just because you feel the effects of your experiences doesn't make it real, this you must be willing to unravel to see the true from the false because the truth will set you free and the false will keep you imprisoned.

If you declare the pains of your experiences are real, then it becomes true for you; but if you deny its effects are factual, then it has no power over you.

The truth will set you free is to confess God is your Father of Love and Light; Christ is your brother of Innocence and Peace; the Holy Spirit is your Teacher and Comforter; the spirit in you is holy, guiltless, and sinless; and Heaven is your home.

And so the truth of this will set you free because you are love, light, life, innocent, sinless, holy, joy, and peace indeed.

The Truth In You

I was born with eyes to see, yet
I was blind, for only the world
born into was I able to see until
I learned to look past it and see
the world from which I rebirthed.

I was born with ears to hear, yet I
was deaf, for it was only the voice
of man and the noise of the world
was I able to hear.

It was this way through my life
experiences until I was willing to
learn and remember to hear and
listen to the Voice of the Holy Spirit.

We are born into a world of
darkness where we all experience
blindness and deafness, but some
people have chosen to literally
be born blind and deaf or both
and they learn to see, hear, smell,
and touch through their senses.

They are no different than we
are because through willingness,
we too learn to see, hear, smell,
and touch through our senses.

For we learn to feel the love of God
in us, we learn to see through the
mind's eye the face of Christ in us,

we learn to hear the peaceful Voice
of the Holy Spirit within, and we learn
to pay attention to the lovely aroma
of Christ all around us.

To be willing to learn and remember
to use our senses to look past the
illusional world and behold the
world of realism is a great conviction
of paying attention to the innocence
and inner peace in you.

For it is only through the calmness
and peacefulness of the mind you
must be willing to accomplish, for
this is a meaningful mission you are
here to do.

For you are a child even if you are
a godzillion years old, which you are,
you are still a child of God and will be
forever.

Here, you learn to use your keen
senses to get past the fences you
put up in your mind to block the
truth from the false.

The truth in you frees you from
blindness and deafness, for blind
and deaf are the false in you that
keeps you in denial of the true you.

The true you is spiritual not physical
be reborn in the spirit where you see
past this world and look upon the real

world through spiritual vision and you
see, hear, feel, and smell the wonders
of Heaven.

Here, you remember Heaven, the
home in which you were born from,
and you see Christ with open arms
and a smile confirming you have
been reborn in holiness and now you
behold the truth in you through Him.

Christ has always told us that to see
Him, we see our Father in Heaven and
to love Him is to love our Father in Heaven
and this is because we are all divinely
connected.

Here, you remember God is your Father,
Christ is your brother, and the Holy Spirit
is your comforter, but you also know
they are much more than this and
through spiritual vision you learn to see
the connection from the Sonship to Heaven
working from the bottom up.

It starts with you and it branches out and
up and so you are the tree in which to free
yourself and your brothers from blindness
and deafness to finally come out of darkness
of a world you don't belong and into the
world you so long.

And so the truth in you is mind and spirit
be willing to embrace it.

Star Child

We have given the name Estrella
to our children since millennia, not
because we are special, but because
we know of the holiness in us, but
for a time have forgotten.

Estrella is the Spanish pronunciation
translated to star in English and child
star is translated in Spanish, chico
estrella.

From the beginning of time every
cultural has given a child the name
Star because subconsciously, we
know of the star we created before
we were born from timelessness into
time.

The star we created is a memoir to
God, Heaven and the Sonship, which
is in you and me.

For a little while we have forgotten
that we are all naturally born stars
because we give the greatest act of
destructive behavior and death that
will never sustain itself forever.

So when we speak of star children, we
are speaking of each and every one of us
because we are all a star child born from
Heaven.

As time crunches the star child in every
single one of us will emerge from memory
loss to memory gain of the star in all of us
and we will draw to one another like a
magnet because the spirit will remember
the star child in you and me.

So every child born nearer to the end of
time will be born with the memory and full
knowledge and understanding in clarity and
certainty of who we are, why we are here,
where we come from, where we will return,
and we have never been alone.

For they will be born with the full memory
of the star in us to help us to remember the
star child within and it has been this way
since time began.

And so the star child in us doesn't make us
special, for it is the holiness in each and every
one of us and as time crunches we will learn
to embrace this as we remember who we are,
where we come from, where we will return and
that God is our Father in Heaven Who permitted
us to miscreate godzillions ago.

I Forgive God

From the day we birth out of Heaven
and born into an alien world we don't
belong, we are born the same, yet we
are blind to this and fail to remember
the body is the armor that guards the spirit.

For you will be taught to value the body
and learn the ways of the world that will
hurdle you deep into darkness where you
become aware that you are lost and spend
a lifetime seeking to be found.

The body is the armor that protects the
spirit, but it's the spirit you will inescapably learn to
cherish and the mind is the world of fear
and darkness you will inevitably be willing
to bring to love and light, yet you are love
and light and this is where you and I are the
same.

On behalf of the Sonship, I forgive God for
permitting us to birth into fear and darkness where
we must be willing to find the way to see
past the body and into the light within that
leads to the golden road of Heaven.

Through self-awareness we become
less careless even though we might
travel various roads to find the barrier
that blinds us to the spirit.

We spend a lifetime believing in the
world we see, for the mind is tangled
and in the confusion of self-deceit, for
we do not realize the spirit of immortality
is imprisoned behind the shield of the
mortal body as we travel all roads that
lead to Heaven.

But, we are pleasantly surprised to find
a glistening golden curtain at the end
of the road we elect to take.

Through all the challenges, obstacles
and hurdles on the path taken, we
can't wait to see what's behind
the sparkly golden curtain, for
everything we've gone through, we
hope for a better world than the one
we traveled through.

When you arrive at the gleaming golden
curtain, you will instinctively know you are
about to see the world from which you came,
at least this is what you are hoping; to know
a better world.

At the base of the glittering golden curtain,
we bow to our knees and lovingly, humbly
and peacefully, we forgive God for allowing
the spirit of love and light to birth out of
Heaven and into a world we are alien to
where we experience the darkness of pre-written
events we asked to experience.

So the glistening golden curtain gently
flows down and you rise to look upon a

world so lovely you can't believe there is
a better world after all, yet you instinctively
know this is your home.

Here, you are a witness to the sparkly
diamonds in the skies of Heaven where
you see beautiful white-winged angels fly
the skies in the fabulous openness of Heaven,
you observe the glistening waterfall streaming
and teaming with abundant of joyful and
playful life.

You hear the lovely hymns of angels, flowers,
grass, plants and trees, you see happy and
peaceful glowing people smiling and greeting
each other in passing.

Then, you gaze upon the golden road leading
to the golden Kingdom of Heaven where Christ
stands with open arms and a welcoming smile,
and you automatically know you are home.

However, you also know you cannot enter
and so you ask what it is you need to do to
re-enter Heaven.

The Holy Spirit guides you and comforts you
to God's threshold where the process of purification and
cleansing begins and it starts with forgiving God, yourself and
your brothers', for letting the speck of darkness
in the heart manifest to the creation of a world
of screams and sorrows we agreed to bring upon
ourselves and each other.

Here, you free yourself and the Sonship
from the bondages of a world you don't
belong, ultimately, you free God to authorize
Christ to hold the sparkly gates of Heaven
open for you until the time arrives for you
to return home.

And so to say, "I forgive God" is the key to
forgiving yourself and the Sonship where
you most certainly will reenter Heaven in
love, light, life, safety, unity, truth, freedom,
joy, and peace. And God Himself will
honor you with the golden crown of
eternity, a recompense to your royalty,
absolutely.

III. The Forgiveness
of Specialness

5. God asks for your forgiveness. He would have no separation, like an alien will, rise between what He wills for you and what you will. They *are* the same, for neither One wills specialness. How could They will the death of love itself? Yet They are powerless to make attack upon illusions. They are not bodies; as one Mind They wait for all illusions to be brought to Them, and left behind. Salvation challenges not even death. And God Himself, Who knows that death is not your will, must say, "Thy will be done" because you think it is. (Chapter 24, *ACIM*)

Memory Loss

Thinking with the human mind,
we think on a puny scale because
the split mind is an undermine of
of who we truly are.

Being born into a world of time
with a split mind wiped out the
memory of who we are and
where we come from, although
it is not lost but for a little while.

We can regain memory loss by
making a decision to be willing to
listen to the Voice of the Holy Spirit,
for by gaining memory with Him
becomes as easy and as pleasing as
breathing.

Living in a world of time is a place
of dark minds, but this only means
we are blind to the memory loss the
moment we are born into an
atmosphere of time.

Memory loss is not forever because
we come from a world where we are
loved and cherished.

In the world of time, the only valuable
thing to remember is God, Heaven, and
the Sonship because God leads you

back to Heaven and it is your duty to
enlightened the Sonship in accordance
to the lead of thy Holy Spirit.

Because when you learn and remember
God is your Father, Heaven is your home,
Christ is your brother, and the Holy Spirit
is your teacher, you learn of your guiltlessness
and this memory is to be shared with the Sonship
because they too are your innocent brothers.

Never force the memory you've been given
upon anyone not willing to listen. Just lovingly,
patiently, and peacefully plant the seed in their
mind of who they are and where they come from,
step back in faith, and let God step in to water the
seed you planted and you've accomplished your
duty in helping them regain the memory of their
holiness and innocence.

This is the best good deed you can give to a
brother, and when their time arrives to
remember, they too will divinely flourish and they will
want nothing more than to share it forward.

It becomes a domino effect to the new comers
born into this world just as it has been since
time began.

Memory loss will eventually become extinct
and memory gain reigns. This is what's important,
for it is a meaningful task you are here to achieve.

And so memory loss of who you are and where
you come from is a temporary thing and memory
gain, God is your Father, Christ is your brother,

the Holy Spirit is your teacher, the Sonship is your holy family, and Heaven is your home, is what will eternally set you free.

III. The Decision for Guiltlessness

16. Say to the Holy Spirit only, "Decide for me," and it is done. For His decisions are reflections of what God knows about you, and in this light, error of any kind becomes impossible. Why would you struggle so frantically to anticipate all you cannot know, when all knowledge lies behind every decision the Holy Spirit makes for you? Learn of His wisdom and His Love, and teach His answer to everyone who struggles in the dark. For you decide for them and for yourself.

17. How gracious it is to decide all things through Him Whose equal Love is given equally to all alike! He leaves you no one outside you. And so He gives you what is yours, because your Father would have you share it with Him. In everything be led by Him, and do not reconsider. Trust Him to answer quickly, surely, and with Love for everyone who will be touched in any way by the decision. And everyone will be. Would you take unto yourself the sole responsibility for deciding what can bring only good to everyone? Would you know this? (Chapter 14, *ACIM*)

Forgive and Knowledge and Understanding Gives

Without forgiveness, you remain in
blindness because to harbor hostility,
bitterness, and hatred of the heart
blinds you and binds you to the
bondages of fear and darkness.

To be willing to forgive is a blessing
because it frees you and your brothers'
from the chains and shackles of fear and
darkness.

Be willing then to learn to forgive and
knowledge and understanding gives the
blessing of forgiveness through spiritual
vision.

For it releases you from the bondages of
tunnel vision where you will see the whole
picture of what you asked for.

Because everything you experience is what
you wrote to endure one to another and
from one side of the world to the other.

So everything we dream, we asked to deem
and Christ tells us, "We receive what we ask"
not remembering the treachery it would bring
the moment we are born from out of timelessness
and into time.

Forgiveness, knowledge, and understanding
gives through the awakening of the whole
picture of what we asked for, and this releases
you from the bondages of hostility, bitterness,
and hatred.

Because forgiveness, knowledge, and understanding
work in unison shining the light on the dream you no
longer wish to deem because you see clearly the
catastrophe of the fear and darkness you made.

It is not necessary to permit guilt to consume you
because God has forgiven you before time began
and this is where your guiltlessness comes in.

To see the guiltlessness of the Sonship and your
own, you must be willing to forgive God for letting
you experience frightful dreams and forgive yourself
and the Sonship for making it and agreeing to be
born into it in order to experience the pains and
sorrows it would bring.

And so forgiveness, knowledge, and understanding
gives you the golden release into calmness and
peacefulness of it all where you recognize the
illusion of what you and the Sonship agreed
to dream.

The Loveliness in You

We are loveless, yet we are loved.
We are homeless, yet we are royalty.
We are senseless, yet we are meaningful.
We are fragile, yet we are powerful.

We are sinful, yet we are holy.
We are fear, yet we are love.
We are joyless, yet we are joy.
We are hostile, yet we are peace.

Nurture the delightful love and light
in you and you regain your memory of the
peace and divine Kingdom of tender sovereignty.

Raise the enchanting divinity in you and
you transform the split mind back to the
wholeness and wholesomeness of your thinking.

Cherish the love, joy, and peace in you,
and you obliterate guilt, fear, and darkness.

Remember there is no such thing as death
because the resurrection, transformation,
and transition is your Heavenly inheritance.

And so be willing to behold and embrace the
loveliness in you just as God created you
and walk alongside of Christ as He escorts
you to your divine Kingdom and enchanting creations
under the sparkly golden openness of Heaven.

The Peace of Completion

It has been a long and arduous road
writing such lovely poems of God's
truth.

In the beginning, it was a struggle, a
wrestling match with God because
knowledge and understanding of His
Holy Spirit's lead had not yet arrived,
yet they were gifts Christ entered with
and laid at my feet; and for a little while,
I failed to see them and so I neglected to
immediately receive them.

In certainty, I see this in clarity and it is a
pleasant blessing to gain full spiritual vision
where instantly I saw them and accepted
them. Soon after, I was honored with the
crown of knowledge and understanding
always follows.

I didn't realize the burden I had been carrying
through my writings of the second edition of
bringing you the significance of your forgiveness
and guiltlessness until I was finished. Here, I softly
felt the blanket of the peace of completion that
oozed upon me.

At the finish line, the heaviness I didn't realize
I was carrying was lifted from me; and in that holy
instant, I knew I had been carrying a yoke of
a load.

Yet it was a lovely yoke that never weighed
me down because while I persevered in my
work at the Holy Spirit's lead, His tender light
outshined the hand of the ego that tried to
hold me down in the hopes I would wear a
permanent frown and toss my inheritance of
the golden crown of eternity God promised me.

When the peace of completion fell upon me,
I saw this clearly and it brought me great joy
to see that I did not listen to the ego's weak
burden it tried to instill upon me.

The ego's darkness is too weak to sustain itself
in me, for God's light is the power in me so the
peace of completion is the glory of God's blessing
of His lovely smile of elation that I persevered in
His glistening, golden, tender yoke, and finished
at the lead of His Holy Spirit.

Through God's urgency and my diligence to
bring to you His lovely poetic messages of your
guiltlessness is of great importance and I am
thrilled that we took a quantum leap here
because this will bring a swift remembrance
to you of who you are and where you come
from and you are not alone and never have
been.

The peace of completion is God's way of
spiritually rewarding me for my vigilance
and diligence in my perseverance with His
Holy Spirit and this is a golden consecration.

And so through your own journey of willingness
and alertness with the Holy Spirit and your walk

alongside of Christ, stick to Them like glistening golden glue of dew; and at the peace of completion, God will pour His blessings of goodness upon you and this will bring you a grandeur of love, joy and peace, indeed.

On This Christmas Day

I think of You at the marina, for I went down to
the river to pray, with my coffee and journal in
hand, in case, I think of what to say on this
divine Christmas day.

For this is the season You were born in, but
I think of You twenty-four seven. O Christ
You are my light, the bright shining star in me,
let others see Your light in them and their
light in You.

For in Your Atonement is the moment, the
eyes open to the senseless and meaningless
clutter the world offers.

O Lord, let it be that we all see Your divine light
shine upon the night obscuring everything
senseless and meaningless to enable us to
see everything that is sensible and meaningful
in all its lovely and holy glory.

And so let it be on this Christmas day and
every day thereof our shining star within
outshines all that is dreadfully senseless,
meaningless and dim from all over the world,
O Lord. In the name of the Kingdom of God. Amen.

Dedicated to Jesus Christ in love, light, life, joy, peace, faith, unity,
safety, royalty, freedom and truth on this Christmas day, December
25, 2017 and forevermore.

Summary

The passion of this book is immense because it shows you how to release the sufferings of Jesus Christ and your own swiftly. At your willingness to take a quantum leap to release Him from the crown of thorns is the most rapid way to see through the fog of darkness and into the clarity of lightness where you will see the world from which you belong. And you will look behind you and see the mirage of the world from which you instinctively know you are not from and this is a fabulous awakening into breath of life! For the delight of the experience in writing it, was on a grandeur scale, in which you can never witness it alone. Working alongside of the Holy Spirit isn't all seriousness all the time, for He has a divine sense of humor! There were times I cried, frowned, smiled, giggled, and laughed, but the ultimate amazement through the whole process was His love, light, tenderness, compassion, understanding, patience, peace, safety, unity and freedom He exhibited through His lead in what was to be written to the divinity of the brilliant act of the King of Innocence and Peace, the guiltlessness in you.

You have never seen anything so lovely until you see Jesus Christ smile! This book speaks of the simplicity of quantum leap where you will be witness to His lovely smile upon you. The intensity of the simplicity and power of quantum leap is beyond anything you could ever imagine until you travel through it with Me. Here, with My assistance, you will swiftly pull yourself out of your own sufferings in any situation and circumstance and the sufferings of others, no matter what form, throughout the whole world in peace through quantum leap. It is important to be patient and remain in calmness in any circumstance because this is the best and instant way holiness enters to help you through. Be willing to release Jesus Christ from the crown of thorns and be a witness as He rises wearing the crown of white lilies you offered Him, glistening golden with a blazing, amazing smile delighted you have chosen to release Him from His sufferings, your brothers' and your own. I hope you permit Me through this poetic truth to take you into spiritual vision and knowledge and we will go through the quantum leap process so tender you will not even know you traveled through it until you realize the spiritual sight given you. Here, you will certainly behold the open doors of bliss to love, joy, peace, freedom, union and safety. To be a witness to the release of Jesus' sufferings from the crown of thorns is to see Him gleam of joy that you have chosen to release Him, yourself and your brothers' from the thorns at every corner of the world. You will witness the risen Christ wearing the crown of white lilies with a lovely smile in beauty and sovereignty, which is the ultimate release into a holy wonder of reconciliation with Him. This is the process of quantum leap into Atonement where you instantly gain spiritual vision and knowledge of who you are, why things happen the way they do, where your real home is, where you will return, and you are never alone. And this is where insanity is restored to sanity and forgetfulness is reestablished to the remembrance of your Father in Heaven. Wouldn't you want to be released from the agonies of your insanity? It would be foolish not to want it!

Holy Spirit
God's Holy Commissioner
(Your Guide, Teacher and Comforter)

The Test of Patience

It was the day after Christmas 2017. At sunrise, I was awakened and was told to go down to the river; Scott's Seafood came into vision. I thought, 'if I must get up this early, I want a white chocolate mocha.' And intuitively, I knew Scott's Seafood does not serve this divine coffee. Nonetheless, once again, I was instructed to go to Scott's Seafood down by the river. For a split second, I wrestled with this divine instruction because I first wanted to go to Peet's Coffee, like I always do, where I am certain they serve white chocolate mocha. Then, swiftly, I instinctively knew my patience was being tested. And it also confirmed what I always instinctively knew that Scott's Seafood does not serve white chocolate mocha. This is why I always went to Peet's Coffee before heading to the marina at Scott's Seafood to pray and write. And, I also knew that my patience was being tested to enable me to see in all clarity and certainty where it is I need to polish the quality of my patience because there is an event that is going to take place that is going to call upon my patience. Anyway, that is beside the point. Nevertheless, I knew I had to follow the Holy Spirit's lead and go where God would have me go. So I did. When I arrived at Scott's Seafood, the first thing I did is ordered a white chocolate mocha and what I already knew was confirmed, once again. They do not serve it. So, I informed them that I was going to go and get a white chocolate mocha and asked them if they are at peace with my returning to their restaurant with it and they said, "Yes." So I peacefully and patiently left to go and get a white chocolate mocha where I had to drive to the other side of the river. As it turns out, it was a blessing. Because when I arrived at Peet's Coffee, she made my white chocolate mocha, handed it to me and said, "Today, your white chocolate mocha is free. Just pay fifty cents for the extra white mocha pumps." I always order extra white choco mocha because I like my coffee nice and sweet. I was persistent in getting my white chocolate mocha and return to Scott's Seafood because I had my journal and pen in hand and that is where I like to go and write. Many times, I sit at the river's edge, pray and write, but on this morning, I sat at the bar to write because I decided I was going to have breakfast. And I will elaborate on that in a moment.

On my way back to Scott's Seafood, my patience continued to be tested. I ended up behind a garbage truck in the middle of the road and the garbage technician was very slow in empting the garbage bins. Finally, he moved his truck out of the way. Then, three parked cars up there was another garbage truck in the middle of the road and once again, I had to stop and wait for him to complete this slow service. Finally, he moves his truck closer to the curb so I can pass. Then, just as I passed him a utility tractor driver was already making a right turn in front of me onto the street I am on and he must have been driving five miles per hour. I said to the Holy Spirit, "Oh my God, Lord, really, are you kidding me?" Ok, so now we are approaching a light signal and I said, "Oh Lord, please let him make a left turn." Because you see, I was going to make a right turn. And to my satisfaction, the utility tractor driver made a left turn. Yay! I was very happy about this, but it was short lived. I make my right turn and thirty feet ahead on this road, I had to make a left turn to be on the road back to Scott's Seafood. So, I make my left turn and the moment I turn around the bend there was a car driving five miles per hour. I began to laugh and said, "Ok, Holy Spirit, I get it. My patience is continuing to be tested." Then, as this driver slowly made a right turn another driver was emerging in front of me onto the road I was on. I took a deep breath and slowly released because this driver too was driving five miles per hour. We finally approached a stop sign at a four way intersection and the driver in front of me paused longer than needed then slowly crossed the road. As I moved up to make my stop another driver opposite side of the four way intersection had the right of way after the car in front of me crossed. So, I remain at the stop sign to let him cross the road, and he does. But, he makes a semi left turn onto the intersection of the road, then he comes to a complete stop right in the middle of the road. He begins to look all around as if trying to decide which way he is going to go. I sat there and suddenly I burst out in laughter and finally, I said, "Ok, Holy

Spirit, I am going to remain in patience and peace just as God would have me be. I am not going to get into the realm of road rage nor am I going to honk my horn. I am simply going to remain in stillness, patience and peace and wait for this lovely man to decide which way he wants to turn." Finally, the gentleman decides to complete the left turn and moves on.

My patience was being tested on this cool December morning because the Holy Spirit is preparing my patience to be fully polished in everything He has taught me. I understood this. For long ago, I asked to become what I teach and preach about and when He brought this to my remembrance, it made me very happy. Because I was able to see and know in all clarity and certainty that God honored what I asked for. So I did everything I was instructed to do in patience and in peace, of course, once I got passed the split second of a wrestling match. Therefore, I passed the test of patience.

So, when I finally arrive back at Scott's Seafood, I walk in with a blazing amazing smile because I passed the test of patience, and I have a white choco mocha, journal and pen in hand ready to write as I have coffee and breakfast. I sit at the bar and order country fried potatoes, sausage and sour dough toast. The bartender said, "Don't you want an over easy egg with your breakfast?" I said, "I usually never order an egg with my breakfast any place I go because over easy eggs must be cooked to perfection the way I like it." She became very interested in this reply and said, "Really, well, how is it that you like your egg to be cooked?" I said, "Well, the white has to be completely cooked and the yoke must be completely cooked as well, but it can't be hard or runny. I have to be able to pop the yoke without it being runny or over cooked. And, the edge of the white must be crispy." She smiled and said, "Wow, ok, you do like it cooked a certain way." I have had lunch and dinner at Scott's Seafood and this was my first time having their breakfast and those country fried potatoes and sausage were the best I ever had. I have had some great tasting ones, but nothing like this. I send my gratitude of my kind thank you to the Chefs' at Scott's Seafood for such healthy and delicious cooking.

And so as it turned out, this morning was a blessing all around, for I got a free white chocolate mocha, a wonderfully flavorsome breakfast, past the test of patience enabling myself to see where it is my patience needs to be polished. So here I sit, at the bar at Scott's Seafood as I write my testimony of this whole morning experience of patience.

I hope this helps you to be mindful that at your willingness to listen to the Voice of the Holy Spirit, you have the divine power invested in you to control your own patience in peace. For life is so divinely good when we listen to the lovely and peaceful Voice of the Holy Spirit. In the name of the Kingdom of God. Amen.

My Heartfelt Thoughts

It is not easy to share the Lord's deepest loveliest thoughts of truth living on a world where many are blind to it. This is where controversy, sabotage, harm, disruption, interruption, quarrel, dispute all these negative thoughts of the ego come into play to try and destroy the truth of God, Heaven, and the Sonship. It is a challenge, a wrestling match between the Lord and us when we are in darkness or even in partial light of true reality of everything. I wrestled with God myself, but in the gentleness of His tactfulness, He did not permit me to wrestle with Him for too long. In doing so, never once did He punish me, threatened me or confine me in order to get me to listen to Him. He just simply waited in love, peace, and patience for my willingness and compliance to learn and remember Him. And through His tender guidance of His Holy Spirit is where I ultimately remembered what I am here to realize, and through sharing my poetic words with you I am fulfilling my duty to the whole Sonship all over the world. And I am very appreciative of His tender tactics and His promise He would ensure I remember my role on this world just as Christ did. He gently releases us from the wrestling match with His love, silence, patience, and peace enabling us to calm ourselves to the willingness of His knowledge and spiritual vision no matter how long it takes. However, if we spend too much time in a wrestling match with Him, it can consume us and we get lost to the truth of what He is gradually unveiling for the opportunity to be a witness to the truth of His true love we do not remember. This is because not only is our faith very little or none at all, as we are in darkness or partial light of truth, we see bits and pieces that the Holy Spirit brings to our remembrance preparing us to see the whole picture of God's grandeur of truth.

As we persevere out of darkness and into the light, God removes the spiritual scales from our eyes a little bit at a time. His gentleness must be this way in order to safeguard the sane part of mind assisting the Holy Spirit to His part of your spiritual awakening from the dream. The Trinity is always working in unison to ensure your success of self-awareness, and as you persevere with Him, you become part of the Trinity, just as well. If God gave us the truth to see swiftly or all at once, it would do no good to the process of the greatest healing of the mind in correcting our sick thinking. However, if you take a quantum leap into the true reality, it becomes a swift elation of happiness to know you do not belong in what feels like eternal pains and sorrows, and the belief in death. On the other hand, you must be at a comfortable place of spiritual vision and spiritual knowledge in order to take a quantum leap because the split brain would not be able to wrap its mind around it because it would be too vast for you to grasp. This is why we can't view the enormity of the universe in all its magnitude concurrently. It would drive our brilliant minds crazy who study it, because they are the ones looking at it firsthand. Their minds wouldn't be able to wrap around what they are looking at and would end up deeper into insanity.

This is another gracious act of the evidence of God's love for us. He knew exactly what His part would be to heal our split mind back to its original wholly state of correction and remembrance of who we are and where we come from. This is the duty of the Holy Spirit. It is vital to invite Him to be your teacher and guide to the golden road that leads to the golden eternity where you will receive your crown of knowledge. It is possible to receive it in time, just as I did, but this depends on how vigilantly and diligently you choose to let the Holy Spirit help you remember the reality of Heaven, who you are, what your role is and where you come from. By the time you receive the crown of knowledge, you would have come to a level of spiritual vision of God's love and truth in you and the Sonship and the innocence and peace of Jesus Christ, your brothers, and your own. Here, your love will merge into the grandeur of God's Love. In the spotlight of His love, your peace and faith is so great that you are not only buddies with the Holy Spirit you remember the lovely friendship of the faith in the King of Innocence and Peace. Faith is just as part of the Trinity as you and I are. In fact, the whole Sonship is just as part of the Trinity as Christ and the Holy Spirit are. She is one of the loveliest friends in God you always had! She shows us all things lovely and true we do not see.

All of God's gifts of goodness are outstanding! Gifts you will no longer want to be blind to and deny once you see the truth. Faith completes the peace of the truth of your innocence. By the time she enters the picture, you would have received the crown of knowledge and ready to go onto the next phase of your spiritual education with the Holy Spirit accompanied by Faith. At this point, you are in a full-blown holy relationship with Christ, a relationship that was lost for a little while now fully restored the instant you removed the crown of thorns from His injured and bloody head and honored Him with the crown of white lilies where you see Him rise in life and beauty with a blazing amazing smile. This is the greatest gift of Atonement we will ever accomplish in a world of darkness, for now we are merged with the Trinity where God willed us to return. Here, we no longer wear eye scales and our sight fully restored to the truth of the Sonship from one side of the world to the other, you included. We have followed the light of Atonement and Christ is the authority of the Atonement that was established for you as He patiently waited for you to be ready to reconcile with Him in love and peace. Atonement is the light of Christ that keeps your path lit up for you to see your way through a world of darkness where faith, love, light, life, joy, safety, freedom, peace and innocence have been neglected. To persevere on the path of Atonement, you continue to uphold your holy relationship with Christ because you entered it with Him first. He guides you to branch out God's love and word of the King of Innocence and Peace to the whole Sonship. The comfort of the Holy Spirit never leaves you because He has safeguarded it through the whole process of your spiritual awakening and will continue to protect it until you are in Heaven where you no longer need His shield. Because once we have transitioned to Heaven, we are forever under the safeguard of God where no darkness can enter Heaven, ever again!

Faith of your peace and innocence will bring to you the things that are unseen, but lovely and true. She brings them to your spiritual vision where you will be pleasantly amazed at what you had forgotten. The remembrance of what she shows you bring about such calmness, because you see the way out of fear and darkness Christ has always told us about in all clarity and certainty. Above all else, value the way out of darkness always in your mind and heart, for what you place your faith in is what will be reality to you. For example, when we put our faith in madness, then that is what our reality will be "madness." If you put your faith in the goodness of God's truth, you see through spiritual vision enabling yourself to find your way back home and will be your reality if you so choose to cherish and value it. Here, you return to what has always belonged to you. It is what we choose to appreciate and give merit too that will manifest into our thought system, therefore, will be real to us. No one wants to make fear and darkness a reality forever, even if you think you do. This is simply plain foolish thinking even if you don't see the folly in it yet. Rest assure one day you will and you will look back and say, "How could I have ever been so blind?"

We say the same thing when we find ourselves coming out of a horrid relationship that we reflect back on. This is just another example to remind us of what we really don't want. Faith can only show you things unseen if you elect to continue to wear the crown of knowledge in humbleness, kindness and peace and let her take you further into Heaven to behold the unseen reality you had forgotten about, since godzillions ago. Carry on with her so you will share the lovely unseen with the Sonship. At this point, you will not have any concern over those who will not believe you, or think you have gone bonkers, because you would have already learned and come to peace with the fact that it is not your job to convince anyone of the truth. It is God's concern to move through them in their own life to help them come to the place in their own spiritual awakening where they will inevitably see the truth about themselves first before they can even behold the truth of God, Christ, the Holy Spirit, Heaven, and the Sonship. It is a burden you do not have to carry and a weight for God to bear for you. For at this point, God needs you to carry a lightweight to help you remain focused on your mission to bring the truth of love, light, life, joy, safety, unity, freedom, faith, forgiveness, innocence, and peace to the Sonship from one side of the world to the next. This is another phase of the evidence of God's Love for you and the Sonship.

IX. The Cloud of Guilt

3. The world can give you only what you gave it, for being nothing but your own projection, it has no meaning apart from what you found in it and placed your faith in. Be faithful unto darkness and you will not see, because your faith will be rewarded as you gave it. You *will* accept your treasure, and if you place your faith in the past, the future will be like it. Whatever you hold dear you think is yours. The power of your valuing will make it so. (Chapter 13, *ACIM*)

To overcome the belief in fear, death, guilt, imprisonment, punishment, separation and judgment, we must be willing to always strive and thrive to reach for forgiveness, the love of God in faith and peace, for He is the love that sets us free. Therefore, to recognize we too are love as one with Him, we set each other free without judgment and bondage because this is what the love of forgiveness does. We all want love, and we spend a lifetime seeking it when in fact love is already in us and always has been. And in fact, because we come from Heaven, we are not only love and light but also royalty, but we do not remember this. Look at the variances on this world and see the majestic of your spirit in light in love as you live on a planet we call Earth that is temporary, not permanent. Here, you will remember the miscreation of the ego we made, how we are all connected and in this dream together. And in the insect, animal, and mammal world, we give royalty names to the behavior of their nature, that is, queen bee, queen ant, lion king, etc., because we subconsciously remember the royalty in us. And even they have a spirit of light and love and one day we all will return to Heaven and live side by side once again in love, joy, and peace in the exquisiteness of Heaven where we create in loveliness and beautifulness sharing our royalties. The misperception of miscreation are glimpses of the illusional world and this is the evidence of miscreation. And what this means is that everything we perceive through the eyes of the devil (ego) is an illusional miscreation regardless the form it rises in or manifests itself in.

And we too are illusion because we too can express bad behavior and this is a miscreation of ourselves, just as well. Keep in mind, everything from the ego's perception is a frightening miscreation. And the misperception of this is that we think it's real. And I'm happy to learn to remember it's all fake! And one day, so will you. In comparison, to create correctly is the evidence of the lovely creations of the real world. To be willing to go all-out in letting go of what you see and flourish in the recognition, appreciation, humbleness, peacefulness, and kindness of the beautification of the lovely unseen is what it means to wear the crown of knowledge.

III. The Borderland

4. Nothing the Son of God believes can be destroyed. But what is truth to him must be brought to the last comparison that he will ever make; the last evaluation that will be possible, the final judgment upon this world. It is the judgment of the truth upon illusion, of knowledge on perception: "It has no meaning, and does not exist." This is not your decision. It is but a simple statement of a simple fact. But in this world there are no simple facts, because what is the same and what is different remain unclear. The one essential thing to make a choice at all is this distinction. And herein lies the difference between the worlds. In this one, choice is made impossible. In the real world is choosing simplified. (Chapter 26, *ACIM*)

As you wear the crown of knowledge, you will be taken to the grandeur of the importance and seriousness of everyone's innocence through the eyes of the King of Innocence and Peace where faith has led you. And you would have learned that it is better not to laugh at another's catastrophes and sustain compassion in one's pains and sorrows. This will enable you to let faith uphold your holy relationship one to another wiping out the guilt of what we created freeing one another to see the importance of the spiritual awakening of innocence and peace. At this juncture, we remember that we are not all at the same place of awakening to spiritual vision and knowledge yet. You have already planted yourself in patience and understanding of this and you will be blessed and appreciated by all those you help get through their unhappiness with love, compassion, and calmness, for you are a witness to their eternal contentment and wellness; therefore, they become witnesses to your own. As I already said before, we are all in it together.

The loveliness of the Trinity, Heaven, and the Sonship, which is you and your brothers and sisters, is such a lovely passion to witness through God's eyes. This book speaks of the simplicity of quantum leap. The intensity of the simplicity and power of quantum leap is beyond anything you could ever imagine until you ask God for it. Here, you can swiftly pull yourself out of your own sufferings in any situation and circumstance and the suffering of others throughout the whole world through quantum leap with Jesus Christ and the Holy Spirit. It is important to be patient and remain in calmness in any circumstance because this is the best way holiness enters as the Holy Spirit enlightens us in the short summary.

Every situation and circumstance we encounter in our lives is a lesson we must be willing to learn from no matter how big or small the lesson is and no matter how kind and tragic it might be. It is all the same. Through awakening in spiritual vision and knowledge, we see the false of every circumstance and the truth of the likeness in you and me. The Holy Spirit will bring to your remembrance all occurrences and settings you prewrote to experience. Faith will continue it by showing you the vision of the comparison of what we ourselves have created in loveliness and beautification that God values and safeguards in Heaven. Everything we prewrote to act out on a world of fear and darkness becomes meaningless because what we see through faith she reminds us that we must not be willing to bring fear upon each other, because it is not real. She shows us the truth of God's love we must be willing to demonstrate one to another like a domino effect. Fear is the opposite of love. If we value fear, then it becomes real to us. If we cherish love, then we remember who God is, who we are, and where our home is. And to offer and demonstrate the love of God is another way to quantum leap from your release from suffering and into spiritual vision and knowledge, which is the greatest gift you can ever give to yourself and one another. This is the boomerang effect. What I give to you I give to myself and it works both ways.

The fabric of the universe is so buoyant all energy will bounce right back to the very mind that sent it. This is what Christ means by, "Give what you yourself would want to receive." He is not speaking of worldly treasures, that is, money, clothes, shoes, cars, houses, furnishing, etc., although to give these things freely without expecting anything in return giving from the heart is a lovely miracle, an act of genuine kindness of charity. Ultimately, He is talking about the loveliness of the core of which you are, love, light, life, joy, innocence, peace, holiness, sinlessness, wholeness, unification, safety and freedom. We must be willing to offer the Love of Christ, His innocence and peace and yours. Be willing to give the ultimate gift of white lilies and you take a quantum leap from bad and negative emotions into loving and positive forces. This is the brilliance of white lilies, the simplicity of quantum leap! Here, you share the essence of your beautifulness one to another without trade or charge, for this is the miracle of God's generosity and yours. Christ has always told us that God gives freely and so too must we. We are in the era of this. We hear plastered all over the television screen through advertisements "…and it's free!" not realizing the power we are giving to the true meaning of "free." Although we have not yet reached the true significance of "free," but we are nearing it because just by repeatedly saying it is where the power in it lies. It will come to the point of literally being given "free" of charge or trade, because the power in just saying it from one mind to the next is immense. As the energy of this phrase hits the buoyancy of the universe, the universe will restore it to its true importance as it sends it back to the minds who say it and it will factually be. Free is of God, it can only be granted, as God would give it. And for us to follow His lead as He would have it be is certainly giving miracles.

III. The Fear of Redemption

6. You must look upon your illusions and not keep them hidden, because they do not rest on their own foundation. In concealment they appear to do so, and thus they seem to be self-sustained. This is the fundamental illusion on which the others rest. For beneath them, and concealed as long as they are hidden, is the loving mind that thought it made them in anger. And the pain in this mind is so apparent, when it is uncovered, that its need of healing cannot be denied. Not all the tricks and games you offer it can heal it, for here is the real crucifixion of God's Son.

7. And yet he is not crucified. Here is both his pain and his healing, for the Holy Spirit's vision is merciful and His remedy is quick. Do not hide suffering from His sight, but bring it gladly to Him. Lay before His eternal sanity all your hurt, and let Him heal you. Do not leave any spot of pain hidden from His light, and search your mind carefully for any thoughts you may fear to uncover. For He will heal every little thought you have kept to hurt you and cleanse it of its littleness, restoring it to the magnitude of God. (Chapter 13, *ACIM*)

IX. The Cloud of Guilt

1. Guilt remains the only thing that hides the Father, for guilt is the attack upon His Son. The guilty always condemn, and having done so they will still condemn, linking the future to the past as is the ego's law. Fidelity to this law lets no light in, for it demands fidelity to darkness and forbids awakening. The ego's laws are strict, and breaches are severely punished. Therefore give no obedience to its laws, for they are laws of punishment. And those who follow them believe that they are guilty, and so they must condemn. Between the future and the past the laws of God must intervene, if you would free yourself. Atonement stands between them, like a lamp shining so brightly that the chain of darkness in which you bound yourself will disappear.

2. Release from guilt is the ego's whole undoing. *Make no one fearful,* for his guilt is yours, and by obeying the ego's harsh commandments you bring its condemnation on yourself, and you will not escape the punishment it offers those who obey it. The ego rewards fidelity to it with pain, for faith in it *is* pain. And faith can be rewarded only in terms of the belief in which the faith was placed. Faith makes the power of belief, and where it is invested determines its reward. For faith is always given what is treasured, and what is treasured is returned to you. (Chapter 13, *ACIM*)

IX. The Cloud of Guilt

4. Atonement brings a re-evaluation of everything you cherish, for it is the means by which the Holy Spirit can separate the false and the true, which you have accepted into your mind without distinction. Therefore you cannot value one without the other, and guilt has become as true for you as innocence. You do not believe the Son of God is guiltless because you see the past, and see him not. When you condemn a brother you are saying, "I who was guilty choose to remain so." You have denied his freedom, and by so doing you have denied the witness unto yours. You could as easily have freed him from the past, and lifted from his mind the cloud of guilt that binds him to it. And in his freedom would have been your own. (Chapter 13, *ACIM*)

Prayer

I pray that you are willing to accept
the Atonement of Christ, reestablishing
your holy relationship with Him first.

And that you are willing to remove the
crown of thorns from His bloody and
injured head and honor Him with the crown of
white lilies in order to reclaim the
peace of His innocence and your own.

For it is only through your willingness
to let Him enlighten you in truth
through your awareness will God
release His authority to allow you
to branch out His Love and true
through faith and peace enabling
you to reinstate your holy relationship
with the figures of the Sonship.

As you are willing to embrace the
unseen of God's truth through Faith,
the light of Atonement will outshine
all darkness that tries to hinder your
awakening to spiritual vision
and knowledge of God's truth.

Through the Atonement of Christ,
He will light up the road you are on
assisting the Holy Spirit in purifying
and cleansing all obstacles you come

up against as you choose to walk in the faith of love, innocence and peace as Christ did.

I lovingly in the grandeur of God's Love, Faith, and Peace send you blessings of your own spiritual awakening in your walk with the Trinity as faith unveils the second phase of your spiritual education.

As I mentioned before, Faith enters entirely at the precise moment you are granted the crown of knowledge lifting the burden of the world off your shoulders and the spearing pains of the heart.

As you move forward in the many delightful creations, you will be shown the grandeur of beauty as a reminder of who you are and where you come from.

Wear the crown of knowledge in humbleness, kindness, and peace as God would have it be and the knowledge of the innocence of the King of Innocence and Peace and your own will never cease.

In the name of the Kingdom of God. Amen.

About the Author

The night I was granted the crown of knowledge was the night I fell to my knees compulsively crying wholeheartedly, for my heart felt it was speared to the agony of the pains and sorrows of the world while I felt the immense weight of it on my shoulders. I could no longer tolerate the pain and hold the weight. As I remain on bended knees, I laid my palms on the floor next to my bed, cried, and pleaded to God to purify the pains of the world from my heart and lift the weight of it off my shoulders, for it was too much for me to bear. God is such a merciful Father, for what seemed like eternity to me was only a fraction of a second when He cleansed the sorrow of my heart and raised the heaviness of the world from my shoulders. For an instant of sobbing over the pains of the world in my heart was immensely sorrowful and carrying the load of the world upon my shoulders was extremely alarming. Because for a split second, what seemed like eternity, I thought I was going to have to live the rest of my life feeling the heaviness of every hurt, dread, and fearful emotion of everyone all over the world as they go through the experiences of their life.

This experience brought me to the full understanding of the knowledge of God's love, joy, and peace we literally share in Heaven for all eternity. This is what true "connection" is to feel the fear or love of everyone from all over the world. God tenderly followed up the cleansing of the pains of my heart and the lifting of the weight of the world from my shoulders with spiritually placing the crown of knowledge upon my head and said, "Well done my child of whom I am well pleased. I have honored you with the crown of knowledge for your vigilance to let my Holy Spirit lead you to the fulfillment of your duty of the deliverance for all the Sonship. Faith has now fully entered waiting your acceptance to let her lead you further into Heaven to bring your work to completion." I cried tears of joy and was shocked that I was given the crown of knowledge. I said, "But,

Father, how . . ." and before I can finish my sentence, He said, "You can receive the crown of knowledge in time. Wear it in peace, humbleness, and kindness and you will receive the golden crown of eternity when you enter Heaven. Tell them about the golden road to Heaven and you will invite many to enter the Kingdom of Heaven where everyone receives the crown of eternity." I was speechless, but to share this with you is breathtaking and heartwarming!

I'm excited that the day will come when you too will learn and remember the truth of what I poetically share with you. Only God knows who will immediately receive His love and who will wrestle with Him for a little while or for too long. I am grateful to Him it is not my responsibility to ensure your acceptance of His truth and love He gives me to share with you, for I have done my part and will continue to do so to the end of my time in the dream. I am looking forward to the day I leave and go back home to Heaven. I already know I am leaving the legacy of His truth and love behind just as Christ and many before and after Him did and it will get to the minds, hearts, and eyes of many. There will be many that will receive my poetic writings of God's love and truth while I am still here, but there will be many, many more who will receive when I have transitioned to Heaven. I am happy to give you the opportunity to read and begin your own way out of the dream and into true reality of God's love. Everyone is entitled to know the truth. There will come the time every eye will see the golden road to Heaven, and every language will confess God's truth of the golden crown of eternity. I urge you to thrive for the crown of knowledge and the golden crown of eternity. To receive the crown of knowledge in time is the most magnificent event you will ever experience!

One day, I was very sad because I was so excitedly and happily ministering to a friend about God's love. There is no wrath in Him and He became very upset. This is where the sadness came in. He started reciting ancient scripture the apostles wrote in the Holy Bible that speaks of God's wrath and the only thing I could do and say is nothing. For the Holy Spirit said, "Remain silent and respect what he chooses to value for he does not yet see the truth." Again, this made me very sad! Because I was so happy and excited to share with my Christian friend that God is true love, there is no wrath in him. I was overly pleased to share this great news with my friend. His nonacceptance of God's true love for us and the true love we have for Him sent me spiraling into sadness. However, God immediately pulled me out of it. He said, "Leave him alone for his time will come to learn the truth." And His instruction was immediately followed up with the direction of the Holy Spirit Who said, as follows:

"Not everyone is going to be as happy as you are Lorenza to learn that God is Love, there is no wrath in Him. This is because the Holy Bible has been around for over two thousand years and many want to hang onto the belief of ancient scripture that speaks of God being a wrathful God because they still want to bring fear upon others. Those who choose not to be delighted that God is pure Love hangs on tight to the ego's thought system, who only wants to destroy God, see you tremble in fear and dead. In humbleness, kindness and peace, respect the belief they choose to value, for the day will come when they let go of ancient biblical writings the apostles chose to write through the ego's perspective frame of red rubies and sparkly teardrop diamonds. Just as your time is here, to confess God is Love, to everyone you minister to and through your writings. God is Love and True and His sparkly diamonds are circular, which is the symbol of completeness and togetherness. Always value the remembrance that everyone's time to learn and remember the truth of God will arrive at their appointed time, and they too will confess God is Love; there is no wrath in Him, and this is only a matter of time."

Just this little note He gave to me to share with you swiftly brought me back into the realm of happiness. I humbly and respectfully withdrew my ministering to my friend remembering to let God do His work in his belief system. For I had planted the seed and now God will water it until truth is fully flourished in his mind.

III. The Fear of Redemption

5. You can accept insanity because you made it, but you cannot accept love because you did not. You would rather be a slave of the crucifixion than a Son of God in redemption. Your individual death seems more valuable than your living oneness, for what is given you is not so dear as what you made. You are more afraid of God than of the ego, and love cannot enter where it is not welcome. But hatred can, for it enters of its own volition and cares not for yours. (Chapter 13, *ACIM*)

On June 10, 2017, I completed the editing of this edition, which was a long and arduous process. I am so happy and in total relief with the peace of accomplishment in preparing this manuscript for submission to my publisher for review. My initial reaction was elation so I poured a glass of wine and sat and listened to Carry Underwood and Vince Gill, *How Great Thou Art*, praising God of the completion of it, but then, I became overwhelmed with sadness and began to cry because I had no one to share my joy with in this great achievement. So to ease my sadness, I decided to listen to Willie Nelson's music and sat and drank my wine, for I desperately wanted to hear *Blue Eyes Crying in the Rain* because for me, this represented Jesus Christ because of His gorgeous ocean blue eyes I was a witness to as I remembered Him as a child. And so this is the reality He presented Himself to me at Heaven's gate knowing I would imme-diately recognize Him, and I did. I also listened to John Lennon's *Imagine* for I wanted to hear his lyrics of the "world we're living for," Heaven. ". . . no hell below us above us only sky. Imagine all the people living for the day. Imagine there's no country it isn't hard to do nothing to kill or die for and no religion too. Imagine all the people living life in peace you may say I'm a dreamer, but I'm not the only one . . . imagine no possession...no need for greed or hunger a brotherhood of man imagine all the people sharing all the world." These are part of the fundamental lessons. God asks we learn and remember to value these lessons through the Holy Spirit and your willingness is inevitable and is only a matter of time. Here, suddenly, peace overcame me then I felt God's presence and He said, "Be happy with the joy and peace of completion there is no one you need to share this accomplishment with, for it is a blessing that will be in its time." I completely understood His kind words of this reminder and peace completely befell upon me indeed! So I sat and enjoyed my wine and eventually went to bed. The number seven is my number, although I was aware it was June, but I thought it was June 7, 2017, for I had not looked at the calendar for weeks. As it turned out, it was June 10, 2017, the day of completion of editing this edition before submitting it to my publisher for review. So out of curiosity, I googled the biblical number ten and this is what I found that I would like to share with you, as follows:

o   The *Bible* numerology code *number 10*. The *biblical* meaning of *number 10* is completed course of time or completeness in divine order. Today, this *number* is used only when referring to any kind of ranking or when describing anything that is near to perfection. *Number 10* is the symbol of matter in harmony (www.astrovera.com/bible-religion/191-bible-number-10.html).

o   This brought me great joy and amazement because I truly felt complete, but it also gave me the inspiration to further assist God in correcting the wrathful beliefs in Him that are untrue. The Holy Bible (*KJV*) tells us of many wraths of God, Zechariah 10:11: "And he shall pass through the sea with affliction, and shall smite the waves in the sea, and all the deeps of the river shall dry up: and the pride of Assyria shall be brought down, and the sceptre of Egypt shall depart away." We are all brilliant writers as I mentioned already. God does not punish. We punish ourselves as the author of our own life script. Now I know God did not punish Egypt and Israel or placed ten horns on the beast, for it is us punishing ourselves for the rebellious nature we chose to create and live in a mortal world where we see and believe in death through dreams. The dream world we created to shatter because the gravity of darkness will never sustain worlds of fear, darkness, and sorrow forever. This is what we must be willing to unravel in our sick, corrupted, and tangled minds of confusion and self-deceit. And when you do this, you will remember how magnificent you really are to come up with such vicious stories of affliction, brilliant, but meaningless because no one likes to suffer. In contrast, the immortal world of the Kingdom of Heaven is life. The bible does tell us that earth is the total opposite of Heaven and through spiritual vision, you see this clearly in every aspect of mortal life. I ask that you be willing to remember that anything and everything wrathful is not of God. It is of the ego, the loveless father we made to experience fear and darkness because all we ever known is love and light. However, you always have the choice to listen to the Voice of the Holy Spirit who will always lead you to the righteous path. Just to enlighten you, "tithing" doesn't have to be ten percent of money. It can be anything, for example, donating your time, clothes, food, service, labor, etc., anything that will provide to others in need of anything and the same goes for offerings.

o   I have always written poetry since junior high school. I had stacks and stacks of journals of dark poetry of the deepest pains within me. Eventually, there was a long gap where I no longer wrote, but it once again flourished when I signed up for the Art of Being class at Wellspring Women's Center. Through the process of attending these classes, I was shocked that I made a huge breakthrough in writing poetry again. This was something I never expected to happen, but it did! And I am very grateful I no longer write of my deepest, darkest pains of my dream experiences because I see clearly how meaningless it truly is. I am all too happy to write of the love and light of God and your own because this is what is meaningful, for it is eternal. It is better to be willing to learn about the loveliness in you rather than dwelling on the mistakes of miscreation and every corrupt and brutal experience is a miscreation. I urge you to invite the Holy Spirit to help you learn of the beautification in you and you will flourish in goodness. Let it be and share it forward upon the Sonship from one side of the world to the next. Go and be a fruitful learner of everything righteous God has planted in you. Let it blossom and enjoy the love, happiness, and peace you spend a lifetime seeking.

"The Test of Fear" poem is an experience I had in Bodega Bay, California, the same weekend I had the experience I am going to share with you here. I am sharing this testimony with you to enlightened you as to how you can take a quantum leap into understanding your own déjà vu's and temptations. God is the authority of quantum leap and the Holy Spirit waits in patience and in peace for His authorization to release to you the answers to what you ask. Faith and patience is of virtue. All the answers to your questions that come through God's Holy Spirit will always be satisfactory because He follows up the answers with comfort and peace of it all. And you would have already mastered the process of spiritual vision and knowledge.

The verbiage style of this testimony is a little different because I was going to implement it as a poem, but I decided to enter it as a testimony without changing the style of the words. And so this testimony has a title, as follows:

The Day I Disappeared

In a past life, she was a published author before the day she disappeared and never reappeared. In the present, she was working on the editing of her second edition manuscript when she felt overly compelled to head to the west coast to work on the editing of her book. So she did. She rented a cabin in Bodega Bay, a fishing village on the Pacific coast and did her best to focus and finish the editing of her manuscript. However, it was a challenge because she was distracted by a deja' vu and the overwhelming temptation to visit Patrick Road in Napa. While she worked on her manuscript, the deja' vu was that she had been in that very village, in the very cabin she rented editing her book.

She prayed and asked the Holy Spirit, "Why is it that I am receiving a deja' vu that I had been here before doing the exact thing, editing my book, in the very village I am in and in the very same cabin I rented?" She further asked, "And why is it that I am exceedingly wanting to visit Patrick Road? Please help me to unravel these experiences so I may remember and understand what's happening." After her prayer, she returned to editing her manuscript and after some time had passed, she received the answer to her questions through spiritual vision. She was shown that in a previous life she traveled to the fishing village of Bodega Bay and rented the very same cabin she is in to work on her second edition when she fell into the temptation of visiting Patrick Road. In the vision, the temptation of visiting Patrick Road was so intense, she could no longer focus on editing her book. So she grabbed her coat and her car keys, and she walked out of the cabin and drove to Patrick Road in Napa. As she drove down Patrick Road, suddenly everything went blurry and poof, she disappeared into nothingness. The vision did not unveil what happened that caused her to disappear. And when she was about to ask what the cause was in her disappearance, the Holy Spirit spoke and said,

- o "You were rebirthed because you agreed to go back and finish writing the books you wrote in your life script you would write and publish. You have the power to not fall into the temptation of going back to Patrick Road in this life time. Do not fall into the temptation of it or you will disappear again and you will be asked to be rebirthed to finish your work."

She is "I" and this was overwhelming indeed! It was a trip to remember what the deja' vu and the temptation was all about. Ultimately, it was a trip to remember what had happened to me in a previous life, but it all made sense to me because I elected to stay connected to God Who releases the authority to the Holy Spirit to unveil the answer to what I ask. The answer to my questions were very satisfying because the deja' vu and the temptation of visiting Patrick Road was wiped clean the holy instant I elected not to fall into it.

And so the overwhelming desire to finish my work overpowered the temptation of the day I disappeared in a previous life. There was no way I was going to be rebirthed only to replay the same life over again because I am ready to finish my work so I can finally return home.

For those who are unfamiliar with Patrick Road, Napa, California, it is known for the legend of the Rebobs, which are winged monkeys that have long fangs and claws. You can google Exemplore or Napa Register for precise details. There are also stories of people disappearing on Patrick Road (YouTube).

Please keep in mind, this is not to bring fear upon you, it is to enlighten you so you can achieve liberty of your own experiences of déjà vu and temptations. In fact, everything I share with you is to help you get through all the merciless experiences we all go through on this merciless world. I ask you be willing to receive it with an open mind and heart to enable yourself to walk through the threshold of all the open doors Christ holds wide open welcoming you to learn and remember who you are, where you came from, why you are here, how you got here, where you will return and you are never alone. In the name of the Kingdom of God. Amen.

O' Father in Heaven, thank you for the crown of knowledge in time. Thank you for Your tender tactfulness to ensure I never steered away from the vigilance and diligence of the truth and love of You and the golden road to Heaven. I pray every soul on earth wills to receive the loveliness of your love and kindness. And they see You will never punish them, threatened them or confine them to the bondages of fear and darkness and they realize that Your goal is to free them from the slaveries of fear they put themselves in. We bring ourselves to the depths of the dark corners of the world by our own asking and making where we demanded You retrieve your light from a part of Heaven so we could know what darkness is like. Let them see it is Your love and light that delivers them out of the shadows of every dreadful encounter and into the loving arms of Your lead to safety, for only through You can we find it because there is no safety on this world, and we made sure of that before we were born into it. O' Father, bless every mind to remember Your humbleness, every eye to see the innocence of the King of Innocence and Peace and their own. Thank You for reassuring me that to be calm in a world of chaos is good and that every tongue will confess Your loveliness at their appointed time. Thank you for being the One and Only True Father in Heaven the Creator of everything lovely, and of your masterpiece of spirit, You adore with a loving mind, tender heart, and compassionate eyes. Thank you for permitting us to behold Your open arms so divinely inviting always ready to cuddle us into Your embracement to the center of Your delightful heart where we abide forevermore under the golden rainbow of Your eternal safety. In the name of the Kingdom of God. Amen.

III. The Fear of Redemption

8. Beneath all the grandiosity you hold so dear is your real call for help. For you call for love to your Father as your Father calls you to Himself. In that place which you have hidden, you will only to unite with the Father, in loving remembrance of Him. You will find this place of truth as you see it in your brothers, for though they may deceive themselves, like you they long for the grandeur that is in them. And perceiving it you will welcome it, and it will be yours. For grandeur is the right of God's Son, and no illusions can satisfy him or save him from what he is. Only his love is real, and he will be content only with his reality.

9. Save him from his illusions that you may accept the magnitude of your Father in peace and joy. But exempt no one from your love, or you will be hiding a dark place in your mind where the Holy Spirit is not welcome. And thus you will exempt yourself from His healing power, for by not offering total love you will not be healed completely. Healing must be as complete as fear, for love cannot enter where there is one spot of fear to mar its welcome. (Chapter 13, *ACIM*)

Author's Recommendations

I highly recommend that when you choose one world from the other you must look at both worlds very carefully and with an open mind and heart in order to see the true world from the false one. As you already know by now, one world is real and the other is fake. One world is made in fear of fear in darkness of darkness and the other is created in love of love in light of light. If you cherish guilt, judgment, punishment, bondage, conflict, self-deceit, and self-destruction, then you will choose the false world; but if you value love, joy, freedom, togetherness, innocence, safety, and peace then you will choose the true world. Whatever characters you treasure and give importance to is the world you create for yourself and others because what you elect to believe and become is what you will teach your brothers'. Again, the world of love, joy, innocence, freedom, unification, safety, and peace is true, the world of fear, darkness, guilt, judgment, punishment, bondage, conflict, self-deceit and self-destruction is false. The holiness, sinlessness, and innocence of the true world is in timelessness, (but can be achieved in time) which is endless and is the embracement of unification and freedom. The ruthlessness of the fake world is the encouragement of guilt, judgment, punishment, bondage, and division for a time and time will come to its end.

Search for love and light within and you will find it, for love and light are you because God is Love and Light and He created you. Seek for happiness in you because it is you for God gave it to you and He is pure joy. Look for the innocence in you because you are guiltless, for the spirit has never sinned because God created you holy and perfect. Look for peace in you because the King of Innocence and Peace has always been with you and in you. Be willing not look to the false world for love, joy, innocence, safety, freedom, and peace because in the fake world these characters are deceitful; therefore, will shatter the love, joy, and peace you invested in your relationships and in yourself. Everyone has their own path to walk to find true love, true joy, true innocence, and true peace. We all spend a lifetime seeking it outside of us not realizing the act of all the fakeness of our search thinking we find it in each other, in the physical sense and in the things of the world when really it's already spiritually anchored in us. Invite the Holy Spirit to join you as you take a good look at both worlds and He will help you identify the true from the false, for it is His priority to help you see through His perspective. Here, you will learn and remember the false world is full of meaningless and senseless ugliness and the true world is meaningful, sensible, and beautiful. And when you see the fabulous loveliness beyond your imagination, you will realize the true world you diligently searched for all your life has always been in you. For you so desperately wanted out of the world of thorns full of shattered dreams and broken promises at every corner of the world.

This is no joke, for God plays no pointless games like all the puny mind games we play with each other making mountains out of molehills trying to find our own way to the golden road of Heaven. Even if we do not recognize it, this is the aim of all of us. Although we spend a lifetime seeking it, we fail to realize we must be willing to bring the Sonship with us, for we cannot enter Heaven alone because that would be pure selfishness and God is all giving and forgave us before we were even born. And so too must we be willing to forgive because forgiveness upholds salvation for you and all those you forgive who will enter Heaven with you. Authenticity of giving is vital, because if you do not allow the Sonship to enter Heaven with you through forgiveness, then you close the door on yourself just as well. This is not God doing this to you. It is you doing this to yourself through your stubbornness to refuse to forgive.

Let the Love of God touch you and let deliverance of Christ rise you up from the chains and shackles of the bondages of a world so fake you can't see past everything it forsakes. Don't let yourself no longer be deceived by the maze of forsaken deeds, for even though you agreed to reenact all the feats you encounter, even the experiences that take you into the depths of hell under your feet you will eventually be released from. Again, if you enter the pits of hell, this is not God doing this to you it's you doing this to yourself. We opted to forsake ourselves and each other. This is why it had to be done in a world of time we created. Time ensures that the world of plays of screams and sorrows will one day come to its end. This is the purpose of time. Time is also God's miracle of Love He sends to the weak foundation of shattered dreams and broken promises to help you in times you feel you cannot endure anymore lashing, slashing, and thrashing of the ego's thought system that feels it's tearing you apart like a little rag doll. You will come to appreciate His love through your miracle because the miracle is the stepping stone to the remembrance of our Father in Heaven. Everyone who has had and who have not yet had their miracle will eventually take the journey through the false world to reach the glistening gateway to the real world of Heaven and everyone will succeed in their voyage taken. It does not matter how big the hurdles seem to be on your way there or how challenging it might seem. Christ will always carry you over, and through what you feel, you cannot bear.

When things become easier for you, remember those are the times Christ lifted you and brought you through. Always appreciate and be thankful and grateful to God's promise. He would never forsake you. Here, you will be gently hurdled into the world of true freedom where you thrive in love, cheer, peace, holiness, and wholeness with God and the Sonship. This is the ultimate moment where the spirit is happy to return to its natural and meaningful habitat and out of the world that goes against its true nature. This is why we are conflicted from one side of the world to the other because earth's environment goes against the essence of who we really are. If you truly and genuinely look at both worlds and weigh fear, darkness, guilt, rejection, and separation on one hand and love, light, joy, innocence, peace, and oneness on the other, the hand holding fear, darkness, guilt, rejection, and separation is so weak it falls to the ground and shatters. There goes what you thought were all your bubbly dreams and unbroken promises we made to break on the weak foundation of fear and darkness that always shatters! But the hand holding love, light, joy, innocence, peace, and togetherness stands because its foundation is built on love, light, acceptance, embracement, and unification. This is why God's promises to you never fractures, cracks, or shatters. This is the joy of His safety He promises you in a divinely lovely world where your peace, innocence, freedom, and safety can never be interrupted because corruption is not permitted in the world of timelessness.

The gravity of the false world is weak because the fake world is dark gravity that houses all kinds of props preprogrammed to destroy and obliterate everything in its path. In contrast, the gravity of the true world is power because its gravity is light and light always outshines darkness upholding all that is lovely for all eternity. This is why all the worlds in the universe are eventually annihilated because its dark gravity can never sustain them forever. We see the evidence of this in our own galaxy and solar system and our brilliant minds who study the universe will continue to see this as they branch further into the vastness of the universe, which they already do. In a nutshell, the gravity of light is the power of God's Love. This is why it is eternal. Therefore, eternal life is real and anything temporary, including the body, is false so earth and everything in it is just a puny imitation of the opposite of what Heaven is, which you will see this in all its clarity and certainty when you take the quantum leap into spiritual vision with the Holy Spirit. Remember this and you will always be able to identify the true from the false, immortality from mortality, and illusion from reality. Wouldn't you rather have a life of immortality? Yes, you would, because as humans, we do want to live forever and be young forever, and we spend a lifetime trying to figure out how to do this as a human. And when we are young, we think we will be young forever, this is the evidence that we are young forever and do live forever, but in the timelessness of spirit.

I lift up the Sonship in prayer from one side of the world to the next that everyone be at peace with the mangled world of shattered dreams and broken promises. Ask our Father in Heaven to help you not blame Him or hate Him for allowing you and the Sonship to make a life full of pains, screams, sorrows and devastations where there is no safety because we created it on a foundation of change and guilt, the gravity of fear and darkness. Change always disturbs joy and peace and guilt always blinds you to the innocence in you and your brothers so you only see cruelty, guilt, punishment, and judgment. The home we made to be born into is a place of exile from Heaven for a little while. And be grateful we are not exiled forever in the vastness of fear and darkness! We made sure the world we created was made on a weak foundation built of the gravity of fear and darkness that cannot sustain a corruptive world forever because it is an illusional life; therefore, it's only but a dream, a dream we must be willing to wake up from. Because when we awaken, we remember God's true love for us and our true love for Him. Remember to be happy when you come to find yourself falling in love all over again with God because even in relations one to another we do the same when we see the relationships we are in falling apart. We do everything in our power to bring wine and flowers, sweetness, and kindness to restore friendships and relationships in the hopes we will fall in love all over again in order to uphold and maintain the lovely relationship we once dreamed. But because it is a dream, these are props made to shatter. Faith, peacefulness, and holiness are a strong foundation in which to build relationships with a genuine touch of true love, kindness, and happiness of your innocence, for they are the gravity of the power of God's love and light and yours combined. Remember to ask God to let you be willing then, to look passed flesh and bones to see the beautiful and sinless spirit in all the Sonship, for this is the opportunity to unite with your brothers' in forgiveness, faith, peacefulness, holiness and wholesomeness that will support your relationships endlessly. Let faith remind you this is possible in time to sustain relationships in togetherness, for peacefulness and holiness are the gravity of love and light and love and light holds everything together forever. Let forgiveness flourish in your mind and heart so you can move forward in the true nature of the innocence in you and the Sonship. For the body is the mortal illusion of life on earth and the spirit is the true eternal life that is immortal and can never be hurt or destroyed neither on earth nor in Heaven because of the ark of God's safety nothing can pierce, spear, breach, or enter it and this is His eternal promise. On behalf of the whole Sonship, I thank God and show my appreciation to Him for being real. For nothing can annihilate the realism of Heaven because Heaven is a home created in love of love in light of light where no dreams or illusions exist. For the shattered dreams and broken promises are only in dreams and let us be thankful, grateful, and appreciative of this because the only thing important is true reality of the immortality, which is the essence of spirit and Heaven. In the name of the Kingdom of God, I send my love, light, wellness, joy, and peace to all the Sonship all over the world. Amen.

My Divine Inspirations

Through the writings of Helen Schucman in A Course In Miracles has been a divine inspiration in my writings. Many of the passages she wrote in her book were parallel to much of what the Holy Spirit had been teaching me through the years. Many of her writings were confirmations to what the Holy Spirit had shown me and taught me. And many of her writings were new things I learned and every new passage I learned, I most certainly brought to the Holy Spirit to guide me through it for wisdom and understanding of it. This is where my relationship with Him began to entirely flourish. Like the golden glistening white vine tightly but tenderly intertwining and never dividing. He is my best buddy through the rest of my duration on earth and it will forever be when I return to Heaven.

At the time as an atheist, I was in a tragic accident on October 22, 2001, in this lifetime. I am not going to go into detail on this experience because it is a whole other book I am working on. And hopefully, I get to finish and publish it before my time to transition from Earth to Heaven. However, I will say this much. There were two spiritual experiences I had that day. The first spiritual experience was hellish and the second spiritual experience was Heavenly, a moment in Heaven where I came face to face with Jesus Christ. When I returned from Heaven to Earth, my entire perception of the puny atheist existence I lived for forty years in this lifetime was squashed by my own memory of Christ and Heaven. This was my miracle God implemented into my life script to honor on that day and at the very hour I asked His miracle to enter before I was even born. In 2001, is when my search for the truth of everything began and it took thirteen years to come across A Course In Miracles. It was in the year 2014 that I discovered Helen's book and it was by pure divine guidance because I certainly was not looking for it because I did not even know it existed. So, Helen's book found me. However, years earlier I asked for it, for I asked Christ for the truth of everything. And through A Course In Miracles is when the second part of my spiritual education with the Holy Spirit began to unravel any and all lingering confusion and uncertainty. However, it did not happen swiftly. It is said that it takes one year to read and study ACIM; however, it took me two years. Because I read it and studied the lessons without judging and analyzing it determined to gain wisdom and understanding of what Helen had written through the guidance of Jesus Christ. Yes, I did wrestle with it, but I did not spend too much time doing that. In other words, every passage I read, and every lesson I studied, I swiftly learned not to spend any time trying to figure out if it is true or not. Rather, I re-read, re-read, and re-studied, re-studied through the divine guidance of thy Holy Spirit. For ACIM is a very deep, deep powerful and fascinating read, at least that is how it was for me. For it took my mind into a whirlwind of a spin where I had to lay it down and rest my mind for a few weeks at a time. Each time I returned to it, I invited God's Holy Spirit to lead me through it. And when He took me through it and I began to absorb it in little doses at a time without my mind spiraling out of control, I absolutely fell in love with it. Because when I enabled myself to embrace what Christ was saying through Helen's writings, spiritual vision and knowledge tenderly entered. And the first thing I recognized is how poetically and divinely lovely Christ speaks. And I fell in love with His divine poetic demeanor in the way He thinks, speaks and writes. I asked Him to teach me how to think, speak, write and express myself through divinity just like Him. Lo and behold, He did. For Christ thinks, speaks and writes in a manner that is ever so divinely kind, humble, poetic, peaceful, tenderly firm and respectful. Ultimately, through my willingness to read and study ACIM without judgment and analyzing it, I enabled God's wisdom and understanding to enter. So, the Trinity honored my request. And when I was ready, the Holy Spirit tenderly hurdled me through quantum leap into spiritual vision where I was able to behold all that I asked to know. And this is definitely a divine trip! And this, ultimately, is why I can write as deep as we have written in poetic form the truth and false of everyone and everything. Because when He tenderly takes you on a universal field trip through quantum leap into spiritual vision, you most certainly will witness the true and false of everything you want to behold and know. And when you read and study ACIM alongside the Holy Spirit without judging and analyzing it *it* becomes…how shall I say? It becomes a parallel spiritual education. I am going to do my best to explain this in a way you are able to recognize what it is I am attempting to get across. When you read ACIM alongside of the Holy Spirit, it truly becomes a divine spiritual education where He will tenderly hurdle you through quantum leap where you will behold through spiritual vision what you are reading. This is where it becomes a parallel spiritual education. Here, you will be witness to the authenticity and duplicity of the two worlds, Heaven, the universe and everything in them, including earth. And to remember the answers to the fundamental questions of blindness is ever so blissful and humbling, because everything you always wanted to know all comes together for you in all clarity and certainty. Yes, you might have questions here and there as you go along, but be free to ask, for your questions will be answered. And they might even be answered before you even ask or before you can finish the question. It's divinely amazing!

The divinity of the Holy Spirit's spiritual trip through quantum leap, ultimately, has been a huge inspiration in my writings. I certainly could not write in divine lucidity and logicality without Him. And you too can learn the truth and false of anything you want to know, for it will divinely be granted to you. In your own search of the meaning of everything, no matter what road you travel and what you read and study, invite the Holy Spirit to join you to permit Him to teach you to remember the true from the false of everything you want to know. Through the years, I had traveled many roads until I found the road for me, but in all actuality, the golden road to Heaven found me where there would be no curves to swerve through and no walls to run into.

And so the ultimate stepping-stone to learn to remember the true from the false was through my divine inspirations of my miracles. This is where I met Christ and it was in that holy moment, I knew He was never crucified; and in a holy instant, I knew Heaven is truly my home. And I am ever so grateful to have been reacquainted with the Holy Spirit Who I did not remember as an atheist, and eventually was divinely introduced to A Course In Miracles. And I am ever so grateful to God that He honored these miracles through my own life script. I highly recommend you converse with God's Holy Spirit, read the passages and study the lessons in ACIM with His guidance so your mind does not go spinning into oblivion as mine did. Even this book, my book you are reading, please take it to thy Holy Spirit for guidance and confirmation. For in your own search for the true and false of everything you read, study and want to know, He will most certainly expose deception and divulge perfection. Learn to listen to His Voice and you will witness and know in all clarity and certainty the true from the false. When guilt and confusion enter, stop and be still and remember that He is God, for every negative force is not of Him.

Through the current of the airflow, I send you grandeur of blessings on your journey to unravel your own life script. Be willing to listen only to the Voice of thy Holy Spirit so you too can behold and know in all clarity and certainty the true from the false of everything you want to behold and know. Listen carefully when others speak, without judgment and without being analytical, for everything positive and lovely spoken and done comes from divinity, which is truth anything else is false. Remember it this way, everything positive is of God and everything negative is of the ego. In the name of the Kingdom of God. Amen.

I. The Message of the Crucifixion

10. We are still equal as learners, although we do not need to have equal experiences. The Holy Spirit is glad when you can learn from mine, and be reawakened by them. That is their only purpose, and that is the only way in which I can be perceived as the way, the truth and the life. When you hear only one Voice you are never called on to sacrifice. On the contrary, by being able to hear the Holy Spirit in others you can learn from their experiences, and can gain from them without experiencing them directly yourself. That is because the Holy Spirit is one, and anyone who listens is inevitably led to demonstrate His way for all. (Chapter 6, *ACIM*)

My Letter to God

Dearest God,

It took me a very long time to listen to You. It took several rebirths and forty years in this present dream to hear Your Voice and be willing to listen. Through millennia of every rebirth and in this present life, many have brought your word to me, but I had a hateful attitude toward You. I was bitter and hostile and didn't want to listen to anyone who spoke of You in my past lives and in this present life. I know this, because had I listened to them in previous lives, I wouldn't be in this one. I would be in Heaven loving and appreciating you endlessly enjoying my position as cocreator with You lavishing in our royalties. Now that I know the truth of You because of my willingness to listen to Your Holy Spirit in the present, I know how they must have felt when I rejected You through them because it is now happening to me. I understand that those who do not receive You through me is because there time has not yet arrived for them to receive Your love and word just as we agreed. Open Your heart to me and shower Your patience upon me, and let me rest in peace to all those who are not willing to hear and see You through me and the lovely poetry books You and I have written together. Bring forward those who are willing to know You and receive Your word of truth in love, light, forgiveness, sanity, kindness, unification, and freedom. Lead them to find me and lead me to find them at the perfect timing we agreed. Help me to remember that I need not work so hard and to stand in faith, patience, and peace so I can easily stay focused on the path of Your love and truth you have me on as Christ and the Holy Spirit stand alongside of me. They are my holy friends now forevermore, and the only two plus You I trust, for, in certainty, the Trinity will never forsake me. Right now, my heart's desire is to be alone with You at the ocean where I wish to be as I continue my work with You. Bless me with the means I need so I may pick up and leave to be alone with You at the ocean scene and breeze. You know my heart's desire and my needs and I gratefully thank You for these gifts You bring to me when the time arrives for it to be. I understand that the work we do is a legacy I will leave behind and I look forward to the grandeur of blessings in my time as confirmation You and I do not work in vain. It will be very nice to see many receive Your love and truth through me before I leave and go back home to You, because before I leave this world to transition into Heaven, I look forward to departing in contentment that your work and mine was not and will not be fruitless. Because right now, the Holy Spirit, everyone, and everything is so silent, I feel so alone. For these past weeks, I have not even heard a chirp of a bird. I look forward to the arrival time when I meet all those who hunger to receive Your love and truth through me and our lovely poetic words.

Father, as You know, I have had my book of the dynamics of my illusional experiences, but also my spiritual experiences on October 22, 2001, and forward on the back burner for a long time and I would like to return to it, complete it and publish it before my time to transition. I invite Your Holy Spirit to guide me in this endeavor and dictate to me what it is You would have me say. For the message I would like to share in the present and leave as a legacy, I want it to be as powerful as You, but loving, tender and sweet just as You are and as You would have it be. In the name of the Kingdom of God. Amen.

Blazing Amazing Smiles

I was contemplating how I could promote this book before it is even published. For months, I had been playing around with RealPlayer doing thirty second fun videos to get to know how it works. RealPlayer offers thirty seconds for free and you can fit seven images in thirty seconds with background music. So I played around with it and figured out that I can even air my voice on it. Finally, the Holy Spirit spoke to me and said, "Blazing Amazing Smiles." And with that, He gave me the vision of collecting and featuring blazing amazing smiles of people from all walks of life including pets in the thirty second videos. And as I played around with this idea is when I figured out I can air my voice and decided to write short poems to recite in the videos as I permit background music to play. Because of limited energy and limited income, I will be uploading one video a month and on the third day of each month for a year as a fun and creative way to promote King of Innocence and Peace, The Guiltlessness In You, A Poetic Truth. This project may or may not be for a season. I am hoping it will grow from short videos to longer videos to continue featuring Blazing Amazing Smiles with longer poems to leave as a legacy for everyone to continue to release Christ from the suffering of the crown of thorns and our own.

Through my writing of this book, I already knew the importance of bringing it to the forefront before it is even published. So when the Holy Spirit gave me the title of the videos to begin with, I was further inspired because then I knew what I needed to do. Through social media, I invited many people to submit their blazing amazing smiles to blazingamazingsmiles@gmail.com to be featured in the Blazing Amazing Smiles videos if they so wish to be featured. I gave a description that the videos are a fun and creative way to promote my book before it is even published that is in publication and I give a brief description of what the book is about. However, I did not get not one reply through social media. Then, I realized I was going to have to do some foot work, and I did. So I visited various establishments talking to people letting them know what it is I am doing as a fun and creative way to promote my book before it is even published, but in the process of publication. And I briefly let them know what the book is about. Because I did not receive any responses through social media, I was not expecting the response I received in talking to people. There were more people supporting this project than not and that was such a divine blessing. The Blazing Amazing Smiles videos was inspired through my writing of this edition and this project continues to be encouraged and led by the Holy Spirit. So, I am hoping that this project is not for a season, for I would like for it to bloom into a legacy so that everyone continues to free Christ, the Sonship and themselves from the world of fear and darkness. And at your willingness to do so it can be achieved.

Those who participated in being featured in the Blazing Amazing Smiles videos will receive a free copy of "King of Innocence and Peace, The Guiltlessness In You, A Poetic Truth" when it is published. I also am hoping to do random giveaways featuring the King of Innocence and Peace portrait wearing the crown of white lilies, no thorns, by: Jenna Frazier. Once again, thank you for your willingness to take part in this divine and creative project led by the Holy Spirit. In the name of the Kingdom of God. Amen.

To all the super stars featured in the Blazing Amazing Smiles videos, please be free to email me with your contact information at blazingamazingsmiles@gmail.com to ensure you receive your free copy of the King of Innocence and Peace, The Guiltlessness In You, A Poetic Truth when it is published. Once again, thank you for your willingness to release Christ from the crown of thorns and for your divine and delightful participation in the Blazing Amazing Smiles project. This is not only a quantum leap into spiritual vision where you free yourself and your brothers from sufferings galore; it makes you a glistening golden diamond star you truly are!

A Delightful Blessing

I am so excited and ever so appreciative
to those who participated in the
Blazing Amazing Smiles thirty second
videos.

I can't thank you enough for such a
delightful blessing where the devil
does not and cannot come a
trespassing.

For God's divine hand is on this
project even if it might be for a
season because it is for a very
good reason.

Yet, it would be a delightful blessing
that at my transition from earth to
Heaven, it be left behind as a legacy
to carry on the release of Christ
sufferings, your brothers' and
your own.

Be willing all you lovely people it be a
delightful blessing, for no one can stomp,
but only for a moment on God's glorious
release from sickness to wellness, the
immortality of sanity.

And so at your willingness to let a
delightful blessing be a domino
effect from one person to the next
all over the world frees you and them
from insanity to sanity in all its glory.

This is a perfect example of what the ego sees and is uncertain

Life asked death,
"Why do people love me,
but hate you?"
Death responded,
"Because you are a
beautiful lie
and I am a
painful truth"

themetapicuture.com

In comparison, this is what the Holy Spirit sees and is certain

Death asked life,
"Why do people hate me, but love you?"
Life responded,
"Because you are a dreadful lie that is blind
and I am a lovely truth that can see."

Lorenza Palomino

VIII. The Vision of Sinlessness

7. Judgment is but a toy, a whim, the senseless means to play the idle game of death in your imagination. But vision sets all things right, bringing them gently within the kindly sway of Heaven's laws. What if you recognized this world is an hallucination? What if you really understood you made it up? What if you realized that those who seem to walk about in it, to sin and die, attack and murder and destroy themselves, are wholly unreal? Could you have faith in what you see, if you accepted this? And would you see it? (Chapter 20, *ACIM*)

VII. The Call for Faith

1. The substitutes for aspects of the situation are the witnesses to your lack of faith. They demonstrate that you did not believe the situation and the problem were in the same place. The problem *was* the lack of faith, and it is this you demonstrate when you remove it from its source and place it elsewhere. As a result, you do not see the problem. Had you not lacked faith that it could be solved, the problem would be gone. And the situation would have been meaningful to you, because the interference in the way of understanding would have been removed. To remove the problem elsewhere is to keep it, for you remove yourself from it and make it unsolvable.

2. There is no problem in any situation that faith will not solve. There is no shift in any aspect of the problem but will make solution impossible. For if you shift part of the problem else where the meaning of the problem must be lost, and the solution to the problem is inherent in its meaning. Is it not possible that all your problems have been solved, but you have removed yourself from the solution? Yet faith must be where something has been done, and where you see it done.

3. A situation is a relationship, being the joining of thoughts. If problems are perceived, it is because the thoughts are judged to be in conflict. But if the goal is truth, this is impossible. Some idea of bodies must have entered, for minds cannot attack. The thought of bodies is the sign of faithlessness, for bodies cannot solve anything. It is their intrusion on the relationship, an error in your thoughts about the situation, which then becomes the justification for your lack of faith. You will make this error, but be not at all concerned with that. The error does not matter. Faithlessness brought to faith will never interfere with truth. But faithlessness used *against* truth will always destroy faith. If you lack faith, ask that it be restored where it was lost, and seek not to have it made up to you elsewhere, as if you had been unjustly deprived of it. (Chapter 17, *ACIM*)

VII. The Call for Faith

4. Only what *you* have not given can be lacking in any situation. But remember this; the goal of holiness was set for your relationship, and not by you. You did not set it because holiness cannot be seen except through faith, and your relationship was not holy because your faith in your brother was so limited and little. Your faith must grow to meet the goal that has been set. The goal's reality will call this forth, for you will see that peace and faith will not come separately. What situation can you be in without faith, and remain faithful to your brother?

5. Every situation in which you find yourself is but a means to meet the purpose set for your relationship. See it as something else and you are faithless. Use not your faithlessness. Let it enter and look upon it calmly, but do not use it. Faithlessness is the servant of illusion, and wholly faithful to its master. Use it, and it will carry you straight to illusions. Be tempted not by what it offers you. It interferes, not with the goal, but with the value of the goal to you. Accept not the illusion of peace it offers, but look upon its offering and recognize it *is* illusion.

6. The goal of illusion is as closely tied to faithlessness as faith to truth. If you lack faith in anyone to fulfill, and perfectly, his part in any situation dedicated in advance to truth, your dedication is divided. And so you have been faithless to your brother, and used your faithlessness against him. No relationship is holy unless its holiness goes with it everywhere. As holiness and faith go hand in hand, so must its faith go everywhere with it. The goal's reality will call forth and accomplish every miracle needed for its fulfillment. Nothing too small or too enormous, too weak or too compelling, but will be gently turned to its use and purpose. The universe will serve it gladly, as it serves the universe. But do not interfere. (Chapter 17, *ACIM*)

IV. The Two Pictures

12. Two gifts are offered you. Each is complete, and cannot be partially accepted. Each is a picture of all that you can have, seen very differently. You cannot compare their value by comparing a picture to a frame. It must be the pictures only that you compare, or the comparison is wholly without meaning. Remember that it is the picture that is the gift. And only on this basis are you really free to choose. Look at the pictures. Both of them. One is a tiny picture, hard to see at all beneath the heavy shadows of its enormous and disproportionate enclosure. The other is lightly framed and hung in light, lovely to look upon for what it is. (Chapter 17, *ACIM*)

VII. The Ark of Safety

7. Your home is built upon your brother's health, upon his happiness, his sinlessness, and everything his Father promised him. No secret promise you have made instead has shaken the Foundation of his home. The winds will blow upon it and the rain will beat against it, but with no effect. The world will wash away and yet this house will stand forever, for its strength lies not within itself alone. It is an ark of safety, resting on God's promise that His Son is safe forever in Himself. What gap can interpose itself between the safety of this shelter and its Source? From here the body can be seen as what it is, and neither less nor more in worth than the extent to which it can be used to liberate God's Son unto his home. And with this holy purpose is it made a home of holiness a little while, because it shares your Father's Will with you. (Chapter 28, *ACIM*)

Prayer

O' Father in Heaven, I humble
myself to You in prayer to thank
you for keeping Your promise to
let me learn and remember Your
promise of love and the return
to Heaven with all the Sonship.

Help them to be willing to receive
Your Holy Spirit so the process of
purification of the heart and cleansing
of the mind may begin to help them
remember Your true love for them and
their true love for You.

Help them to remember their willingness
to be new will bring them face to face with
the preciousness of forgiveness who upholds
salvation for all parties involved in a
scuffle where she brings peace of mind and a
painless heart to all the craziness and hurts
we think we do one to another.

I appreciate and am forever grateful
Heaven is no dream and your promise
to every soul on earth never shatters
because the enormity of your love and
light is the power in You and them.

You are the one and only true Father
in Heaven Who holds everything
together with the love of your light,

for You are the eternal gravity of
everything lovely.

Thank you for letting me remember
this at the appointed time I gave
myself to recall the importance of
You, Jesus Christ, the Holy Spirit,
the Sonship, and Heaven.

Through my spiritual learning with the
Holy Spirit, thank You for reminding me
that the Sonship is part of the Trinity
along with the lovely gifts You offer to
us twenty-four seven.

I look forward to the day every eye
will see and mind free to confess the
truth of You in them and them in You.

I know it's a matter of time because
we are in the illusion of time where every
mind will come to wellness and every heart
will be at peace with releasing the imprisoned
spirit to transition back into timelessness where
Heaven awaits their homecoming.

Help them to realize in the faith of
Your grace no one can take another's
life because the body is the shield to the
spirit and spirit is life.

Through Your Holy Spirit, let them
learn and remember the guiltlessness
of the Sonship and their own to help
them enter forgiveness through the light
of the peace of the Atonement of Christ.

Through faith and hope, let them remember
they have been forgiven before they were born
and that no one is doomed in a world full
of gloom and it is OK to love, forgive, and unify
the relationships that brought the act of devastation
be restored to love, joy, unity, freedom, safety, and peace.

For all the devastation is an act a play of ancient
occurrences we can get through as we gaze through
the maze and fall in love all over again with the
holy Trinity and the holiness in each other.

Thank You Father in Heaven for keeping
Your promise to all the Sonship.

In the name of the Kingdom of God. Amen.

VII. Attainment of
the Real World

1. Sit quietly and look upon the world you see, and tell yourself: "The real world is not like this. It has no buildings and there are no streets where people walk alone and separate. There are no stores where people buy an endless list of things they do not need. It is not lit with artificial light, and night comes not upon it. There is no day that brightens and grows dim. There is no loss. Nothing is there but shines, and shines forever." (Chapter 13, *ACIM*)

IV. Your Function in the Atonement

3. When you have let all that obscured the truth in your most holy mind be undone for you, and therefore stand in grace before your Father, He will give Himself to you as He has always done. Giving Himself is all He knows, and so it is all knowledge. For what He knows not cannot be, and therefore cannot be given. Ask not to be forgiven, for this has already been accomplished. Ask, rather, to learn how to forgive, and to restore what always was to your unforgiving mind. Atonement becomes real and visible to those who use it. On earth this is your only function, and you must learn that it is all you want to learn. You will feel guilty till you learn this. For in the end, whatever form it takes, your guilt arises from your failure to fulfill your function in God's Mind with all of yours. Can you escape this guilt by failing to fulfill your function here? (Chapter 14, *ACIM*)

VII. The Call for Faith

7. The power set in you in whom the Holy Spirit's goal has been established is so far beyond your little conception of the infinite that you have no idea how great the strength that goes with you. And you can use *this* in perfect safety. Yet for all its might, so great it reaches past the stars and to the universe that lies beyond them, your little faithlessness can make it useless, if you would use the faithlessness instead.

8. Yet think on this, and learn the cause of faithlessness: You think you hold against your brother what he has done to you. But what you really blame him for is what *you* did to *him*. It is not his past but yours you hold against him. And you lack faith in him because of what you were. Yet you are as innocent of what you were as he is. What never was is causeless, and is not there to interfere with truth. There is no cause for faithlessness, but there *is* Cause for faith. That Cause has entered any situation that shares Its purpose. The light of truth shines from the center of the situation, and touches everyone to whom the situation's purpose calls. It calls to everyone. There is no situation that does not involve your whole relationship, in every aspect and complete in every part. You can leave nothing of yourself outside it and keep the situation holy. For it shares the purpose of your whole relationship, and derives its meaning from it. (Chapter 17, *ACIM*)

VII. The Call for Faith

9. Enter each situation with the faith you give your brother, or you are faithless to your own relationship. Your faith will call the others to share your purpose, as the same purpose called forth the faith in you. And you will see the means you once employed to lead you to illusions transformed to means for truth. Truth calls for faith, and faith makes room for truth. When the Holy Spirit changed the purpose of your relationship by exchanging yours for His, the goal He placed there was extended to every situation in which you enter, or will ever enter. And every situation was thus made free of the past, which would have made it purposeless.

10. You call for faith because of Him Who walks with you in every situation. You are no longer wholly insane, and no longer alone. For loneliness in God must be a dream. You whose relationship shares the Holy Spirit's goal are set apart from loneliness because the truth has come. Its call for faith is strong. Use not your faithlessness against it, for it calls you to salvation and to peace. (Chapter 17, *ACIM*)

II. The Coming of the Guest

2. You have accepted healing's cause, and so it must be you are healed. And being healed, the power to heal must also now be yours. The miracle is not a separate thing that happens suddenly, as an effect without a cause. Nor is it, in itself, a cause. But where its cause is must it be. Now is it caused, though not as yet perceived. And its effects are there, though not yet seen. Look inward now, and you will not behold a reason for regret, but cause indeed for glad rejoicing and for hope of peace. (Chapter 29, *ACIM*)

Your Willingness to Admit

Your life has become unbearable and unmanageable because you do not believe that a power such as God is greater than yourself in the physical sense but equal to you in the spiritual sense because He created you as His clone. You believe He cannot restore your sanity, but if you choose to align your will with His, He aligns His will with yours as you understand it before you were even born. Your willingness to admit you were wrong in searching for a mortal existence for yourself and accept your immortality and the Atonement of Jesus Christ, a quantum leap to combine your light with His and atone with your brothers for all the wrongdoings you have ever said, done or thought of, is everything. Forgive God for letting you transform from immortality to mortality and confess to Him that you are ready to have Him remove the evilness from your mind and heart. Humble yourself to Him in prayer and it becomes easy to humble yourself to the Sonship. Receive every memory God brings to your remembrance of every evil deed you ever said, thought of or done and let the cleansing and purification process begin through your repentance in prayer. Forgive yourself and atone with every person you ever harmed or thought of harming in your mind and heart. Lift them up in prayer as an amends to your brothers, for power is in prayer. Pray for the knowledge of your will that it be given to you in restoration of your wrongful thinking. Receive the quantum leap into spiritual vision to see beyond this world and gaze upon Heaven as a remembrance of where you come from. We all must forgive each other no matter what we do because we must free one another from the chains and shackles of the ego's sinister prison we bondage each other to through guilt, judgment, punishment, and imprisonment. Right now, we are living by ego standards and we must be willing to break free from it restoring the mind from split to whole and live in the unification of holiness, sinlessness, kindness, joyfulness, peacefulness, freedom, and safety. Through forgiveness you can obtain this. Be willing to admit what you made to experience because it becomes easier to see what you had asked for before you were even born. Accept it as what it is so you move forward in patience, comfort, and peace with God's Holy Spirit, for He will gently take you through the quantum leap process, but your willingness is everything, for without it, you are nothing and you have nothing. No longer choose to be nothing and have nothing as a mortal and embrace your immortality and take the journey to wellness of mind and love in your heart and let your light combine with Christ where God shines His love and light upon you and through you. Here, your light beams under your feet with each step you take, every word you say, and each gesture you make.

And so your willingness to admit what you have made to experience in your life becomes bearable and manageable in your mind and heart where you meet stillness and calmness in the bliss of holiness, guiltlessness, love, joy, peace, safety, unity, and freedom where you are the Son of God He showers with endless love and royalties for eternity. In the name of the Kingdom of God. Amen.

IV. The Little Willingness

5. You merely ask the question. The answer is given. Seek not to answer, but merely to receive the answer as it is given. In preparing for the holy instant, do not attempt to make yourself holy to be ready to receive it. That is but to confuse your role with God's. Atonement cannot come to those who think that they must first atone, but only to those who offer it nothing more than simple willingness to make way for it. Purification is of God alone, and therefore for you. Rather than seek to prepare yourself for Him, try to think thus:

I who am host to God am worthy of Him.
He Who established His dwelling place in me created it as
He would have it be.
It is not needful that I make it ready for Him, but only
that I do not interfere with His plan to restore to me my
own awareness of my readiness, which is eternal.
I need add nothing to His plan.
But to receive it, I must be willing not to substitute my
own in place of it. (Chapter 18, *ACIM*)

III. The Altar of God

1. The Atonement can only be accepted within you by releasing the inner light. Since the separation, defenses have been used almost entirely to defend against the Atonement, and thus maintain the separation. This is generally seen as a need to protect the body. The many body fantasies in which minds engage arise from the distorted belief that the body can be used as a means for attaining "atonement." Perceiving the body as a temple is only the first step in correcting this distortion, because it alters only part of it. It does recognize that Atonement in physical terms is impossible. The next step, however, is to realize that a temple is not a structure at all. Its true holiness lies at the inner altar around which the structure is built. The emphasis on beautiful structures is a sign of the fear of Atonement, and an unwillingness to reach the altar itself. The real beauty of the temple cannot be seen with the physical eye. Spiritual sight, on the other hand, cannot see the structure at all because it is perfect vision. It can, however, see the altar with perfect clarity.

2. For perfect effectiveness the Atonement belongs at the center of the inner altar, where it undoes the separation and restores the wholeness of the mind. Before the separation the mind was invulnerable to fear, because fear did not exist. Both the separation and the fear are miscreations that must be undone for the restoration of the temple, and for the opening of the altar to receive the Atonement. This heals the separation by placing within you the one effective defense against all separation thoughts and making you perfectly invulnerable. (Chapter 2, *ACIM*)

Who We Truly Are

For a time, we are but puny and synthetic humans
on a speck of blueness out in the vastness of the
intergalactic darkness.

Join with me to look beyond the vast field
of the cosmos to enable yourself to gaze
upon the white skies glistening golden. For
I am your savior and so you too are mine.

The madly backward and downward steps taken
on the world of blueness brings about sadness,
for the subconscious starves to move forward
and skyward because it knows it's the natural.

*Like a starving fox squirrel wildly searching
the ground just to get a speck of a seed to feed.*

Be willing to ascend from out of the blue bubble.
For don't you know "blue" is the clue?
Escape its chaos and slip into silence before
the blue ice melts.

Swiftly little children!

Rise alongside of me, embrace your immortality,
be ready to transition from Earth to Heaven beyond the
vast darkness to enter the grandeur of holy lightness
glistening golden.

For this is where our home is.

And so godzillions ago, we forgot who we truly
are, join me in memory to enter your divine sanctuary,
for we are each other's savior to the glistening golden
altar, Christ within, and this is how it has always been.

III. God's Witnesses

1. Condemn your savior not because he thinks he is a body. For beyond his dreams is his reality. But he must learn he is a savior first, before he can remember what he is. And he must save who would be saved. On saving you depends his happiness. For who is savior but the one who gives salvation? Thus he learns it must be his to give. Unless he gives he will not know he has, for giving is the proof of having. Only those who think that God is lessened by their strength could fail to understand this must be so. For who could give unless he has, and who could lose by giving what must be increased thereby?

2. Think you the Father lost Himself when He created you? Was He made weak because He shared His Love? Was He made incomplete by your perfection? Or are you the proof that He is perfect and complete? Deny Him not His witness in the dream His Son prefers to his reality. He must be savior from the dream he made, that he be free of it. He must see someone else as not a body, one with him without the wall the world has built to keep apart all living things who know not that they live. (Chapter, 29, *ACIM*)

Absolute Love, Freedom and Atonement

Wouldn't you want absolute love, freedom and atonement? True love, freedom and atonement is needed among all the people on the world. Through the release of Jesus Christ from the crown of thorns is to honor Him with the crown of white lilies and we free Him, ourselves and our brothers from sufferings galore. Here, we shall be free from every aspect of fearfulness, darkness, selfishness, carelessness, helplessness, hopelessness, loneliness, homelessness, sadness, pettiness, pettishness, ruthlessness, hatefulness, wickedness, insanity, separation, starvation, bloodshed and greed. For we cannot reunite with Christ and one to another under the veil of the dreary circle of fear and darkness. For it is only through the glistening golden circle of righteousness can we reunite with Christ and each other under the veil of God's love, light, life and truth. So be willing to learn to remember there is no need to put a value on all the things the world offers. Nor is there any need to put up borders at every corner of the world, because in the end, anything and everything the world offers is ever so meaningless, senseless and shallow. Why? Because it all withers, rust and turns to dust. For only through forgiveness can we release our dark minds from the dreams of chains and shackles of the ego's sinister prison. For what is most profoundly meaningful is to remember that through your willingness to release Christ from the crown of thorns, you are His savior, as well as He is yours. He and you are also my savior and so too am I His and yours. As I said before, we are all in this ruthless dream together. This means we are all connected and we always have been and always will be no matter how deep we slip into the madness of insanity. We temporarily have memory loss and are momentarily insane. However, we can regain memory and sanity if we so wish to do so. Remember, we already went through the phase of temporal life of releasing Christ from the cross. We are now in the era to release Him from the crown of thorns.

To be yearning to be His, your brothers' and your own divine savior is the sovereignty of being miracle minded through every righteous deed ever so hallowed. For this is everlasting love, light, life, truth, freedom and atonement, absolutely. Through willingness is where forgiveness, holiness, wholeness and wholesomeness enters. This is a great achievement we must be striving to complete in readiness where the holiness of love, light, life and truth fully enters. These are the holy fundamental divine qualities of humbleness, happiness, kindness, peacefulness, faith and patience, the pure blissfulness of safety, unity, sanity, royalty, love, freedom and atonement. Here, all of Heaven rejoices, drums roll, trumpets blow, cymbals ring and angels sing, "bravo little children." For our compliance to achieve the greatest deed to release from the temptation of the greed of the dollar and we tore down the borders to be our brothers savior. Greed and ungodliness set into motion, grieving, thieving, crushing, hating, killing, judgment, punishment, imprisonment, depression, insanity, homelessness and starvation. The fundamental behaviors of the dreary circle full of frightful and sorrowful feats.

Yet, there is no need for anyone to suffer under these ruthless and senseless laws and conditions when we can easily choose to be miracle minded by giving everything freely and forgive everyone doing what they do to survive the unforgiving, cruel world and be their savior. For you are their divine brother and savior, even if you don't remember this. The goal of the Holy Spirit is to help you recall the miraculous divinity and sanity in you and I am all too happy to assist Him in this endeavor. However, to be compliant is everything, for without it we achieve nothing. Our subservience to be miracle minded, is to put into practice, an offering to everyone needy ever so speedy through the process of quantum leap. For our obedience to love, forgive, redeem and atone is everything. Remember, we come from the Kingdom of Heaven where God showers His love and royalties equally to all the Sons of God. As a result there is no need for greed or to steal, kill and destroy, for no one is deprived of anything and everything. Be willing to return to miracle minded thinking where we move forward and skyward beyond anything and everything fear and darkness offers. For this is what it means to escape a world spiraling deeper into a backward and downward spiral, where the chains and shackles of the pit of the ego's sinister prison prevails. Be willing to rise into the glistening golden circle of love, light, life and truth of your celestial sparkly golden temple, the holiness of miracle thinking.

And so be willing to forgive in authenticity and lovingly accept and embrace everyones differences, regardless the form it rises in. Be jolly and in amity when you give freely without charge or trade. For this is ideally completely, concretely, graciously, heartily, miraculously and intensely, but tenderly meaningful, dutiful and worshipful. This is the ultimate earthly glory you will ever receive in a ruthless kingdom where everyone thrives on fearsome stories and achievements. The greatest act is to follow and honor God's grandeur plan of His laws of forgiveness and redemption, which puts into motion a domino effect, the power of miracles. This is the divine sovereignty to transform the whole darkened world into a holy kingdom. For this is the glory of the glistening golden light of love, life and truth, ever so extraordinary, inspirational and absolute love, freedom and atonement, indeed.

III. God's Witnesses

3. Within the dream of bodies and of death is yet one theme of truth; no more, perhaps, than just a tiny spark, a space of light created in the dark, where God still shines. You cannot wake yourself. Yet you can let yourself be wakened. You can overlook your brother's dreams. So perfectly can you forgive him his illusions he becomes your savior from your dreams. And as you see him shining in the space of light where God abides within the darkness, you will see that God Himself is where his body is. Before this light the body disappears, as heavy shadows must give way to light. The darkness cannot choose that it remain. The coming of the light means it is gone. In glory will you see your brother then, and understand what really fills the gap so long perceived as keeping you apart. There, in its place, God's witness has set forth the gentle way of kindness to God's Son. Whom you forgive is given power to forgive you your illusions. By your gift of freedom is it given unto you.

4. Make way for love, which you did not create, but which you can extend. On earth this means forgive your brother, that the darkness may be lifted from your mind. When light has come to him through your forgiveness, he will not forget his savior, leaving him unsaved. For it was in your face he saw the light that he would keep beside him, as he walks through darkness to the everlasting light.

5. How holy are you, that the Son of God can be your savior in the midst of dreams of desolation and disaster. See how eagerly he comes, and steps aside from heavy shadows that have hidden him, and shines on you in gratitude and love. He is himself, but not himself alone. And as his Father lost not part of him in your creation, so the light in him is brighter still because you gave your light to him, to save him from the dark. And now the light in you must be as bright as shines in him. This is the spark that shines within the dream; that you can help him waken, and be sure his waking eyes will rest on you. And in his glad salvation you are saved. (Chapter 29, *ACIM*)

Quantum Leap Into Spiritual Vision

Look and see, for there is no limit as to what you can achieve when you let thy Holy Spirit lead, not through physical eyes, but through spiritual sight. For the spirit will remember the life that is coming is already before us, waiting to behold and know all the prewritten episodes of life on Earth and on other worlds throughout the whole universe and dimensions.

Let the worlds open up through the mind's eye and we can see through quantum leap into spiritual vision. Be willing to look more closely with the guidance of thy Holy Spirit and we find the eyes to see and the memory of what we already know.

And so quantum leap into spiritual vision, which is the quantum leap effect, is where you will behold and know everyone and everything you have always known. For you and the Sonship are cocreators of the universe and everything in it. Just as the Sonship are the Sons of God and cocreators with God of everything lovely and true. But we can only witness and reacquaint our memory of the factual and the fabricated through spiritual vision with the guidance of thy Holy Spirit. For as God's Holy Commissioner, His goal is to make sure you remember, everyone are your brothers no matter the form of each figure on earth and in the universe. This will enable you to learn and remember that the Kingdom of Heaven is your royal inheritance because you are forever a child of God, as well as all.

In the name of the Kingdom of Heaven. Amen.

CPSIA information can be obtained
at www.ICGtesting.com
Printed in the USA
BVHW022122260919
559558BV00018B/110/P